CHAPTER ONE

NATURE'S INVITATION

'The peculiar formation of the great Caledonian valley, – long, deep and comparatively very narrow, and occupied by a regular chain of inland lakes and extensive arms of the sea – had long suggested the idea of a canal which by connecting the whole might afford the means of a navigable communication between the opposite sides of the island.

Indeed so marked were its features in this respect, that it must have been difficult to escape the conclusion that Nature had irresistibly invited the hand of man to the completion of such an undertaking.'

So wrote a Victorian commentator in the 1840s in a description of the Caledonian Canal. We appreciate his sentiment yet any topographical examination of the terrain of Scotland would suggest that nature's invitation could be extended to a number of locations where narrow land barriers separated Scotland's seas, even where there are no 'inland lakes' (sic).

The number of places named 'tarbert', gives the clue to the indented nature of Scotland's coastline and to the number of possible invitations extended by nature to the hand of man. A tarbet or tarbert (*tairbeart* in the Gaelic) is an isthmus – a narrow stretch of land between two stretches of open water. It also came to mean a portage – a land bridge over which it was possible, with some considerable effort it has to be said, to drag a curragh or birlinn from sea to sea rather than sail many wearisome and dangerous miles.

There are tarberts, both east and west, on Harris, Jura and Kintyre. And they lie between Lochs Eil and Linnhe in Lochaber, between Lochs Sunart and Linnhe and between Lochs Long and Lomond.

As far as we know no-one saw any commercial advantage in a canalized connection between the Harris or Jura tarberts. However, linking the Kintyre tarberts was several times proposed (once as late as 1846) and could have given serious competition to the route of what we now know as the Crinan Canal. The Norwegian king, Magnus Barefoot, in the 11th century, had his galley dragged from the Atlantic to Loch Fyne at Tarbert and thereby claimed to have 'sailed' round Kintyre. His object was to establish that the peninsula was one of his 'islands'. Malcolm Canmore granted the Norwegian's claim to add Kintyre to his collection of Hebridean islands.

The tarbert to Loch Sunart is six miles long and qualifies as a 'glen'. A canal there would have provided more direct access to the Atlantic from Fort William than the journey down Loch Linnhe and north through the Sound of Mull or south round the Ross of that same island.

In 1801 the engineer Thomas Telford, in one of his surveys in the Highlands, considered making a canal from Loch Eil across to Loch Sheil at Glenfinnan and then to the Atlantic at Kentra on the Ardnamurchan peninsula. This would also have provided a shorter access to the Atlantic ocean from Fort William than sailing the full length of Linnhe and rounding Mull.

Both of these plans were of course ancillary to the

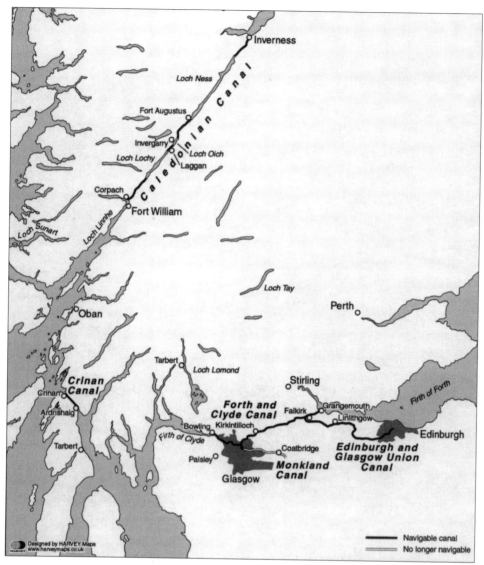

The Canals of
Scotland.

great adventure of creating a waterway through the Great Glen and would have been an additional strain on the public purse that was underwriting the Inverness to Fort William project. Neither was acted upon. The invitation was declined.

The two-mile strip of land between the deep waters of Loch Long and those of Loch Lomond was not seen as a significant technical barrier by those who determinedly promoted a route from the Clyde to the Forth by exiting from the south-east corner of Loch Lomond. They wanted to build a 'battleship canal' across the carse of Stirling to the east coast. The existing Forth and Clyde Canal was to be superseded by a one-level canal which would allow Great Britain's capital ships ease of access from the North Sea to the Atlantic. This was an echo of an earlier idea which had been used in the promotion of the Caledonian Canal during the early 19th century's 'French' wars.

The concept was current in the 20 years up to World War I although the idea of joining Loch Lomond to the Forth via the Endrick had first been advanced in 1764 by Smeaton. The Stevensons, of lighthouse fame, undertook a survey and recommended the Loch Lomond-Loch Long route in 1889. A 1917 proposal took the canal through the suburbs of modern-day Stirling. Another route, 'The Direct Route', from Yoker to Grangemouth was actively promoted by the Mid-Scotland Ship Canal National Association almost up to the onset of World War II. The association took itself very seriously and was supported by representatives of the great and the good, including some senior naval officers. Again nature's invitation was spurned; perhaps because stationing battleships at Scapa Flow allowed both east and west coasts to be readily patrolled as well as offering ease of access to the north Atlantic?

Nevertheless Scotland's narrow waist between Clyde and Forth, the six or seven miles of Knapdale that split the Atlantic from Loch Fyne and the Clyde and the lengthy geological fault that is Glen Albyn or Glen Mor all presented the opportunity to cross the country from sea to sea.

The Forth and Clyde Canal linked those two rivers and its title was therefore as logical as it was descriptive. Crinan, (once and originally Port Righ) was the western destination of the journey across Kintyre and the title 'Crinan Canal' served it well. The Edinburgh and Glasgow Union Canal, a cumbersome title mostly abreviated to the 'Union', certainly joined the two main cities, but why the 'Caledonian Canal'? Why not the 'Inverness and Fort William Canal', thereby following previous geographical examples? An early advocate of the canal referred to it with some accuracy as the 'Strathlochy Canal'. It was Thomas Telford who preferred to call it 'Caledonian'. It seems it was to be the grandest canal in all Caledonia and should be named as such. We must grant that he was correct about that.

Commerce and the attraction of carrying materials and goods by ship or barge (the most efficient transport technology of the 18th and early 19th centuries), at low unit costs, would provide the compelling logic for taking up nature's invitation in these three instances. These waterways were built, not for pride in constructing 'the world's first sea to sea canal' but because the time was right. Scotland was on the march intellectually and scientifically in the late 18th century. Scotland needed new transport facilities, particularly for the Lowlands, to meet its upsurge in technical innovation and industry from the 1760s onwards.

Curiously Scotland's first canal was made to serve God rather than Mammon. Andrew Wood had distinguished himself in the service of James III by repelling an English fleet from the Forth and also withstanding their seige of Dumbarton. He was knighted and given lands at Largo. Around 1495 he had a canal constructed that allowed him to be conveyed, each Sunday, in his admiral's barge from his house to church (the outline of the quarter-of-a-mile-long ditch can still be seen). The pomp and circumstance of his arrivals were no doubt forgiven for the regularity of his attendances.

Mankind had been building canals long before Wood's conceit, indeed for the best part of three millennia. Irrigation canals were in use in the Middle east in the 7th century BC and the Persian King Darius connected the Nile to the Red Sea 200 years later. The Chinese, who in the middle ages were to build the spectacular 700-mile-long waterway from Huai-an to Peking, were active around the Yellow and Yangste rivers from the 3rd century BC.

Exactly when man had first appreciated that the buoyancy of objects in water eased his transport needs is not clear. Archimedes (285–211BC) had certainly articulated the principle that a solid immersed in water would be lighter by the weight of the water that it displaced. Whether this scientific rationalisation was applied to cargo and fighting vessels or not, the practical results were there to see. It might not have been understood that the frictional loss between water and a rough surface wetted by water was much lower than frictional loss between early axles and wheels and those wheels and rough roadways. Nevertheless it was clear for all to see that a horse could pull a hundred times the load in a barge that it could in a cart.

As we might expect from their many other engineering and architectural works the Romans were active in the canalization of rivers throughout their European empire largely for the purposes of military transport. Tacitus (56–120AD) described a project in which was to be realised 15 centuries later as the Canal du Midi. In the 1st century AD Marcus Livius Drusus connected the Rhine to the Yssel. Probably the first canals on the mainland of Britain were the Roman links from the Cam to the Ouse and the Nene to the Witham perhaps with the intention of reclaiming the fens as much as providing military transport.

The technical feature that is most associated today with canals — locks and lock gates — were to emerge in Europe in the 12th and 13th centuries as the continent moved towards renaissance from the Dark Ages. Appropriately enough, at a place called Damme, a lifting gate was constructed in 1180 to control the water flow where the Brugge canal entered the sea.

In Italy around the same time, the Naviglio Grande was being constructed (1179–1209) to service the great city of Milan. The canal was later to carry marble for the erection of Milan's Duomo. It was for work on improving this canal that Leonardo da Vinci (1452–1519) is credited with the invention of the mitre gate which replaced the lifting gate at the San Marco lock at the junction of the Naviglio Grande with the Martesana Canal. He was commissioned to design the canalization of the river Afronte (to drain the Pontine marshes near Rome,) and also of the river Arno in

1503. For this later project (never even commmenced) he devised a system of locks on the tributary streams to connect the small towns of the valley with Pisa. It is conceivable then that the two-leaved gate pointing upstream into the direction of water flow, which was thereby able to withstand higher water pressures than the gate which closed flat, could have come from his fertile imagination.

In medieval times in the commercially active area we now know as the Low Countries where the geography lent itself to water-borne transport, an integrated system of rivers and canals was so developed as to have been the most important method of inland transport. At the junction of the canal from Utrecht to the Lek river (completed in 1373) there were two lock gates and between them a basin in which the water level was controlled by the operation of the two gates. Thus the 'pound lock', so familiar a feature today in most canals, was invented.

Twenty-five years later the Stecknitz Canal was completed. It fell 40ft from Lake Mollner down to Lubeck and when it was extended south to Lauenburg on the river Elbe, through another 40 ft drop and two locks, it became possible to take barges from the Baltic to the North Sea.

It was not until construction of the first short section of the Exeter Canal in 1564–66, designed to improve the navigation of the river Exe, that mainland Britain saw its first pound lock. (The canal was under two miles and had a single lock but it underwent major extensions in the 17th and 19th centuries). It was virtually 200 years later that the canal age proper began in England with the Bridgewater Canal.

Continental Europe, particularly France, had continued to provide technically sophisticated examples of the expansion of the use of the canal as a means of communication. The Briare Canal, which was completed in 1642, rose 128ft to a summit before falling 266ft through a total of 40 locks in joining the Loire to the Seine. Even greater perhaps was the Canal du Midi of Baron Riquet de Bonrepos. Through 26 locks it rose 206ft, had a three-mile summit and then fell 620ft by way of a further 74 locks. It was 150 miles long and its most daring innovation was the 500-foot-long Malpas Tunnel at Beziers. The greater part of the work was carried out between 1665 and 1681. Thus was the Bay of Biscay connected with the Mediterranean via the rivers Aude and Garonne and another great sea to sea passage became possible.

Coal, the fuel which literally drove the machines of the Industrial Revolution, was to be the cause of beginning of the canal age in Britain. (The desire for cheap coal was what made the citizens of Glasgow and Edinburgh support canal projects). The Duke of Bridgewater desired to reduce the cost of delivery of coal from his estate at Worsley to the growing town of Manchester. A well-travelled man, he looked to the continental models. (He had been impressed by the Canal du Midi and wished to have a canal made for his purposes.) He turned to one James Brindley for advice and the age of the canal and the civil engineer was about to begin in the United Kingdom.

For the next half century, until the arrival of the railways and Stephenson's *Rocket,* canal mania swept the country. Inland water transport became the preferred and almost the fashionable option, for the captains of the Industrial Revolution. There was scarcely a section of country, north and south of the border, where schemes for canals to improve local transport, were not investigated.

In Scotland, in the half century after the failure of the Jacobite cause in 1746, there was a period of astonishing creativity. Intellectually, architecturally, philosophically, agriculturally and scientifically the country bounded forward. In the epoch, generally known as the Scottish Enlightenment, Scotsmen became world-renowned for their advances in their chosen fields of activity. William Smellie edited the first edition of the *Encyclopaedia Britannica,* the concept of two Edinburgh printers, Bell and Macfarquhar. Adam Smith practically 'invented' economics by his publication of *Wealth of Nations,* Robert Adams made Scottish architecture the most influential European style and David Hume was considered the greatest philospher of the day. Joseph Black discovered latent heat, James Hutton advanced the science of geology, the Hunter brothers at Edinburgh University made Scottish medical training the most advanced in Europe and James Watt took the steam engine to a higher plane of efficiency.

Through the consolidation of the ancient run-rig system into larger tenant farms, the agricultural 'Improvers' increased Scottish food productivity beyond recognition in the Lowlands. People left the land, where they were no longer required, and headed to the cities where the steam was powering the mills and factories. An improved transport system was needed to take them food to live on, raw materials to work on and then to take their products to markets. The canal was seen as just such an improvement. With the exception of the publically funded Caledonian Canal, the construction of which was more politically than economically motivated, the building of the Forth and Clyde complex, (including the Monkland and the Union canals) and the Crinan, was driven by a market economy.

The estate owners, the merchants and the manufacturers needed advice on how and where to make the much talked of canals. A group of practical, often self-taught men, were prepared to provide the answers to their questions. They called themselves 'engineers'.

CHAPTER TWO

THE ENGINEERS

The promoters of the Scottish canals had similar motives to those of the Duke of Bridgewater — they wanted modern improved transport systems. They were men of letters and wealth, rather of science, and had a want of technical advice. They needed 'engineers'. They may not have fully understood what was meant by an 'engineer' but they appreciated that they had to call on specific skills to survey the possible routes for their canals and put a price on their construction. Once approval had been obtained from parliament for their projects, someone who could mark out the line to be followed by their canal and supervise its construction was required.

They called on James Watt for example. Greenock-born Watt was closely involved in the daily management of the excavation of the Monkland Canal from 1770 to 1774, (and he had previously surveyed its line), but he also undertook surveys of possible routes for the Forth and Clyde, Crinan and Caledonian canals. Watt's reputation today rests on his improvement of the Newcomen steam engine but he was a instrument-maker 'to trade'. His invention of the separate condenser in 1765 vastly improved the efficiency of steam engines but while he was building a test engine and applying for a patent, which he obtained in 1769, he set himself up as a land surveyor. His experience on the Monkland Canal was not a particularly happy one. (He found supervising contractors an uncongenial and difficult business.) He made the correct decision in 1774 that fame and

fortune lay with the improved engine and he left Scotland and canal building for Birmingham. His firm of Boulton and Watt later supplied three steam engines for the building of the Caledonian Canal.

Nevertheless during his eight surveying years he mapped out canal routes for the Forth and Clyde (1766), the Monkland (1769), and the Crinan (1771). Between 1773 and 1774 he explored routes for the Caledonian, the Campbeltown to Machrihanish and the Crieff to the Tay canals. He provided costings and timescales for the completion of these projects and all were eventually built except the one from Crieff. For the Monkland he was commissioned by the magistrates of the City of Glasgow and he was given leave of absence from its construction to work for the Commissioners of the Annexed Estates on the other two 'highland' canals.

How does a successful scientific instrument maker turned inventor set himself up as land surveyor and win prestigious commissions like these? One assumes that the application of 'scientific method' to the solution of problems offers the clue. Or was it a case of the one-eyed man in the land of the blind? Canal building, at the time, was new to Scotland but acquired expertise in the art could be found in England in the work of earlier canal engineers like Brindley.

By all accounts James Brindley (1716–72) left no written records of how he designed and constructed his canals. This is not only true of his ten miles of canal for the Duke of Bridgewater, with its tunnel and

James Watt (1736–1819)
Of world-wide renown for his improvement of the Newcomen steam engine, Watt surveyed and partially built the Monkland Canal, and prior to 1774 undertook surveys for seven other canals in Scotland. He went into business with Matthew Boulton and their steam engines were used for pumping in the construction of the Caledonian. This statue stands in the entrance of Strathclyde University.

William Jessop (1745–1814)
Possibly the foremost canal designer of the late 18th and early 19th centuries, Jessop was a pupil of John Smeaton and responsible for the design and construction of 11 canal projects. He supervised Thomas Telford on the Ellesmere and Caledonian canals. The latter was completed by Telford after ill health forced Jessop to withdraw from the project in 1812.

aqueduct, but also of his later work on the Grand Trunk Canal. A grand total of 360 miles of canals are attributed to him and not a drawing or calculation has remained. He began his career as a millwright and engine builder and was self-taught as a civil engineer.

The beginnings of the profession of civil engineering may be traced to the foundation in France of the École Nationale des Ponts et Chaussées in 1747 which followed from the creation of a separate Corps in 1716 for the building of bridges and roads. Separate that is from the well established Corps of military engineering.

The professors of the École wrote treatises on materials, machines and hydraulics that became standards in Europe and aspiring engineers learned to read French to benefit from them. In this sense many of the growing group of mid-18th century engineers in Britain were self-taught.

As we have noted, talented craftsmen like Brindley, a millwright, became a canal builder par excellence. John Rennie, born in East Lothian in 1761 and also a millwright built the Kennet and Avon Canal, the original Waterloo Bridge and was to play a significant part in the building of the main Scottish canals. Thomas Telford, (1757–1834), a stone mason from Dumfriesshire, apart from his many other accomplishments, will be remembered in Scotland for his work on the Crinan and Caledonian Canals.

Yorkshireman John Smeaton, (1724–92), certainly called himself a civil engineer but had started life as an instrument maker like James Watt. Smeaton founded the Society of Civil Engineers in 1771, 24 years after the establishment of the École Nationale des Ponts et Chaussées. The Institute of Civil Engineers was established in 1818 and Telford became its first President. The purpose was to exchange information and to allow the young engineers to learn thereby from their experienced elder colleagues.

We are used to casually referring to Smeaton or Rennie as 'the builders' of the Forth and Clyde or the Crinan, or talking of the Caledonian as 'Thomas Telford's canal'. But in truth their role was more often what we would today consider as that of a consulting engineer. Their's were the tasks of delineating the concept, giving evidence to promote an enabling act through parliament, issuing broad guide-lines before the start of the construction process and periodically, say once or twice per year, supervising the progress towards completion. The consultants were often involved in the supervision of more than one major project at any time. Telford, for example, was involved, amongst other projects, in improving Aberdeen harbour up to 1812 when he was 'building' the Caledonian. There was a whole body of men, the resident engineers, unsung heroes today, who got their boots very muddy in the actual business of cutting the canals. Thus Robert Mackell on the Forth and Clyde, John Paterson on the Crinan, and on the Caledonian Canal the Davidsons (Matthew and James), John Telford and Alexander Easton are worthy of a place in history. Watt's dual role of consulting and resident

engineer on the Monkland was unusual for its time (and did not in any case last very long) and the broadly similar one of Hugh Baird on the Union sprang from his position as surveyor on the Forth and Clyde.

For the last 40 years of the 18th century John Smeaton and William Jessop (1745–1814) were recognised by their contemporaries as the leading figures of the engineering profession, in an almost apostolic succession, Jessop having been apprenticed to Smeaton. It was from one of these two that the House of Lords heeded evidence before passing bills and to whom the subscribers of the canals turned for initial designs and approval of their ultimate execution.

Smeaton travelled in the Low Countries in 1754 studying canals and harbours and he brought his knowledge and experience to the rebuilding of the Eddystone Lighthouse in 1756–9 before he took charge of the construction of the Forth and Clyde Canal a decade later. At least when the Trustees for Fisheries, Manufactures and Improvements in Scotland (set up in 1727) paid for the 1764 report of a survey of a route for a canal between the Forth and the Clyde they gave the job to the man recognised as the country's foremost civil engineer of the day. The report was presented and signed by 'John Smeaton, Engineer and Fellow of the Royal Society'. He rode over the ground in the summer of 1763 and gave an oral report in August that year, during which he made favourable reference to the Canal du Midi as an example to be followed for the link from Forth to Clyde.

There had been earlier surveys for this canal. Robert Mackell and James Murray, for example had produced one in 1762 for Lord Napier of Merchiston but this was not acted upon. Mackell again, this time with James Watt, in 1766 produced routes and costings for the City of Glasgow which desired a route that entered the Clyde at the Broomielaw. The Carron Iron

Company joined the debate and promoted yet another route which accommodated its interest in being directly connected to the proposed canal. Smeaton's second report of 1767 was the basis on which the enabling Act of Parliament for the project was drawn up after the Carron interests were compensated for withdrawing their alternative proposals, with a payment of £1,500.

The act received the Royal Assent in March 1768 and Smeaton became the chief engineer of the undertaking. Mackell's reward was to be made the resident engineer and work started in June 1768. Still the debate on the route would not die down. A report over the names of Brindley, of Bridgewater fame, Yeoman (another FRS) and Golborne kept the argument for a cut to Carron alive even after digging had commenced. Smeaton, with the strength of an Act of Parliament behind him, publically defended his views. The Carron argument he stated 'is artfully wrote but from beginning to end is full of the grossest Mistakes and Misrepresentations.' Work continued on his chosen route.

Smeaton had time to 'inspect' Watt's work on the Monkland in 1770 and his suggestion for increasing the depth of the canal by additional banking was acted upon. Work had got under way in June 1770 after the passing of an enabling act in the April. The Glasgow magistrates led the subscribers to the project who quickly adopted the cheaper of his two proposals; a scheme for a lockless canal which would be linked to the city by a waggon-way. Watt agreed to supervise the digging and so became both chief and resident engineer. Glasgow was not inclined to pay for two engineers when one would do, though no doubt Smeaton submitted a fee for his inspection!

With two major canal constructions progressing in the Lowlands by 1770, the Glasgow magistrates, with

the bit between their teeth, decided that a canal across 'Cantyre', (sic) would promote trade between the city and the Western Isles. They petitioned the Commissioners of the Annexed Estates to have a survey made. Watt was employed and offered the alternative of Loch Gilp or west Loch Tarbert as the Clyde estuary terminus without stating a preference.

No action was taken but the concept resurfaced at intervals in the 1770s and 1780s. Encouraged no doubt by the imminent completion of the Forth and Clyde a proposal was put to the British Fisheries Society to have Watt undertake a new survey. In the event it was John Rennie, experienced canal builder of Kent and Avon fame, who was employed by the Duke of Argyll and the Earl of Breadalbane to make another survey.

In 1792 Rennie costed two routes neither of which used Tarbert. That to Portree, as Crinan was then known, was adopted as the basis of the Act of Parliament in 1793 and work began in 1794. John Paterson became the resident engineer under Rennie's supervision.

Rennie's services were much sought after in Scotland at this time. He carried out surveys for many projects which like the Dee valley (1802) and the Arbroath to Forfar (1817) canals did not come to fruition. His 1800 investigation of the practicality of Saltcoats to Glasgow canal, after several re-appraisals, one of which was made by Telford, eventually became the Glasgow-Paisley-Johnstone Canal. Rennie's Aberdeenshire Canal however was completed in 1805.

Rennie was also employed in 1797 by the magistrates of Edinburgh, who wanted a canal to get coal to their city more cheaply. He had to choose between the four routes for a Leith to Glasgow canal that a survey, commissioned by them in 1793, had produced. Naturally Rennie recommended a fifth which was to pass by Cumbernauld. Great debate and dissension among vested interests and the stress of the wars with revolutionary France caused the lengthy postponement of any decision.

In 1813, Hugh Baird, who had been appointed surveyor of the Forth and Clyde Canal in 1806 and who was later to conduct a critical survey of the reservoirs of the Crinan Canal, produced a design for a canal to link the capital, not Leith, to the Forth and Clyde at Falkirk. Rennie's concept was dusted down and advanced as more desirable and the debate raged. Thomas Telford came down on Baird's side in 1815 and eventually the parties were reconciled. An act was passed in 1817 and work on the Edinburgh and Glasgow Union Canal, as a 'tributary' of the Forth and Clyde, with Baird as engineer, began in 1818.

Watt's 1773 survey for a possible canal through the Great Glen, carried out with the object of assisting the fishing industry, had been set aside by the government of the day. Watt was conscious, as were others who proposed similar schemes in 1785 and 1793, of the problems to navigation posed by the prevailing westerly winds which were contrary to a north to south passage in those pre-steam propulsion days. By the end of the 18th century however government was concerned with wider social problem of emigration from the Highlands and its possible effects on recruitment to Highland regiments, on whose qualities, since the '45, the army had become dependent. If government was aware that it was dealing with the aftermath of the social and economic effects of the early Clearances it showed no sign of it. Thomas Telford was commissioned to study the causes and propose solutions.

By 1801, when Telford started his survey, he had experience of being in charge of public works in Shropshire for 15 years. He had made his reputation on the Ellesmere Canal (the designs for which he was

Thomas Telford (1757–1834)
He began his career as a mason and by study made the transition to architect and engineer. After his work for the British Fisheries Society in the 1790s, he was asked by the government to undertake a survey of roads in Scotland. From this emerged the policy to build the Caledonian Canal and over a period of 20 years he was responsible for the construction of over 900 miles of roads and 120 bridges in the Highlands.

required to submit to Jessop for approval) where cast-iron troughs were used to carry water over the aqueducts at Chirk and Pontcysyllte. His proposals to ameliorate the social and economic causes of emigration were not concerned only with the canal but with the construction of roads, bridges and harbours in the north of Scotland. He proposed improvements to the infrastructure of a countryside which however was becoming denuded of its people, at a rate of 10,000 per year at that time, due to economic reasons that he could not address. He consulted widely on the matter of a canal and got positive responses but the deciding factor was possibly political – a canal would protect shipping from the depredations of French privateers.

Enabling acts were passed in 1803 and 1804 and a

committee, known as the 'Commissioners', was appointed to report to parliament. Jessop, who had 13 major canal constructions to his credit by this time, was appointed consulting engineer by the Commissioners. Telford, who reported to Jessop, was paid three guineas per day (£3.15) while Jessop was paid five guineas (£5.25) per day. It was Jessop, who unlike Telford had previous experience of building sea-locks, who finalised the route and costed it. He and Telford jointly signed the annual progress reports to the Commissioners until 1812 when poor health caused him to withdraw from the project. (The Kilmarnock and Troon Railway, Scotland's first public railway, which opened in 1811, was the last major construction which Jessop saw to completion.) Most of the section, from Fort Augustus to Loch Lochy, which brought the Caledonian to completion, was finished solely under Telford's supervision.

For all of this developing knowledge and experience not one of these major Scottish canals, the Forth and Clyde and its branches, the Crinan or the Caledonian was opened within the cost or the timescale that was originally planned (see Appendix II). Rennie, whose opinion had been sought in the early planning stages for the Caledonian, thought that it would cost over £600,000 proved to be nearer the mark than either Telford or Jessop.

At this remove, the two years estimated for the building of the Crinan, compared with the eight that it actually took, and that under severe pressure for completion, looks optimistic but comes into perspective when it is considered that the Caledonian took from 1803 to 1822 (at nearly twice the cost) and the best opinion of the day was that it would take no more than seven years. Baird's appointment to the post of engineer for the Union Canal specified a five-year building period and an overall cost of £240,500. The time limit was nearly met but the final cost was over £460,000.

There were extenuating circumstances of course. Changes were made, sometimes for practical and sometimes political reasons, during construction to the lines the canals took, and to their operating depths. Mackell's proposal of 1770 to take the Forth and Clyde nearer to Glasgow, two years after digging had begun, involved the expense of building the Kelvin Aqueduct. But the biggest problem, for all the skills of the surveyors, was their lack of knowledge of soil mechanics and of a systematic method of assessing the geology of the areas through which their diggings were to proceed. Telford did take test borings along the line of the Caledoniam Canal in 1804–05, (They cost £600 out of a total expenditure of over £900,000), yet he still covered himself by reporting that until the ground was actually opened – 'we are unable to specify particular exceptions'. Watt, too, in surveying for the Monkland, took drillings where the ground looked 'suspicious' but still he got caught out by what was virtually quicksand at Coatbridge. It is noteworthy that James Hutton (1726-97), the Edinburgh lawyer and agriculturist and a shareholder in the Forth and Clyde, published his seminal work on geology in 1785, *after* years of serving on the Forth and Clyde committee and being closely involved in the practical problems of its construction.

This is not meant as a harsh judgement upon them for the study of soils did not start to be developed into a science until the mid-19th century. But reading their progress reports to their subscribers there is a constant theme of being taken aback by the difficulty of the terrain and their surprise at what they found, rock instead of clay for example on the Crinan route, when they broke the surface. Dealing with the Dullatur Bog on the Forth and Clyde, for they knew well that it was there, was a considerable headache. After the walls of the cut sank into the mire they solved the problem, at some cost in time and money, by basically filling the bog in to a depth of nearly 50ft. For all our 21st century sophistication in these and related matters, we still evince little surprise today when we hear of a major construction project exceeding its original cost estimates.

The effects of these cost increases and time delays were threefold. First, since the companies formed to construct and operate the canals had a capital sum paid up by subscribers, which was usually based on the engineers' estimates, money often ran out with the canals only partially completed. Raising additional capital often presented major difficulties. Second, the subscribers faced annoying delays in getting a return on their investment the longer their money lay fallow in a non-profitable enterprise. (The subscribers to the Forth and Clyde were more fortunate than most for their canal started to earn tolls section by section as it crept westwards from the Forth, to Kirkintilloch for example, which was reached in 1773.) All of this strained the patience and the financial resources of those who invested and led to the third effect; less than best construction practices being adopted in the desire to speed up completion.

CHAPTER THREE

THE SUBSCRIBERS

Unwittingly, the Jacobite rebels of 1745, were to contribute timely and crucial financial support to the development of Scotland's canals. The fate of those of the Scottish nobility and clan chiefs who were 'out' in 1745, and who escaped capture and execution, was exile and the forfeiture of their estates. Over 40 estates were forfeited within days of Culloden and later some 13 large estates were inalienably annexed to the Crown. Until 1784, with the passing of the Disannexing Act, (which legally forgave the rebels and returned their estates for the payment of outstanding debts), their properties were managed by the Commissioners of the Annexed Estates.

The Annexing Act of 1752 provided that the profits derived from the estates were to be applied to developing them but money was also diverted to 'civilise' the Highlands by integrating the area with the rest of the country. Schemes for the development of industry and fisheries in the area and for the improvement of roads and agriculture were to be the remit of the Commissioners. They were to apply the rents and profits 'for the better civilizing and improving the Highlands of Scotland and preventing Disorders there for the future.' In this way the Highlands were to become relatively more prosperous and therefore loyal to the crown.

For over 30 years the Commissioners applied funds to the building of roads, bridges and even inns for those who travelled in the Highlands. With the passage of time the purely anti-Jacobean principles became diluted and they considered and supported many projects peripheral to the original purpose. They acted in a manner that perhaps has its parallel today in the disbursement of National Lottery funds to good causes, in the Commissioners' case to the founding of schools and the planting of trees. The development of harbours, ferry services and canals, fully met with their approval.

With the proceeds of the sale of the Annexed Estates, in some cases back to their original owners, the Barons of the Exchequer lent £50,000 to the Forth and Clyde Canal Company in 1784. On its repayment they promptly loaned half of it out to the Crinan Canal Company. As noted previously the Commissioners had responded positively to petitions to pay for James Watt's surveys for routes for the Crinan and Caledonian canals in 1771 and 1773 respectively. Even after the planning for the Forth and Clyde was underway the Commissioners were petitioned by the Convention of the Royal Burghs for money to allow a deeper canal than that envisaged in the enabling act, to be dug.

The legal process for starting a canal company in 18th-century Britain began with holding a public meeting to gauge support for a project to construct a specific canal. Support was confirmed by individuals undertaking to 'subscribe' for shares at a stated price. This price multiplied by the number of shares was the anticipated, mostly wrongly anticipated, cost of construction.

The price of a single share was usually fixed at £50

or £100 pounds (this latter sum roughly equivalent to £26,000 today) or even higher. An amount of this order, whether in single or multiple applications was not readily affordable in the late-18th century except by the nobility or merchants. (A university professor might have been paid £150 per annum at this time.) Scotland was not considered a wealthy country but between 1768 and 1793, some £236,000, equivalent to around £61,000,000 today, was called for in the initial subscriptions for the building of the Forth and Clyde, the Monkland and the Crinan canals (the canals cost a great deal more than this by the time of their completion). The successful businessmen and the landed aristocracy in Scotland responded by diversifying their interests, the former from merchanting and the latter from re-investing only in their estates. Yet a large proportion of the money came from noble and mercantile classes who had their residences in England.

Not all the money was put up at once but it was drawn off as the building progressed. It was not unknown for some of the initial subscribers to lose their enthusiasm for the project or decline to pay, leading to shortfalls in the capital required. Powers could be taken under Scots law to forfeit shares and charge interest on outstanding calls. Shareholders motives for investing ranged from altruism (frequently stated in the reasons for proposing the idea, but in reality, fairly rare) to the expectation of profit and dividends.

Once public support had been so demonstrated the next step was to promote and guide a bill through parliament setting up the canal company and describing its purpose, location, powers to take water supplies and to levy tolls. It was not unusual for the tolls to be precisely defined with upper limits put on the levels of dividend that could be paid to shareholders, to curtail 'profiteering' (this debate on the

balance between the needs of suppliers and consumers was a public issue in Scotland at the time and was to find world-renowned expression in the publication in 1776 of Adam Smith's *Inquiry into the Nature and Causes of the Wealth of Nations)*. This form of public debate, and the debate could be lengthy and contentious as in the case of the Forth and Clyde Canal, was in essence an early form of the current process of obtaining planning approval. It could be a cumbersome procedure and necessitated separate acts, for changes in canal routing, for example. Changes in the Forth and Clyde were regulated by 13 separate acts in the 60 years of the reign of George III. Once the act had received Royal Assent the first call on the subscribers for cash was made, engineers and managers were appointed and digging began.

The subscription for the 'great canal', Smeaton's preferred option for the Forth and Clyde, was opened in London in 1767 and soon £100,000 was promised. The act of 1768 authorised the issue of shares at a value of £100 each up to an initial limit of £150,000. (Smeaton's estimate for a 7ft-deep canal was £147,000). There was a provision that if this sum was insufficient a further subscription could be put in place to raise an additional £50,000. The list of proprietors was a roll-call of the 'great and the good' of the day in Scotland; three dukes, two marquesses, 17 earls, 15 knights of the realm and the Provosts of the two cities to be joined by the enterprise. Lord Queensberry was elected chairman of the company. The Dukes of Bedford and Marlborough led the English contingent who were outnumbered approximately ten to one among the 125 subscribers. The Dundas family, led by Sir Lawrence, who had lands at Kerse at the eastern end of the canal, held 20 per cent of the shares.

The success of the English canals, beginning with the Bridgewater in 1761, was such that they became *the* thing to invest in, rather like the electronic information technology based companies in the 1990s. They opened up exciting new vistas in the communications field, and with thoughts of getting in on the profitable ground floor the well-to-do rushed to invest. The landed gentry had their rents to redeploy and Scotland's merchant classes sought new uses for their profits.

Trade with the Low Countries, the Baltic and transatlantic colonies had established fortunes, especially in the tobacco trade. Tobacco lords, like Alexander Spiers and John Glassford, were prominent in subscribing to the Forth and Clyde, (which they saw as aiding their Baltic trade) and the Monkland. These merchants were well positioned to exploit the deposits of coal and iron (which were often found on the estates of the aristocracy) to establish industrial centres in the lowlands of Scotland. They knew the value of sea transport and saw the advantages of also having inland water transport. The prospect of Scotland's first canal and one that would join east and west was an enticing one.

The Carron Company was already established (1759) and it fought to have its position recognised in the design of the Forth and Clyde Canal. James Watt's engines meant that steam-powered linen and cotton mills could be taken to the centres of population so there was no need any longer to take a workforce to where free, but variable, water power could be found. Demand for cheap coal led the way.

Not all of the Forth and Clyde's subscribers met their commitment when the call came for hard cash and the problems of Glasgow's tobacco trade during the American War of Independence, (with its embargo on American goods), meant that raising the original commitments, never mind extra funds, was difficult. The City of Glasgow however, had paid all but £50 of

the £1,000 to which it was committed.

Work stopped in 1775 when the canal had reached Stockingfield because the company needed another £109,000 to clear its debts and complete the canal, the calls on subscribers being £39,000 in arrears at this stage. The Royal Bank's support had been essential for the canal to progress up to this point and its cash-compt loan method, an early form of overdraft, was the mechanism for advancing the money. In the mid-18th century this form of banking was unique to Scotland and many enterprises of the industrial revolution benefitted from it. The loans were at what was, at the time, regarded as the modest rate of four percent but there was a quid pro quo – the Royal insisted that the workforce was paid only with its notes.

There was interest throughout Scotland in saving the canal and petitions were organised, with the support of the Convention of Royal Burghs, calling for the injection of public monies. Despite the fact that the canal was by this time earning tolls and could provide security for loan repayments, the Commissioners of the Annexed Estates refused to authorise a loan and it was not until 1784, after a change of government and the sale of the annexed estates, that a loan was forthcoming from the Barons of the Exchequer, who managed these funds. It was subsequently repaid out of profits in 1799.

The making of the Forth and Clyde broke ground in a quite literal sense and in a metaphorical sense it was to do the same in the important area of company accounting. The canal was the largest financial enterprise seen to that date in Scotland and the question of how it was to account to its subscribers for the use of their money required that a financial reporting system had to be devised and widely circulated. Eventually a satisfactory system evolved after much shareholder scrutiny and criticism, and in 1815, 29 years before the first Companies Act became law, the annual accounts were published. This was possibly the first recorded instance in Scotland of the veil of secrecy surrounding a company's financial affairs being lifted. (See Appendix VIII)

The act forming the Monkland Canal Company was passed in April 1770. It had been promoted from the outset by various commercial interests in the City of Glasgow because it would 'be of great advantage to the trade and manufactures in the city' by reducing the delivered price of coal. The coal was to come in from east of the city from the north Lanarkshire pits. Since the Lord Provost of Glasgow was James Buchanan, the tobacco trader, who had bought an estate at Drumpellier, the choice of these pits was not surprising!

The preferred route was the lockless nine-mile channel from Sheepford to the mansion of Jermiston, (about a mile outside Glasgow), via 'Cotesbridge' (sic) and Drumpellier. Watt had costed this plan at £9,653 (the precision of those 18th-century estimates never ceases to amaze!) and the proprietors sought to raise £10,000 in shares of £100 each to pay for construction and the expense of promoting a bill through parliament. They allowed themselves the contingency of raising another £5,000, if necessary, by a second subscription. It was, indeed, to become necessary but it proved impossible to raise when the Company ran out of cash in 1773. Local landed interests, through whose estates the canal was to pass, Dick of Gartsherrie (in the environs of today's Coatbridge), and Dougal of Easterhouse, readily bought shares, as did Lord Provost Buchanan and Spiers, Glassford and Ritchie, (three of the famous 'Four Virginians', the most important men in the tobacco trade). The Trades House of Glasgow, the incorporations of wrights, bakers, masons, fleshers, etc and the university all invested. The funding of the Monkland was a purely Scottish exercise. One name on

the list of proprietors which was to be significant in the future was that of the merchant William Stirling. It was his partnership which contributed to the raising of new capital in 1782 which took the canal past the seven-mile mark where it had stopped in 1773 when the original £10,000 had been exhausted.

An attempt to raise an additional £1,000 from the original subscribers in 1780 failed; almost certainly because the canal, in its shortened form, was losing money and perhaps because the war with the American colonies (1775–83) was having disastrous results on the tobacco trade. (Provost Buchanan went bankrupt in 1777 and had to sell the Drumpellier Estate). The original shares were sold in 1781–82 at heavily discounted prices; roughly at about 30 per cent of their £100 value. Ten of the 101 shares remained in the hands of the Town and Trades House of Glasgow and the remainder were taken by individuals, principal among whom were the Stirlings.

New shares at a cost of £150 were raised and sold, taking the capital of the 'new' company to £15,000. The result was the completion of the waterway to Blackhill and the two partners of William Stirling and Sons and their fellow clansman Andrew, whose pits on the canal bank produced up to 30,000 tons of coal annually, became the principal shareholders. These three men eventually owned the canal outright and funded the canal's improvements over the next 20 years. Given that the company paid no dividends until into the 1800s it must be assumed that the Stirlings were happily making enough on their sales of coal to regard the canal as a means to an end and of secondary financial importance as far as a return on their investment was concerned.

Having determined from Rennie's survey that the cost of the Crinan was to be £69,000 and having described in a prospectus the advantages in opening a

The Barons of the Exchequer

Over £100,000 was raised in 1784 under the Disannexing Act. This sum was paid by families for the repossession of the estates that had been forfeited after the 1745 rebellion. The largest disbursement (see line 2) from this sum was to the Forth and Clyde Canal Company. Note also that the Earl of Breadalbane was given £200 for building a bridge over the River Lyon. (NAS)

route between the Clyde and the Western Isles, the promoters of the act set about raising the capital in the form of £50 shares.

Some 270 individuals responded, among them 48 with the surname of Campbell, led by the biggest Campbell of them all, John, the fifth Duke of Argyll, who subscribed for 20 shares. Other Scottish notables, the Marquesses of Lorne and Tweeddale, the Earl of Breadalbane and Sir Archibald Edmonstone similarly subscribed for £1000. Four of the Wedgwoods from

The Seal of the Crinan Canal Company
The seal carries the 1793 date of the passing of the enabling act for
the construction of the canal. It appears that the loaded barge is
being towed from a tunnel but this is artistic licence. From
surviving documents it would appear that at no time was a tunnel
contemplated. (NAS)

Etruria contributed £2500 having no doubt seen the
advantages that Brindley's canals had brought to the
potteries. Almost immediately Rennie revised the cost
estimate to £107,700 to accommodate a change in
depth to 15ft and the extra sum was rapidly subscribed.
'Canal mania' was at its height.

More than half of the subscribers had addresses in
England, (accounting for roughly two-thirds of the
shares) and all the proprietors' meetings were held near
London, in the same St. Albans tavern where the Forth
and Clyde investors had held their meetings. The
Western Isles supported the prospect of improved
communications between there and Glasgow and
money came from Colonsay, Lunga, Coll, Gigha,
Shuna and Mull. Macneil of Barra, MacLeod of

MacLeod and the Easdale Slate Company (the Earl of
Breadalbane was a shareholder) were also subscribers.
The City of Glasgow and its Chamber of Commerce
put up £300 between them. One John Rennie, with an
address in London, subscribed for two shares. Could
this have been our engineer showing his belief in the
concept by hazarding £100? Certainly he worked in
London for many years and died there in 1821.

The Crinan took a lot longer to build than
Rennie's estimate of two years and by 1799 the proprietors of the unfinished canal were in financial
difficulties. The first subscription had fallen short by
some £14,000, an additional call was unsuccessful, and
the banks refused support. The canal was saved when
the Barons of the Exchequer (in effect the treasury)
advanced a £25,000 loan at five percent interest after
being partly persuaded that Baltic traders taking an
'inside' route through the canal would be safer from
French privateers.

This allowed the canal to be opened in 1801 but at
a depth of only eight feet and with some of the
construction not completed. Future tolls were
mortgaged to the exchequer to secure the £25,000. The
canal was completed by 1809 when it was rescued by
another £25,000 from the exchequer, on the same
terms, after disastrous flooding in 1805 had closed it.
More flood damage and another closure in 1811
resulted in another appeal for support to the
exchequer. Effectively control was taken away from the
proprietors in 1816 and by an Act of Parliament it was
vested in the Commissioners of the as yet unopened
Caledonian Canal. It was logical to do this as it was
important to keep the Crinan open as a feeder for the
Caledonian for Glasgow to Inverness marine traffic.
The government was of course also underwritng the
cost of the Caledonian. The Exchequer had Telford
survey the Crinan's repair needs and provided another

£19,400 to allow it to be reopened in a fit state in 1817.

By now some £74,000 of public money had been invested in the Crinan Canal and the proprietors had put up £117,500. The return of the control of the canal was conditional on all these loans and interest on them being repaid. The canal was not profitable enough to accomplish this. Later the burden was added to by the condition that operating losses incurred be added to the sums due. The outstanding debts were never repaid and the subscribers lost control and all their investments. The Crinan Canal had passed into public ownership and there it has stayed.

There really was never any question that the Caledonian Canal would be in other than public ownership. Its building was undertaken as a government initiative. Part of Telford's sweeping review of 1801 of how to reverse the trends of depopulation of the Highlands, it accounted for £350,000 of the £650,000 that he proposed be spent on improving the economic conditions of the Gaels. Despite the promotion of the idea of the canal through the Great Glen by various people from the 1720s onwards, no group of entrepreneurs had come forward with money to invest in such a venture. A commercial demand for a bulk transport service had underwritten the Forth and Clyde and Monkland, but it was Prime Minister Pitt's concerns for the future of recruitment to Highland regiments and the prospect of moving ships of war, especially large frigates, rapidly from west to east coasts that drove forward the construction of the Caledonian. It has to be remembered that at this time Britain was at war with France and the victories of Trafalgar and Waterloo were in the future. Even the blow dealt to the Franco-Spanish fleet in 1805 did not substantially reduce the French ability to harrass British coastal trade and commercial shipping with their cruisers and corsairs. It was to fight these that

John Campbell (1762–1834)

John Campbell, 4th Earl and 1st Marquess of Breadalbane, was typical of the aristocratic subscribers to the Crinan Canal. No doubt he was interested in transporting slate from the quarries on the island of Easdale. He also promoted a canal, which was not built, from Loch Earn to Perth for the movement of limestone. Canals must have been in the genes for the 5th Earl was involved in the 1840s in plans for canals to link the south end of Loch Lomond with the Forth and Clyde through the Vale of Leven. He promoted a canal from the north end of the same loch to the south-west end of Loch Tay. Neither of these projects was fulfilled. (NGS)

Britain commissioned its frigates and Pitt wanted the canal for their passage from sea to sea.

Nor was the intellectual climate of the times necssarily hostile to government intervention of this nature. Adam Smith in his *The Wealth of Nations* had argued that it was one of the essential functions of government to construct public works, into which category the Caledonian Canal certainly fell. Another essential was the defence of the nation and the two could be happily married in the promotion of the canal.

The benefits to merchant shipping of avoiding the perils of the Pentland Firth were promoted in the preamble to the enabling act of 1803 but the dimensions of the canal were fixed by the size of His Majesty's frigates. The size of the locks was fixed at a length of 162ft, a breadth of 38ft with a depth of 20ft to accommodate a 28 gun frigate. The draft of a 44 gunner was uncomfortably close to this depth and its length and beam of 185 and 41ft respectively were just too big for the new canal. To accommodate such vessels would, it was estimated, cost another £47,000 in construction costs.

A second act of 1804 provided for subscriptions to be made and for the Commissioners to put shares of the canal on the market once the canal was completed. But shares in the Caledonian were never floated. Much later, in 1840, after the future of the Caledonian and the Crinan were reviewed by a select committee, an unsuccessful attempt was made to place the management of the canal in the hands of private enterprise. An offer to lease the waterway free of rent to any appropriate joint stock company did not attract any takers and the government, unwilling to close the canal, had to provide finance to make the needed repairs. Another attempt to 'denationalise' in 1858 was equally unsuccessful (two years later the result was the same when

the Commissioners tried to move the financial burden of the Crinan to private enterprise). David MacBrayne, the shipowner who had run services on both canals, did propose to lease both the Crinan and the Caledonian in 1881 but the Commissioners rejected his offer. The Caledonian Canal, with its 'subsidiary' Crinan Canal, remained, and have remained since, nationalised concerns.

The Edinburgh and Glasgow Union Canal, (the Union), had a long gestation. The idea for a linking waterway between Glasgow and Edinburgh had been discussed, surveyed, debated and postponed since about 1791. By the time the 1817 act for a canal from Edinburgh to 'at or near Lock Number Sixteen' on the Forth and Clyde, the railway age was fast approaching unbeknownst to its subscribers. But at the time, in the canal sector, the Forth and Clyde and Monkland were well established and successful, the Crinan was struggling and the Caledonian's construction was nearing completion. So better late than never. And anyway Edinburgh's coal, carried from Lanarkshire by the Monkland and by road was 'too dear'.

A sum of £240,500 was raised in £50 shares and the act empowered the subscribers to seek an additional £50,000 if it became necessary. This was prudently £5,500 above the estimated building cost and in addition to the large contingency built into the estimate, seems to indicate that some of the lessons of optimistic budgeting on the other canal projects were being learned. The Lord Provost of Edinburgh invested as did local coal owners like Maxwell and Livingstone and a Nabob, Robert Downie. His contribution was significant enough to ensure that he became chairman of the managing committee and the basin at the western end, where the two canals joined, would be called Port Downie.

Alas the £50,000 had to be drawn down by 1821,

three years after work had started, and this after the same sum had been raised in exchequer bills a year earlier. Future tolls were given as security, exactly as the Crinan proprietors had done with somewhat similar results. By 1823, after a difficult first year of operating, another £50,000 was obtained from the exchequer, who thereafter refused further support. By this time £461,760 had been spent on the canal of which the original subscription was only just over half of that sum. Each £50 share, therefore, carried a debt burden of £46. Although the Union made profits, and sometimes paid dividends, it gradually fell into arrears in paying off the annual interest and capital of its debt. In the 1840s it did not have the financial strength to fight railway competition or meet heavy repair costs necessary to maintain the waterway (see chapters 7 and 9).

When it was taken over by the Edinburgh and Glasgow Railway in 1849, those shareholders who had not discharged their part of the debt, about one third of them, received £5 per share while those who had coughed up over the years got £33.33. But then the latter had invested £96 for the privilege while the former had only put up their £50! They got their payment in railway shares. No matter which way the

outcome is examined, subscribing in the Union Canal had not been a licence for printing money but at least after 1849 they got dividends on the railway shares.

The subscription for the Union Canal brought to an end the age of major Scottish canal developments (the half-mile-long Forth and Cart, opened 1840, cannot be considered as 'major'?). The Forth and Clyde and Monkland configuration (these two canals amalgamated in 1846, with an exchange of shares from which the Monkland proprietors did rather well) continued to be profitable and attract support for its technical improvements. But from the 1830s onward 'railway mania' took over from 'canal mania'.

Eventually the Forth and Clyde proprietors, worried about the exhaustion of the mineral supplies in their catchment area, sold out profitably to the Caledonian Railway Company in 1867 (see chapters 7 and 9).

In 1825 the Stockton and Darlington Railway opened. In 1830 the Liverpool and Manchester Railway started using George Stephenson's designs for the railroad and locomotives. It was this line's scheduled passenger and goods services which truly opened up a new era of competition to the canals for traffic and capital.

CHAPTER FOUR

THE NAVIGATIONS

Background

Unlike roads and railways, which can rise and fall relatively simply with the geographic features through which they run, canals cannot cope easily with anything but moderate gradients. Admittedly there were some dramatic changes in level, at, for example Beziers on the Canal du Midi, but the canal engineer usually sought as level a line as possible for his waterway. Smeaton, Watt, Rennie *et al*, followed this golden rule in choosing their routes, with, in the first instance, an eye to ease of construction. The theodolite had been around for two centuries so they had the basic scientific instrument for planning their routes but it is noteworthy that our instrument maker, James Watt, refined the device in 1771 during the construction of the Monkland.

Operational and maintenance costs were always of concern but in the days before the railways arrived, canals offered such advantages over roads for the movement of bulk commodities that speed through the canal was not a primary consideration. In any case since the motive power in both cases was literally one horsepower, there was little difference in speed. There was an enormous difference in the tonnage carried by a canal barge compared to a road cart. Locks slowed the transit through the canal but were necessary to traverse the hills and valleys and so the time taken to pass the locks was accepted by the engineer with equanimity. Nevertheless he sought to maximise the stretches between locks because time and money were saved in reducing their number to a minimum.

It is axiomatic that vessels cannot travel through water at speeds that can be achieved by road or rail vehicles but on one Scottish canal water transport regularly lost out to 'shanks' pony'. En route from Glasgow to Inverness, Victorian passengers, sacrificing comfort for economy, would disembark at Ardrishaig and walk to Crinan to connect with the Oban steamer in less time than it took to sail through the canal's 15 locks.

Locks and their number were a determining factor in the construction cost of any canal which had to change levels over its course. In their original schemes, the Monkland and the Crinan were the same length of roughly nine miles. The 1769 estimate for the Monkland was £10,000 while the cost for the Crinan was calculated at £69,000 in 1793. The difference was not caused by price inflation over the period but was due significantly to the fact that the Crinan was to have 15 locks and the Monkland none. Building a lock took time, skilled labour and expensive materials. 'It is,' said Watt of the cheaper of his two proposals for the Monkland, 'much easier to find people who under-stand removing of earth than building locks ... ' Of Jessop's first estimate of £475,000 for the Caledonian, the most expensive item at 36 per cent of the total, was the cost of lock building. The locks had to be made with care and precision and this was carried out by the elite of canal building — the stonemasons. Hand-dressed stone bonded with Italian mortar (pozzuolana cement was imported from the Naples area) was the favoured method.

The conventional wisdom, experience or simply tradition, seemed to indicate that a rise of eight to ten feet was the practical limit for a mitre gate lock. It may have been decided that this depth of water was the limit of pressure that could be safely contained by the wooden gates of the day. Although as we shall see it was decided not to risk a ten-foot rise on the Caledonian at Laggan where two smaller locks were built. But then the locks on the Caledonian were three times the surface area of the next largest, those on the Crinan.

The size of the lock (and other canal parameters) was planned to accommodate the sea-going ships of the day and therefore the engineer did not have to look at more fundamental considerations in planning his canal. This was certainly the case for the Forth and Clyde, the Crinan and the Caledonian but it was not the case for the Monkland which was conceived as a purely inland waterway. The Monkland proprietors kept an eye out for the development of the Forth and Clyde and considered as early as 1770 the possibility of joining their canal to it. Watt was sent to investigate but as it was not then at all clear where the Forth and Clyde would enter the Clyde, they decided to leave that consideration aside. Had a junction been planned Watt would simply have made his canal the same profile as the Forth and Clyde. With no specific ship design in mind he examined the ability of channels of various sizes to take barges of differing deadweight capacity. He concluded, rightly, that a small canal would cause the barge operating costs/ton carried to increase relatively, and make the smaller canal less attractive to the user (his detailed calculations have survived.) He plumped for a canal to take a 20 ton deadweight barge which would be 60ft long drawing 30 inches of water and

produced a navigation which could take craft much the same length as on the Forth and Clyde but narrower and shallower.

The lock was only one weapon in the engineer's armoury. He could build masonry viaducts to carry water over river valleys if distance was to be saved and the viaduct was less expensive than a series of locks. The Kelvin Aqueduct on the Forth and Clyde and the structures of the Almond Aqueduct and Avon Aqueduct of the Union are regarded today as major engineering and architectural artefacts in Scotland's landscape but they were built for practical purposes.

An adequate supply of water was fundamental to the operation of the 'summit canal'. The summit canal seeks to maximise its length at its highest geographic level to speed transit and to provide water which will flow down through the canal to operate the locks throughout its length. All three main Scottish canal systems, if we take the Forth and Clyde-Monkland-Union configuration as a unity, were of this type. Seeking a water supply, from natural sources such as rivers, burns and lochs, was uppermost in the engineers mind when planning his canal. Indeed the Act of Parliament which authorised the building of the canals specified that the canal companies were given power to take water from named sources or to create supplies by the building of reservoirs. Smeaton was authorised to take water for the Forth and Clyde from any source within ten miles of the canal's route, for example. And of course once he had obtained his supply he had to make provision for dispensing of it safely at the lower levels once it had served its purpose. The management of water is still a primary task of canal operators today.

Water loss through leaks and seepage was always of great concern and the artificial channels were protected against erosion and leakage by 'puddling';

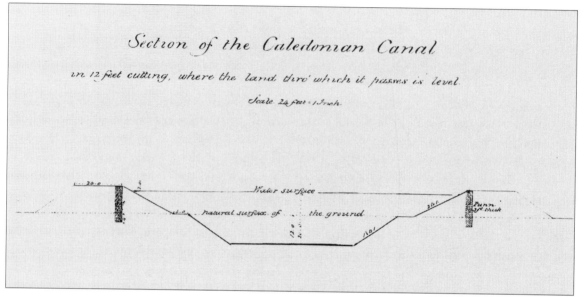

Profile of a Canal
This drawing, signed by Jessop in 1804, shows the typical sloped sides of a canal. The angles, marked '1½ to 1' and '2 to 1', are approximately 30 degrees. The excavated earth was to be used to make up the banks to achieve a water depth of 24 feet. (ICE)

the art of pounding clay on the canal bed to form a consistency impervious to water. The canals used thousands of tons annually in maintaining their watertight systems. The Monkland is recorded as consuming 15,000 tons of clay in 1875, a significant amount in a canal only ten miles long. The Forth and Clyde puddled the same quantity in 1885. Sections of the canals were 'run-off' to allow these repairs to be carried out. These canals were very busy during this period which may account for the high usage and around 5,000 tons annually would have been a more normal figure. Cast iron troughs had been used in the construction of the aqueducts over the Ceiriog and Dee valleys but this technique was not used in Scotland except on the Union canal. The puddling and the

digging of the channels was entrusted to a spade-wielding fraternity known as the 'navigators', who were highly skilled earth-movers. They have come down to us the 'navvies', a term perhaps less used today than it once was, for unskilled labourers.

The channels were not simply rectangular shaped troughs dug in the ground. They were generally twice as wide at what was to be the canal surface as they were at the bottom (the Forth and Clyde was 60ft wide at the surface and 30ft at the bottom). The Crinan varied according to the terrain and was reduced from a surface width of 84ft wide to 56ft through rocky ground. (See Appendix III.) Whether or not this profile was a rule of thumb or scientifically derived, it made good practical sense. Clearly a vertical canal side would be vulnerable to erosion and being undermined. A sloping surface to the canal bank (the angle was usually around 60 to 65 degrees) provided a supporting buttress. Watt's first scheme for the Monkland was based on an angle of 45 degrees because 'as the soil is in general strong, clay will I *imagine* (author's italics)

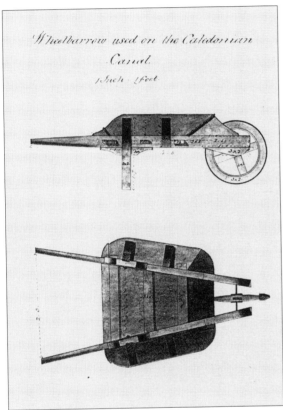

A Wheel Barrow
Even although mechanical devices such as steam dredgers and pumps were to be used in the building of the Caledonian the consultant engineers found it necessary to design more basic equipment. This is Jessop's concept of a wheel barrow. Telford also designed tilting carts for discharging spoil. (ICE)

The Lowlands

The engineering task that Smeaton and Mackell undertook in making a channel from the Forth to the Clyde can be stated simply. They had to mark out and dig a channel for about 38 miles west from the Forth, take the cutting up 156ft above sea level to a plateau (more or less) which ran from modern-day Banknock to Stockingfield in Glasgow, then take it down again to the Clyde at Dalmuir (the western destination was planned as Dalmuir but subsequently changed to Bowling). They achieved this by constructing 39 locks, of an 8ft rise, 20 to the east of the summit area and 19 to the west. They created the Townhead reservoir, near to Kilsyth, to feed the summit with water and built Scotland's first major aqueduct, the Luggie Aqueduct, at Kikintilloch. Its 50ft span was later to be put in the shade by a larger construction over the Kelvin. The Union canal's aqueducts over the Almond and the Avon and at Slateford were to be even larger.

Digging began in the east in June 1768 and by November the sea lock, at what was to become Grangemouth, was ready. With up to a thousand men working on the project the cutting had progressed nine miles to the west by January 1770 and six months later James Watt was sent off by the Management Committee of the Monkland to buy 50 spades and 20 wheel barrows so that he could get down to work at Sheepford. Watt's task was the simpler of the two. His canal was smaller, shallower and only nine miles long and he had no locks to build. He did however have to construct eight bridges to carry existing roads as he progressed eastwards.

By 1771 all the digging east of the summit on the Forth and Clyde had been made and the Townhead reservoir was begun. At the same time Watt was working on his reservoir at Drumpellier Moss for the

be sufficient to keep them from falling in.' In the event the angle in the Monkland, where the final channel profile was 32ft at the top, 16ft at the bottom and with a depth of 4ft, was nearer 30 degrees.

And so our engineers navigated their way across country, in the words of their contemporary, Robert Burns, through the 'mosses, waters, slaps and styles' of the rough Scottish countryside.

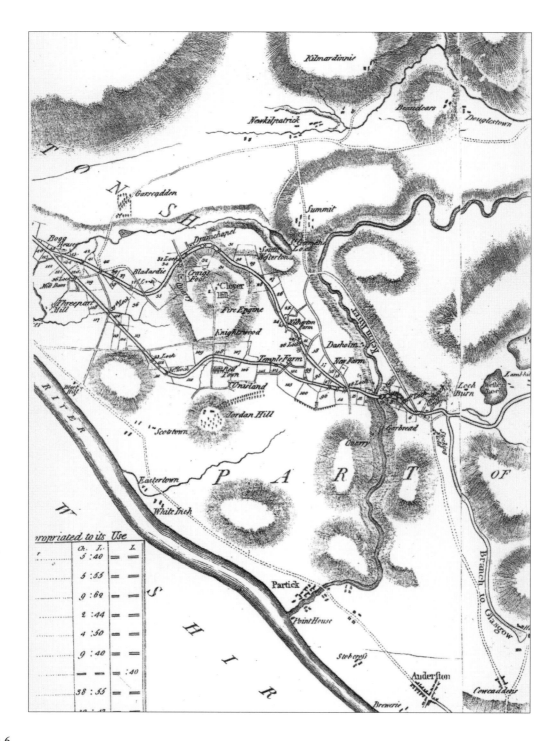

(Left). The 'New Line'
The extension of the Forth and Clyde beyond Glasgow was referred to at the time (1780s) as the 'new line of the canal'. Two routes from Maryhill to Boghouse were considered and the northern one was preferred round 'Cloyer Hill', now known as Cloberhill. Note that Anniesland was then referred to as 'Onisland'. (GLA)

(Above). Ferrydyke, near Dalmuir
At this spot is an example of a bascule bridge. They were to be found the length of the canal. ('Bascule' may derive from the French, 'bacule' meaning a see-saw.) They cantilevered upwards at both sides of the channel to allow vessels to pass. This was an essential feature of a waterway which had been built for the passage of sea-going vessels with masts. The bridgekeeper's cottage is to be seen beyond. The canal company supplied company houses for lock and bridge operators. (JRH)

Monkland having reached Coatbridge. He put his cut to practical use by shipping coals from pits to the east to Langloan. But at this point in time attention on the Forth and Clyde was diverted to discussions about a new route which would take it nearer to Glasgow.

Mackell argued that to swing further south from Kirkintilloch to come within two miles of the City would save construction time and money even if it meant having to cross the River Kelvin. His view was accepted and a new act was steered through parliament

(Above and opposite). Grangemouth Basin
North Basin Street at the eastern terminus of the Forth and Clyde, *c.*1900. The sea lock lay beyond in the Old Harbour. This section and all along Dalgrain Road to the west was infilled in the 1960s, necessitating the building of a new sea entrance during the Millennium Project. (FK)

to allow the changed route to be put into effect.

In 1772 Watt was beginning to run out of money, which was always slow in being released by his committee. He had spent £8,000 over his £20,000 budget for land purchases. Nevertheless he had reached Queenslie and coals were barged to Netherhouse in the 60-ft long by 10ft-wide barges which he had caused to be made. By contrast Mackell was able to allow sea-going vessels of 50 tons burden to reach Kirkintilloch by August 1773 and had begun to work on the Stockingfield basin, north of Glasgow. This same year was to see the departure of the two principal engineers.

Smeaton's departure from his supervisory role over Mackell was not unexpected as he had offered to go two years earlier to save his salary costs. Once the Dullatur Bog problem had been overcome, the canal partly opened and the Townhead reservoir filled, he went with the Company's thanks but sounded a warning about the costs incurred to that date.

Watt resigned in July 1773 having completely exhausted the finances available in reaching modern-day Barlinnie. The canal was measured as seven miles and 15 chains (or 330 yards) long; about two miles short of its intended destination. He was hopeful that the canal would be well used but was thankful to go ('I would rather face a loaded canon than make a bargain,' he wrote). He was unhappy with the quality of the work done admitting that, 'The work is done slovenly and our workmen are bad and I am not sufficiently strict.' The Monkland was not to have the subsequent

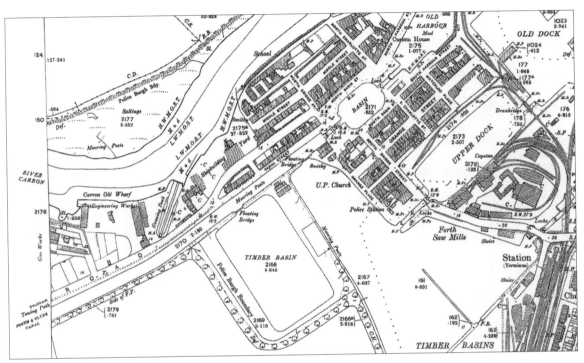

repair troubles that others had and while there is enough evidence that other canals suffered from the same quality problems Watt was the only engineer to be so outspoken about the subject. It was to lie in this unfinished state for ten years.

By the beginning of 1775 the Forth and Clyde held five feet of water as far west as the Stockingfield basin and there it stopped to allow the cutting to the south towards Glasgow to be made. This was stopped in 1776 because the company was deeply in debt but by the end of 1777 the Glasgow branch had reached the basin at Hamiltonhill and there matters rested. Glasgow was connected to the River Forth.

New funds were sought but it was not until 1784 that Pitt's intervention resolved the situation with the loan from the proceeds of sale of the Annexed Estates. By this time the Monkland had been re-financed, at the instigation of the Stirlings, and had been extended to Blackhill, but of course at a level nearly 100ft above the Forth and Clyde.

Mackell had died in 1779 and Robert Whitworth, a pupil of James Brindley, was appointed to drive west to Bowling with a budget of £59,000 (a sum of £6,200 was included for the Kelvin Aqueduct, but inevitably it cost nearly 40 per cent more). The point of entry to the River Clyde, which by this date had a deeper channel than in 1768 when the canal was first planned, had been reconsidered. However there was still only about four feet of water at the Broomielaw. The opening of coal pits at Bowling (where there was around ten feet of water at high tide) swung the argument away from an entry at the Broomielaw and also from the original proposal of Dalmuir. Until such times as the Clyde was deepened the shipowners of the 1790s found the tideless canal a more reliable way to get to the city of Glasgow than the river itself.

The Monkland Canal at Coatbridge
Coatbridge was seldom to be found on maps before about 1840 but it became an important transport and industrial centre. The Monkland runs from the top left corner to near the bottom right of the picture. Coming in from the top to meet the main canal is the Dundyvan branch and the Gartsherrie Branch runs off to the bottom near the right-hand edge. Both of these branches, and a third at Langloan further west, were built to service the iron industry that made Coatbridge so important in the second half of the 19th century.

Port Dundas
A 19th-century lithograph of the Forth and Clyde at the Port Dundas Distillery. Distilleries were a feature of the canalsides. Apart from transport facilities, the canals provided water for the processing.

The years 1785–6 were significant for the futures of both the Forth and Clyde and the Monkland. The Forth and Clyde extension needed an increased water supply and the planned new reservoirs lay to the east of Glasgow and just north of the Monkland. If the Monkland could be used as a conduit of these new supplies then the expensive business of the joining of the reservoirs to the Forth and Clyde could be avoided. Plans were therefore laid to join the two canals. The Monkland was clearly going to benefit from offering through traffic to Glasgow and beyond. The Forth and Clyde would benefit from using the Monkland as a water supply and from direct access to the Lanarkshire coal and iron deposits. The Monkland management set about designing locks at Blackhill to effect the junction and an eastward extension to bring down water from

the Calder river involving locks at Sheepford. The Forth and Clyde planned to link up at Hamiltonhill but this idea was eventually translated into the development of a basin, to be called Port Dundas, to the east of Hamiltonhill. Acts of Parliament were passed in 1790 to give both companies the powers to effect the link and by June 1791 Port Dundas had been built and joined to Hamiltonhill. Four months later the cut to Blackhill was complete offering a four-foot depth from Port Dundas and the first boat from the east came through. By 1792 the Monkland had made the link to the Calder and, in November 1793, Blackhill locks — four sets of double locks, each lock giving a twelve foot drop — were opened. Three months earlier one of the Stirlings' colliery boats had made the first journey from the east to Blackhill. Work had also started on the

Bowling
Here at the western terminus of the Forth and Clyde, the Outer
Basin and Customs House are seen from the sea-lock. The railway
bridge in the background was not there originally and crosses the
channel which leads to the Inner Basin.

(Top and above). The Maryhill Aqueduct
The aqueduct is viewed from the east at Lock 25, the last of the
sequence of four which starts the Forth and Clyde on its descent
from Glasgow towards Bowling. The unique curvature of the walls
of the four arches is clearly visible. Completed in 1790 it was
described as being in a 'truly romantic' situation over the valley of
the Kelvin!

Crinan in 1793, so it was a busy year in the Scottish canal scene; but three years before the Forth and Clyde had reached Bowling.

In July 1790 a company barge sailed the 12 miles from Glasgow to Bowling down 156ft through the fine set of five locks at Maryhill, each with its own turning basin, passing the Kelvin Dock between locks No 22 and 23, where the first puffers were to be built in Swann's yard in the 1850s, and across the then, and even now, much admired Kelvin Aqueduct. When viewed from above, its horizontal 'arches' which stress the structure to take its water burden can be seen. This principle had first been used earlier on the single arch Luggie Aqueduct, near Kirkintilloch.

Another nine locks between Drumchapel and Yoker dropped the barge down to Clydebank and onto the fairly level stretch to Bowling where, with great ceremony, a barrel of water from the Forth was emptied into the Clyde to symbolise the final joining of Scotland's two great rivers. For the first time it was possible to traverse Scotland from sea to sea. The voyage from Glasgow to London via the canal was now 450 miles compared with the journey of 800 miles round Land's End. It was a matter of great significance

The Union Inn
The Union Inn, pictured recently on a day cold enough to let swans walk on the frozen canal, stands near where the junction of the Forth and Clyde and Union canals once was. Port Downie, on the Union, would have extended eastwards from the front of the inn to the foot of the junction locks.

that, although the size of the locks placed a restriction on the vessels that could make this journey, there was no limit on the headroom. The use of bascule, or lifting bridges at the road crossings, had seen to that.

The Union Canal, or to give it its full title, the Edinburgh and Glasgow Union Canal, had a long gestation period. So long a time that it was only completed a few years before the start of the railway age that would make it obsolescent. By the time that

the Forth and Clyde had opened in 1790, the debate about which line the Union should take ought to have been solved. There was no point in building a channel to run parallel to the Forth and Clyde just to join Leith and Edinburgh directly to Glasgow (coals from Lanarkshire could reach the east coast by coming down the Forth from Grangemouth to Bo'ness or Leith). But routes to the Clyde continued to be argued over and Rennie obliged with surveys in 1797–8 although nothing was resolved. Baird, engineer of the Forth and Clyde, suggested joining Edinburgh to 'his' canal at Falkirk in 1813 but the good burghers of the capital considered this was no more than a ploy to enrich the Forth and Clyde shareholders. Eventually Thomas Telford was asked to adjudicate and he came down on the side of Baird's Falkirk link.

The Camelon Locks
Part of the flight of 11 locks that rose for 110 feet from the Forth and
Clyde to the level of the Union. They were filled in during the
1930s. They accomplished what the Falkirk Wheel does today. These
11 locks were the longest chain in Scotland. (FK)

The Falkirk Tunnel
The tunnel was the major construction feature, dug through the
necessity of having to go round the Callender estate of William
Forbes. The arches of the entrances were of dressed stone.
The rest of the tunnel is rough hewn as the modern lighting in
the interior shows.

Baird's 32 mile route followed the contours of the
countryside west to Broxburn, then north to
Winchburgh and then west again to Linlithgow and
Falkirk and required no locks to be built; except that is
for the 11 needed at the extreme western end for the 115
foot drop to the Forth and Clyde at Lock 16. In
preferring Baird's route Telford had suggested that the
link be made on the Forth and Clyde summit at
Wynford Lock (No. 20) but his idea was not adopted.
It would have 'saved' two or three locks since the
difference in levels at Wynford would have only been
86ft, roughly 30ft less than at Lock 16, but the canal
would have needed to have been extended some five
miles further west (the idea of such a link was revived
from time to time but never acted upon).

Lockless as it was for its journey from Edinburgh

to Falkirk, the canal crossed river valleys and many roads. The main engineering effort became that of building 62 bridges, five minor and three major aqueducts, a tunnel 696 yards long, and the Cobbinshaw Reservoir, at West Calder, to supply water (the Cobbinshaw water supplemented the flow of the River Almond, the main water source). The first sod was cut at the Edinburgh end by the shareholding Mr Downie, in March 1818 at the Edinburgh end and most of the masonry work was soon in hand, including that on the substantial flight of 11 locks at Port Downie. It did not catch the imagination in the manner that the smaller flight of eight on the Caledonian, which had been completed in 1811, did. They became known as 'Neptune's Staircase' but the Port Downie Locks carried no such imaginative title down to posterity.

Indeed it is the aqueducts that are the glory of the Union Canal. But the glory came at a price. Sadly they cost £21,000 over budget; a fact that became apparent in 1820 when more money had to be raised. Apart from the Pontycysyllte Aqueduct, the Avon is the largest in the United Kingdom. Its 810-ft length straddled the valley of the Avon, south-west of Linlithgow, with 12 stone arches 86ft above the river. Like the other two it was designed by Baird with the advice of Telford and used cast iron troughs for the channel. By comparison the Almond Aqueduct (over the valley of the river of that name near Broxburn) and the Slateford Aqueduct (above the Water of Leith in Edinburgh itself), both with eight arches at around 75ft high, are 420 and 500ft long respectively.

There was no technical need to build the tunnel to take the canal through the Callender estate at Falkirk but it was the price that had to be paid to be allowed to cross the ground. Mr Forbes the owner of Callender House wished his eyes to be shielded from the view of commercial traffic on the canal and so the channel was

(Above and opposite). The Avon Aqueduct (Union Canal)
The largest of the Union's three major aqueducts, the Avon is 810 feet long and its 12 arches carry the canal 86ft above the valley of the River Avon. Telford advocated the technique of lining the channel with iron troughs, a technique which had first been used on the Ellesmere Canal, and this was adopted. (RCA)

(Top left). The Almond Aqueduct
This five-arched structure carries the Union some 76ft above the pleasant valley of the River Almond. It is the shortest of the Union's three major aqueducts at 420ft long.

(Above left). The Almond Aqueduct
Two horses wait to have the tow-line re-connected to a full barge which has just crossed the Almond Aqueduct. The picture, *c.*1890, suggests that this barge was operated by a man and woman crew and that such a load required a two-hp traction 'engine'. (ED)

(Top right and above right). The Slateford Aqueduct
The most easterly of the three great Union aqueducts, the Slateford, once in the countryside, is now in the busy west of Edinburgh. Its eight solid masonry arches carry the canal 75ft above the main road from the city to Lanark.

taken underground. The Callender estate has strong Jacobite connections; it was the forfeited ground of the Livingstones, Earls of Linlithgow, when Forbes bought it. Just to the west of the tunnel is the site of Charles Edward Stewart's last victory in 1746. The channel was 13ft wide with a 5ft towpath and the air draft was 12ft over 6½ft of water depth. The tunnel was therefore a not inconsiderable excavation for the navvies with the

The Prince Charlie *Aqueduct*
So called because Charles Edward Stewart is reputed to have sent his demand for the capitulation of Edinburgh from his encampment near here. This structure lies east of the Slateford Aqueduct and carries the Union over the city's busy Slateford Road. (JRH)

simple tools of the day.

In January 1822 a party of inspection sailed from Edinburgh to the tunnel but could sail no further as it was not ready to accept water. Indeed the tunnel was the last section to be completed and held up the finishing of the whole canal. Four months later a boat carried flagstones from Denny to Port Hopetoun, as the Edinburgh terminus was known, to complete the first ever west to east passage. There was no ceremonial carriage of a cask of Clyde water to the capital.

The Union had taken four years to build and was one of the better examples of a Scottish canal being completed expeditiously and well. The main system of Lowland canals was now in place. The Union was commissioned in the same year that the opening of the Caledonian completed the Highland system.

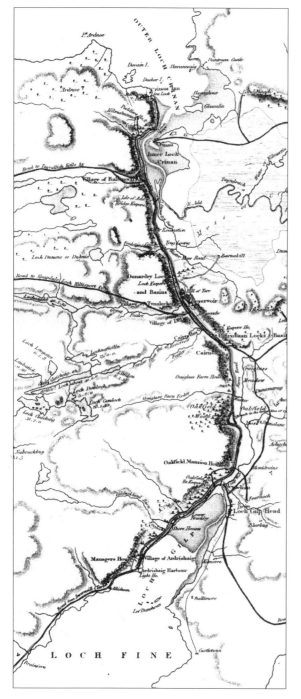

The Highlands

The task before the two Johns, Rennie as Chief Engineer and Paterson as Resident Engineer, in building the Crinan 1793 did not seem all that daunting. It was one of the shortest routes of any that had been considered in Scotland. It was to be a mere nine miles in length, compared with the 38 planned and built for the Forth and Clyde. It was only to require 15 locks to get it up and down the 69ft that the summit reach was above sea level. The Crinan plan was for a water depth of 15ft. Smeaton and Mackell had taken eight years to bring a shallower cut from the Forth to Stockingfield even though they had built more locks. The most recent experience was that of driving the Forth and Clyde the 12 miles from Glasgow to Bowling which took from 1784 to 1790. Again there were more locks and the Kelvin Aqueduct, but even so maybe it was rather optimistic to allow only two years for the completion of the Crinan, all things considered?

Serious work began in 1794 using a steam engine, the purchase of which the managing committee had approved earlier in the year. The running debate about the final depth of the canal was not resolved (at 12ft), until January 1795 but in any case progress was slow

(Left). The Crinan Canal
This map of the Crinan was published in 1848 as part of the annual report made to the House of Commons on the Caledonian Canal. The two canals were by that time under common supervision. It dates from 1823 when it was made under the direction of Thomas Telford who had overseen major repairs to the Crinan in 1816. (NAS)

(Opposite). The Crinan Summit
The summit reach stretches eastwards out of the top of the picture. Locks 9 to 13 at Dunardry occupy centre stage. Adjacent to Lock 9 can be seen the remains of the once-covered dock where the passenger vessel, *Linnet*, could be laid up and repaired. (RCA)

Ardrishaig
This 20th-century view of Ardrishaig from the air clearly shows the harbour, basin and Locks 2, 3 and 4.

The Basin at Crinan
Looking north over the basin at Crinan the final approach round the hill to Lock 14 and the sea lock (No. 15) can be seen. The basin is strangely empty of vessels but *Linnet* is lying at the quay outside Lock 14.

because of the tardiness of subscribers in putting up their cash. In fact the supply of water to the summit from the handful of small lochs and lochans, mostly to the south of the canal line, was to prove inadequate in providing an operating depth of more than eight or nine feet.

By March 1796 it was obvious that the waterway would not be complete by the end of the year and the best that was hoped for was that the cutting from Ardrishaig to the summit level at Cairnbaan would be finished. Apart from the financial constraints it was proving difficult to make the expected progress because of the difficulty of obtaining supplies of stone and skilled labour, particularly masons, in what was then remote Argyll. Indeed labour shortages in general were a constant theme in Paterson's reports to his committee; that and the difficulty of the terrain which was proving to be a mixture of peat bog and rock.

By 1798 Rennie had to tell his shareholders that

because of unanticipated difficulties in cutting through rock the canal width would not be uniform over its length. It would be as much as 28ft narrower at the Crinan end. He also declined to estimate a completion date until he was told how the shortfall in subscriptions was to be corrected. Lack of rock in other areas meant that the foundations of seven of the locks had to be floated on timber piles. He did indicate that at that stage he considered £22,000 was needed to open the canal.

As the workmen struggled with the embankment at Bellanoch throughout 1799 a loan of £25,000 at five

(Opposite). 'Estimate of the Expenses of making a canal from Inverness to Fort William'
This document, from the archive of the Institute of Civil Engineers, is signed by both Jessop and Telford and puts the construction cost at over £474,000 with an additional £13,000 for land purchase. (The final cost was over £900,000.) The major item (36% of the total) is the expense of building locks.

Estimate of the Expence of making a canal
from Inverness to Fort William &c.

	£
Excavation of the Canal 21 Miles 18 Chains	142,970
Extra Cutting and Embanking	20,922
Cutting new courses for Rivers &c	14,061
For Dams & Weirs across the Rivers &c	3,685
Deepening Loch Oich and the Rivers below Bona Ferry	17,830
Building 23 Locks	171,321
Building 24 Bridges	34,766
Culverts and Aqueducts	4,612
Coffer dams, cutting Rock, Steam Engine, Pumping	29,234
Contingencies	35,150
£	474,331

W. Jessop

Purchase of Land	13,000

Thos. Telford

Entrance to the Caledonian Canal at Corpach
With Ben Nevis brooding in the background a twin-funnelled
paddle steamer lies outside the sea lock while SS *Cavalier*, (built
1883), is in the lock itself. *Cavalier* was built specifically for a round-
the-Mull Glasgow to Inverness service. (AB)

per cent per annum was negotiated with the treasury
which held a mortgage on the canal through the
Barons of the Exchequer. Even this proved to be
insufficient as, for example, the wages of the masons
rose by a third as the labour market developed a bias in
favour of the seller. The pressure to start earning tolls
to repay this led to the premature opening of the
waterway in July 1801 before it was possible to achieve
the planned operating depth. Only eight feet of water
was available over the length by the spring of 1802 but

at least income was being earned from vessels of such a
draft as could be accommodated.

Work was to continue on the supply reservoirs
until 1809 to improve the water depth and the Crinan
was declared 'complete'. But meanwhile the canal had
been closed from January 1805 until July 1806 to repair
flood damage which had destroyed the banks near
Oakfield. The lack of income and the repair costs
worsened the financial difficuties for the shareholders.
The 'usual' labour shortages had by then been exacer-
bated by the competition of the building of the
Caledonian, work on which had begun in both the
Inverness and Corpach areas in 1804.

Between the passing of the 1803 and 1804 acts for
the Caledonian, after which construction began, Jessop
had revised Telford's cost estimate of £350,000 to one

of £474,000 substituting masonry for Telford's proposed turf in the construction of the locks. Both estimates excluded the cost of land acquisition (Telford claimed that some land had been offered free). The 1804 act had specified cash being advanced for the work at the rate of £50,000 per annum and that indeed was to be the rate of the flow of cash from the treasury. Though it was not explicitly stated this certainly implied that Telford's original time span of seven years was more likely to be ten. As a result of this cash restriction work was planned annually within the limit of the grant. In some early years work was stopped on the middle section, around Fort Augustus for example, when the annual budget had been spent. The numbers of 'navigators' employed varied if technical problems were encountered or material costs rose, so that the annual budget could be balanced. Usually it was assumed that there would be no work in the winter months (in any case the Highlander traditionally was unused to working in the winter), but even in the remaiming eight months the availablility of labour varied with the demands of spring sowing, peat cutting, fishing in the summer and autumn harvesting.

Telford, with Jessop's approval, appointed two Resident Engineers, Matthew Davidson in the east at Inverness and John Telford (no relation), in the west at Corpach. Their remit was to proceed towards each other to close the 60 mile gap between them. The logic was that machinery and materials could be transported to the interior as the seaward sections were completed.

Of the 60 miles between Inverness and Corpach,

Neptune's Staircase
Such is the scale of the Caledonian that it is best appreciated from the air. The continuous flight of eight locks at Banavie, completed in 1811, is one continuous masonry construction of about 500 yards in length. (RCA)

(Above). The Locks at Fort Augustus
While not as dramatic as the sequence of eight locks at Banavie, the five at Fort Augustus still have their own grandeur. At this point the canal is raised some 40 feet from Loch Ness on its way to the summit at Loch Oich. Completed in 1820 these locks were the last major undertaking completed before the canal's opening in 1822. (RCA)

(Opposite). Muirtown Locks, Inverness
A basin was built at Muirtown, below a series of four locks, to service the town of Inverness. Swing bridges, rather than lifting bridges as on the Forth and Clyde, were used on the Caledonian. One of these is seen beyond the lock. Also visible on the right of the lock gate is the capstan arrangement, with the bars stacked in place, that was used to operate the lock gates. By 1819, before the canal was fully opened, sea-going vessels were plying between Inverness and Fort Augustus. (AB)

only 23 miles were to be canal. The rest, 37 miles and 41 chains, in the terminology of the time (there being 80 chains to the mile), was natural waterway. Loch Ness, 23 miles long, Loch Oich four miles and Lochy ten miles, were to be joined by man-made channels. Eventually 28 locks were required to rise to and descend from the summit reach 106ft above sea level. Twenty-five locks were planned, three more became necessary before the opening in 1822 and an additional regulating lock was added in 1843 to make the 29 we know today. Loch Lochy fed the locks to the west of Laggan and Loch Ness those to the east of Fort Augustus. Loch Oich had to supply only nine from the summit reach and consequently water supply was not a problem. The Caledonian was, however, to be the deepest and widest of all Scotland's canals with its

dimensions approaching double those of the Forth and Clyde.

At the western end the rise from the high water mark at Corpach was a steep 80ft with a dramatic 50ft in the last quarter of a mile to Banavie. The eight locks built here were to become famous as 'Neptune's Staircase'. The fall from the summit at the east end of Loch Oich was more gradual with a 54 foot drop to Loch Ness at Fort Augustus and the final descent to the sea began 30 miles further east at Muirtown. The technical problem of making the summit reach was to exercise Telford greatly but that problem and its solution were a decade in the future.

By 1807 the construction of the Muirtown basin, was well advanced and in the west work had begun on Neptune's Staircase. Consequent on his victories at

Jena and Austerlitz, Napoleon enforced a trade embargo on Britain through his 'Continental System' and as the price of Baltic timber rose the number of men employed on the cuttings was adjusted downwards in 1808–9 to balance the books. Work on the central section was postponed but nevertheless three of the locks at Banavie were completed in 1809.

At about this time work on improving the reservoirs to supply water to the Crinan summit reach had begun and in early 1809 this was completed. These were a series of lochans the principal of which were Loch an Add, Dial Loch, Gleann Loch and Loch na Faolinn and Loch Bharain to the south of the line of the cutting and Loch Bharain to the north. The canal was declared 'finally complete', albeit at a depth of nine feet, in August of that year.

Jessop and Telford reported in May 1810 that some £303,100 would be required to complete the Caledonian, £265,400 having already been spent. Cost estimates were then beginning to exceed the originals by around £100,000 and that still did not include the claims for compensation for disturbance from local landowners or the cost of purchasing their land. A year later the two engineers were proudly referring to the completion of the 'great chain of locks at Banavie'.

The year of 1811 was a pivotal time for the Highland canals. Construction had recommenced on the middle section of the Caledonian and Loch Lochy had been reached from the west by way of four aqueducts. Mechanisation had made its effect at Corpach and was about to at Loch Doughfour in the east where much dredging was required to bring it to the level of Loch Ness. Jessop designed a dredger which cost £6,200 and was powered by a Donkin steam engine. A Boulton and Watt engine was used for pumping, so James had a hand in the building of another Scottish canal. Regrettably the Crinan had to close as the Clachaig reservoir bank collapsed after a gale and the rush of water wrecked the gates at Lock 6.

The Crinan was patched up and re-opened in January 1812, thanks to yet another treasury loan, but real doubts existed about the canal's viability and talk

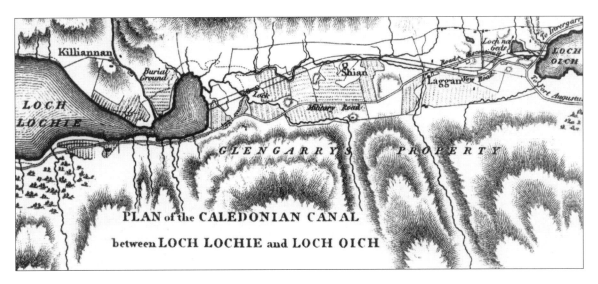

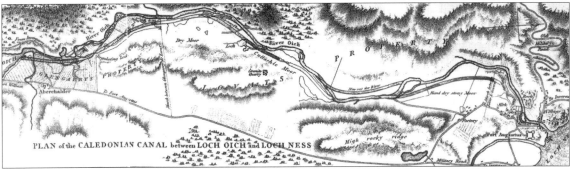

of its abandonment was taken very seriously. Both government and Telford saw the Crinan as a feeder route from Glasgow and the Clyde for the Caledonian. A closed Crinan would, they thought, seriously prejudice the success of the Caledonian. Both canals were in effect being run from the public purse and so the treasury requested that the Commissioners of the Caledonian Canal make Telford available to assess what was needed to make the Crinan reliably operational. Telford's 1813 report was highly critical about the state of the Crinan but expressed, (not surprisingly), support for the concept. Baird of the Forth and Clyde reported separately on the state of the reservoirs the

(Opposite). Clachnaharry Sea Lock
Considerable difficulties were experienced building this entrance to the Caledonian from the Beauly Firth. This was resolved by the local engineer, Matthew Davidson, building 400-yd embankments on the mud of the firth from quarry spoil. This provided the solid foundation to contain the outermost lock seen here. (RCA)

(Above). Progress on Building the Caledonian
Telford was required to make an annual report to the House of Commons on progress towards the completion of the canal. In part, this he did by reproducing engravings of the line of the canal on maps of the area. The Loch Lochy to Loch Oich section shows the line of the Laggan Avenue. It appears not to be shaded but actually is coloured in yellow indicating the work had begun at this part. Brown was used for sections completed and green for parts not then begun. (NAS)

CRINAN CANAL
IN SCOTLAND.

IT is long since the Dangers and Difficulties attending the Navigation round the Peninsula or *Mull of Cantire*, in Argyllshire, suggested the importance of a Canal by which these Perils might be avoided; and in 1792, a subscription was opened for that purpose.

This Canal is now finished, from *Loch Crinan*, on the West, to *Loch Gilp*, on the East, communicating with the Firth of Clyde; and the Masters of the Vessels which have gone through it acknowledge the great facility and safety of their Passage: Advantages that are open to all Vessels navigating the West Coasts of Scotland and England, and East and North Coasts of Ireland, besides affording them immediate Shelter from a stormy Sea, and an Opportunity to be laid dry to repair Damages.

The Length of the Canal, from Sea to Sea, is Nine Miles.
The present Depth of water is Eleven Feet.
The Locks are Ninety-Six Feet long, and Twenty-four Feet wide, *in the Clear.*

'From Sea to Sea'
A handbill, printed in London and widely disseminated, announcing the opening of the Crinan across the peninsula of 'Cantire'. (NAS)

dams of which he suggested needed raising.

While this was going on Telford was also under pressure to explain the cost over-run on the Caledonian as by this time £468,000 had been spent. His detailed rebuttal of the criticisms concluded that a completion date of 1817 was possible if another £235,000 was made available. He was able to point to the completion of a total of 18 locks, including the Muirtown basin and locks and the Clachnaharry sealocks with their substantial and innovative 1,470-ft long embankment, as considerable achievements. This was indeed substantial progress but the central section of the waterway still posed problems.

Having reached Lochs Ness and Lochy and with 'only' the stretch from Fort Augustus to Laggan, roughly 11 miles, to be made, it might be thought that the worst was over. However this final stretch was to

take as long again as the rest of the canal. The cutting at Laggan, the passage through Loch Oich itself and the flight of locks at Fort Augustus all proved to be problematic.

It did not help that MacDonnell of Clanronald and Glengarry, Alexander Ranaldson of that ilk, who regarded Loch Oich as his private fishing water, opposed the building of the canal, mostly by legal means but in one instance by physical force. He was one of a body of objectors, another was Cameron of Locheil, who sought high prices for the sale of their land and for disturbance to their amenitites. One claimed that the construction of the locks as unnatural barriers would put the fish off breeding. Some £50,000 was paid in compensation. Glengarry got £10,000 for his land but failed in his claim of ownership of Loch Oich. Locheil was paid £8,800 for his fisheries. Needless to say the two lairds turned an honest penny felling and selling timber for use in the construction of the canal.

By 1814 the detailed plans for the Fort Augustus locks, built on a problematic gravel base, had been completed. Later Telford was to decide to channel straight down the middle of Loch Oich (rather than dig along the south bank) and to abandon the idea of a towpath for this stretch. It would be 1820 before the staircase of five locks, accommodating a change of level of some 40ft at Fort Augustus, was completed. In that year Henry Bell, of *Comet* fame, began a steamship service, with SS *Stirling Castle*, from Inverness to Fort Augustus. A coach was available at Fort Augustus to travel onward to Fort William for sea connections through the Crinan for Glasgow. It had become possible to pass through to Loch Ness from the east in 1818 and there was a growing sailing vessel trade by 1819. At about this time, at the other end, the Corpach basin had come into use and vessels were discharging and loading there regularly.

But before this there were further problems with the Crinan and the need to finish the Caledonian at all was seriously questioned. After the defeat of Napoleon it was argued that the naval requirement for a canal had vanished and in any case it was costing too much and taking too long to finish. The controversy was to rumble on until the canal actually opened and there was real doubt that parliament would continue with its annual advances (no payment was made in 1820, for example). Pushed on to the defensive, Telford in 1816, had committed himself to completing the canal in 1819, but it would cost another £175,000. This was brave of him as leaks had developed at Torvaine and the two miles of deep cutting at Laggan to connect Lochs Oich and Lochy had yet to be made.

In December 1816 Telford had had to make another inspection of the Crinan as bad leakage due to

poor initial puddling was occuring at Bellanoch. As a result the Crinan was closed for repairs from March until November 1817 and, as reported earlier, the commissioners of the Caledonian were required to assume responsibility for the management of both canals. Henceforth the Crinan profits, if any, were for the account of the Barons of the Exchequer. The improvements went further than stopping the leaks and included repairs on all the locks and deepening the Ardrishaig entrance.

It had been planned originally that the eight locks at Banavie would allow the level of Loch Lochy to be raised by 12ft and that this would save on lock building at the Laggan end where there was known to be rock. Instead a lock was made at Gairlochy in the hope that time and money would be saved at Laggan. The water level was thus raised but the result was a weak point in water volume control and a second Gairlochy lock was constructed in 1843, after a near disastrous flood nine years earlier, put the area west of the first lock at risk. The ground at Laggan proved to be so intractable that the Laggan avenue was cut to a bottom width of only 30ft, compared with the 50ft of the rest of the waterway, but only two lock gates were needed to change down to the raised Loch Lochy. The Loch Oich channel was then dredged and the Laggan staircase was finished in 1822.

The formal opening took place in october 1822 when two ships set off from the Muirtown basin to the sound of cannon fire. The night was spent at Fort Augustus and joined by *Comet II* the convoy proceeded to Fort William where there was another salute, bonfires were lit and free whisky consumed by the populace. A dinner was given by one of the commissioners to the travellers. Thomas Telford was not present. Glengarry was.

CHAPTER FIVE

PASSENGER SERVICES

Passengers and freight. People and coal. They run like the waft and the weave of the cloth of the canals' story. They were the commercial basis of their existence. From the moment each canal opened for trade it carried coal and people preferred the smoothness of the waterways to the rough and tumble of the roads.

In the year of 1836, just before they went into battle with the railways, the Lowland canals carried 376,264 passengers as shown:

Forth and Clyde	197,710
Monkland	33,400
Union	127,292
Crinan	17,862
	376,264

In addition a total of 423,000 people used the 'Paisley', the never-completed Glasgow to Ardrossan canal, which served Glasgow, Paisley and Johnstone from 1811 to 1881. This means that over three quarters of a million passengers, or the equivalent of every man, woman and child in the counties of Edinburgh, Lanark and Renfrew, used these canals. At the time the population of Scotland was just under two and a half million. The canals certainly kept the Scots on the move.

The passenger trade on the Forth and Clyde lasted nearly 40 years until the railway competition forced all of the Lowland canals out of the business. The Forth and Clyde carried passengers as well as freight in their

'tracking boats' when they introduced them in 1783. These were smaller than the canal scows being 50ft overall with a beam of 14½ft and were not at all comfortable for the travellers. In 1801 a total of 1,650 persons was recorded as having been carried on the all-purpose tracking boats and this must have continued to rise because, after some experimentation, the decision was made to make specific provision for travellers. A regular timetabled service was provided in craft designed for passengers only and solely with comfort in mind.

The service began in 1809 when a single vessel, a 'passage boat', made one trip in either direction from Glasgow (Port Dundas) to Lock 16 to link with the Edinburgh stagecoach. The number of customers that year rose to 15,877. The income was £1,318 and a contribution to the overall profitability of the canal of £455 was produced. The tracking boats, the purpose of which was really to carry general goods, only had a small passenger space but the passage boats had a cabin, steerage and a dining-room. Meals and refreshments (wine and strong ale) were served during the journey and newspapers and magazines were available. And there were water closets. The journey from Port Dundas to Lock 16 was accomplished in five hours at a steady speed of nearly 5 mph by means of relays of teams of horses.

As a result another boat was introduced in 1811 and the number of journeys increased to four. The income and the passenger numbers rose to £3,046 and

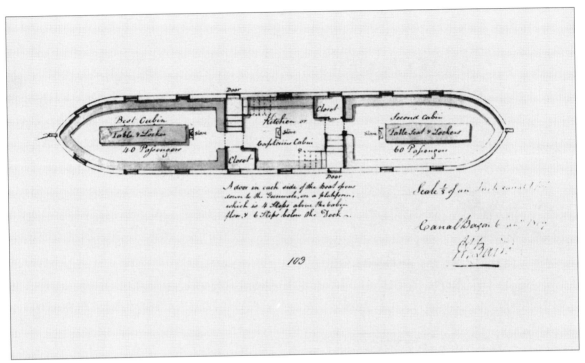

The First 'Passage' Boat
In 1809 Hugh Baird, Engineer to the Forth and Clyde, put his signature to this design for a passenger boat. Only 40 first-class passengers were carried in the 'Best' cabin while 60 were accommodated in much the same space in the second cabin. It is not known whether these lesser mortals were allowed to use the same closet as the more fortunate 40. (ED)

36,701 respectively. An alternative route to the capital was offered in 1816 with a coach from Lock 16 to Grangemouth and a steamer to Leith organised by the London, Leith, Edinburgh and Glasgow Shipping Company (this arrangement was discontinued after the opening of the Union Canal in 1822 as it was assumed the journey would be completed by canal). By 1819 there were four boats, three making a return trip and the other making a single transit from Lock 16 to Grangemouth. The numbers carried rose steadily, exceeding 117,000 in 1833 (see Appendix IX for details of the numbers of passengers on the Forth and Clyde over the life of the service).

The Monkland had started a Sheepford to Glasgow passenger service in 1813 and soon had three passage boats operating on the two-and-a-half-hour-journey and charged one shilling and six pence (£0.075) for a single journey.

Night boats, introduced in 1824 by the London, Leith, Edinburgh and Glasgow Shipping Co., for the Port Downie to Port Dundas trip, helped swell the numbers. For example, of the 117,086 passengers who used the canal in 1833, a total of 25,111 travelled at night. To save the time of locking down from the Union to the Forth and Clyde these passengers walked down the hill to Lock 16. The income from the overnight business was divided equally between the Union and the London, Leith, Edinburgh and Glasgow Shipping Co. At this time coaches were used to link Wyndford

CANAL PASSENGER BOAT.

(Left). A Swift Passage
A handbill from 1830 giving details of the Glasgow to Edinburgh service on the Forth and Clyde and Union, which was soon to be expanded by the introduction of a second vessel.

(Above and opposite). A Swift Passenger Boat
An example of the 'swifts' which were designed for speed. It was claimed that they could reach speeds of seven miles per hour, about double that normally achievable by horse 'tracking'. Pairs of horses, driven on by a liveried postillion, were used and changed at regular intervals of about eight miles. Similar boats were also used on the Paisley and Monkland canals. *Vulcan*, built on the Monkland in 1819, was Scotland's first all-iron ship. She could carry 200 passengers on the two-and-a-half hour trip from Coatbridge to Glasgow. A replica has been built and may be seen at the Summerlee Heritage Park at Coatbridge. (ED and NL)

lock on the Forth and Clyde to Stirling, Alloa and Kincardine and these fares supplemented the passenger trade income.

By this time of course the steam locomotive had made its entrance to the Scottish transport scene and the Committee of Management were beginning to wonder how to combat the speed advantage offered by the railways. It was over this period, from about 1828 to 1832 that the Forth and Clyde experimented with steamships like *Cyclops*, *Manchester* and *Lord Dundas* and the catamaran-type *Swift* (see Chapter 8). The *Swift* had made the Port Dundas to Port Hopeton round trip in an average of just under seven hours or a

speed of around eight mph. Committee-man, Thomas Graham, Esq., was much exercised by this problem of passage boat speed. He conducted a detailed exercise to study the causes of delay, and while it yielded not much at all by way of speed improvements, it has left us with an interesting account of a horse-drawn transit of the canal from Port Dundas to Kirkintilloch one day in 1833. A summary is given below.

The passage boat had to proceed northwest along the Glasgow Branch to Stockingfield where it turned east onto the main canal line. His journey took one hour, nineteen minutes and fifteen seconds and he suffered, so

he said, 'intolerable delays' which amounted to five minutes and twenty seconds! The average speed was about six mph and the increase in speed by saving the five minutes would hardly have brought average up to that of even the earliest railway.

Between Port Dundas and the first bascule bridge they had to slow down to negotiate a wood raft unloading on the trackside of the canal and to then pass a sloop loaded with dung. The tow rope had to be passed over the stationary raft or gathered inboard, with a consequent loss of speed until the horse was re-harnessed. This practice was necessary at all the bascule bridges. While the horse was walked round the end of the bridge the tow rope had to be taken inboard and then thrown ashore again once the obstacle had been rounded. While it is not recorded if the sloop was under sail it would appear that the passage boat took the edge off its speed as a precaution while passing her.

A coal boat discharging on the trackside and a laden sloop travelling west again caused a loss of time before the second bridge. All went well until they had to stop at Stockingfield to take on five passengers (one man, three women and a child) and at the next bridge six passengers were set down. Then they moved to the other bank to allow the passage of another sailing vessel. Time was made up (apart from slowing for the rope handling) at

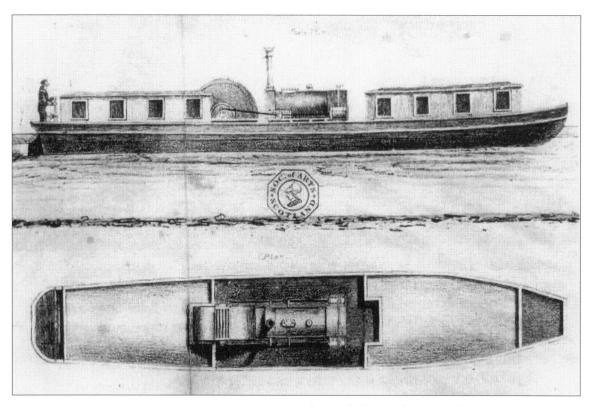

Lord Dundas
In the 1830s it was believed that steam-propelled passenger boats would meet the anticipated competition from the railways. The *Lord Dundas*, which was designed to maintain a speed of six miles per hour, was introduced to the Forth and Clyde. She was of a twin-hulled, catamaran-type construction with a central paddle wheel. But for the aft cabin she is reminiscent of her earlier relative *Charlotte Dundas*.

the next bridge. At the next two bridges, however, picking up two passengers and then disembarking 'two ladies and one child', getting round another scow loading on the trackside and passing another deep-drafted sloop, caused further delay. Fortunately a full eight minutes of uninterrupted progress were then made to Kirkintilloch!

Graham's report gives a picture of a busy canal in the pre-steam age. Clearly access to the canal banks at any point that was convenient for the loading and discharging passengers and materials was taken for granted by those who paid their tolls.

Of course the six mph made on this trip was typical for the passage boats of the time and nearly double that achieved by loaded scows. But then the passage boats were smaller and lighter and served with relays of pairs of horses operating at a trot. Graham does not record if his trip was made in one of the new, lighter, high-speed passage boats, introduced in 1833, based on the design that was operating so successfully on the Paisley Canal, but the implication is that it was one of these.

The Union's passenger traffic was greatly influenced by its link with the Forth and Clyde but within the canal there was local traffic centred on Linlithgow and Falkirk. From the very first a daily passage boat operated for the Edinburgh to Glasgow travelling public. The through-fare of seven shillings (£0.35) was shared, 54 per cent going to the Union as a greater mileage was travelled on the Union than on the Forth and Clyde. Competition from the Edinburgh to Glasgow stagecoach companies soon saw the fares reduced. The speed achieved by coach was much the same as that on the canal, although the canal journey was more comfortable; but it seemed to be a price-sensitive market. The Union's passenger service did not ever enjoy an untroubled existence and was not always profitable even before the opening of the Slammanan and the Edinburgh and Glasgow Railways (see Chapter 9). Nevertheless by 1835 there were six passage boats running to Glasgow with more than 124,000 people using the service annually.

In 1840 the opening of the Slammanan Railway as far as Causewayend, just west of the Avon Aqueduct, was welcomed by the Union management in the hope that this new railway and canal route would become the most popular method of travel with the Glasgow and Edinburgh public. However stagecoaches were soon running from Causewayend and the anticipated benefits did not materialise. But the real problem for the Union and Forth and Clyde passenger traffic came with the opening of the Edinburgh and Glasgow Railway in February 1842. This railway ran on the south

side of the Forth and Clyde and parallel to it as far as Falkirk. There it crossed over the Union and ran on its north side as far as Winchburgh and took a more direct line to Edinburgh rather than follow the meandering path of the canal through Ratho. It could not have been in more direct competition with the two canals. Suddenly the journey time from Haymarket in Edinburgh to Queen Street in Glasgow was cut to two hours.

Almost overnight the Glasgow and Edinburgh stagecoach companies went out of business. The canal companies responded to the railway threat by cutting the fares. There was a successful precedent for this. In 1831 the Monkland had reduced its rates from £0.075 to £0.033 when the Garnkirk and Glasgow Railway opened. This matched the second-class fare on the railway and the Monkland managed thereby to defend and even improve the level of its business (this railway not only allowed people to get to Glasgow, but also fed goods from Lanarkshire to the east via the Forth and Clyde). Some 25,100 people had travelled from the Coatbridge area on the Monkland in 1831; by 1836 this number had increased to 33,400 and to 38,000 in 1843 and a modest profit was being made from the traffic (but the Garnkirk and Glasgow carried 119,000 in 1834). Optimistically the managements of the Forth and Clyde and the Union thought that they could see off the railway competition and were convinced that low passenger rates would be ruinous to the Edinburgh and Glasgow Railway which at that time had no great goods traffic.

Passenger fares were cut in 1842 and again 1844 and the following table and Appendices IX and X demonstrate that considerable business was attracted to the Forth and Clyde. Unfortunately it was loss-making business. Before this, as Appendix X shows, it had yielded healthy surpluses (see Table 1).

TABLE 1. *Forth and Clyde, Passenger Income, 1840–47*

Year	Average Fare	Number of Passengers	Income	Operating Costs	Profit/(Loss)*
1840	£0.071	192,120	£13,728	£8,646	£5,082
1841	£0.067	127,681	£ 8,604	£5,799	£2,805
1842	£0.051	154,213	£ 7,863	£6,816	£1,047
1843	£0.050	113,720	£ 5,636	£4,320	£1,316
1844	£0.022	200,694	£ 4,498	£3,771	£ 727
1845	£0.023	226,269	£ 5,135	£4,838	£ 297
1846	£0.028	163,928	£ 4,540	£5,295	£ (755)
1847	£0.023	137,570	£ 3,174	£5,321	£(2,147)

* Stated simply as income less expenditure

No doubt the opening of the Slamannan Railway partly explains the drop in passenger numbers in 1841 and the fare cut in 1842 demonstrates that many were not prepared to pay the premium for rail's speed (third class by rail was £0.2 and steerage by canal was £0.1). The Edinburgh and Glasgow retaliated and the canal rates were halved with a dramatic increase in traffic in 1844. By this time the wisdom or otherwise of the price war was being thrust on the canals' managements. Numbers of passengers were broadly similar for 1840 and 1844 but a drop in profit from £5,000 to £700 was clearly unacceptable. To put this in context, with the average surplus on the Forth and Clyde over the 1840/7 period being £33,400, a £7,000 drop represented a difference of 20 per cent in the money available to pay dividends to shareholders.

Similar trends were being observed on the Union and for the same reasons – fare-cutting leading to increased passenger numbers and less profit. Without being specific it was being reported at their 1844 annual general meeting that passenger numbers were up on the previous year's total and in 1845 'passenger numbers were nearly treble those of 1843'. This was quite remarkable considering that on the Forth and Clyde, the performance of which was bound to influence that of the Union, numbers had only doubled. However by 1846 the Union was beginning to negotiate an amalgamation with the Edinburgh and Glasgow Railway.

The overnight sleeper service was withdrawn in 1846 as people just simply were not using it. No-one wanted to sit up overnight when the alternative was a two-hour journey during the day. Indeed as the prices between the two modes equalised the seven-hour canal trip also became less attractive even during the day and numbers of passengers on the waterways fell year by year (in January 1847 the Union took only £1.45 in fares for the month!). Losses on the service could not be sustained and the passage boats were withdrawn from both the Forth and Clyde and the Union at the end of

March 1848. The Forth and Clyde had run up a loss of £1,000 in the first quarter of 1848. The final straw was probably the opening in 1848, by the Caledonian Railway, of a line from Glasgow to Edinburgh via Carstairs. The Caledonian, understandably, could not stand still in the face of the Edinburgh and Glasgow's initiative.

The Garnkirk and Glasgow Railway had opened a station at Coatbridge in 1842 and ran five trains per day to Glasgow. By 1845 the numbers using the Monkland passage boats had fallen back to the 1831 level of 25,000 and losses were being incurred there as well and it too pulled out of the trade. Within a few years the Edinburgh and Glasgow Railway was carrying 200,000 passengers per annum and turning over £50,000 from doing so. It had clearly won the war.

To all intents the managements of the Lowland canals were out of the passage-boat business by 1848. However both on the Monkland and the Forth and Clyde permission was given for private individuals to take the financial responsibility for operating a single passage boat to provide a service to canal-side communities. The want of a canal service would have been badly felt on the banks of the Forth and Clyde where there was no rail service along a line between Glasgow and Falkirk until the Kelvin Valley Railway opened in 1879. Limited services between Sheepford and Blackhill on the Monkland and Port Dundas and Lock 16 on the Forth and Clyde were established.

In 1860 the Taylor family, which had been involved in the passenger trade since 1848, substituted the steamer *Rockvilla Castle*, for a traditional passage boat on a run from Port Dundas to Castlecary. In outward appearance she was very much a passage boat with a lum and she could carry 86 people. With the railways well established there must have been an element of travelling for pleasure rather than necessity

Fairy Queen
A crowded *Fairy Queen*, the first of that name, built in 1893, is ready for a cruise on the Forth and Clyde. The setting is a few miles in fact, but many in appearance, from the industrial Glasgow that her passengers are seeking to escape. (JRH)

in using this relative slow route. However the service ran all year round and few would have spent their leisure time on the canal in a Scottish winter. The *Rockvilla Castle* was withdrawn in 1881 when the Taylors retired from the trade.

Twelve years elapsed before another passenger service commenced. This time it was the Aitken family, one of whom had served with the Taylors, who began a service. Their series of 'Queens' (see Appendix XI), became a Forth and Clyde institution. They ran summer-only-purely-for-pleasure excursions. They kept the canal in the public mind and eye if they were

never particularly significant to its commercial well-being. These excursions, regarded with great affection by the west of Scotland public, ran from 1893 until 1939 although the period of greatest popularity was the decade before World War I when they had three steamers operating.

On the western and northern edges of central Scotland the Crinan and the Caledonian had many years yet to run without opposition from the railroads. Indeed in the year that the Forth and Clyde was closing down its passenger trade the Crinan was approaching its peak in number of passengers carried.

Given the technical problems that the Crinan operators had in the early years the 'opening' date of 1801 is somewhat misleading. There really wasn't enough water until about 1809 and then in 1811 it closed for a year for repairs. The Caledonian Canal commis-

sioners were asked by the Crinan's creditors to supervise rectifying the more serious deficiencies. This was done between 1816 and 1818 and it was only after this time that a pattern of trading and use of the canal emerged. The most significant, as far as the travelling public was concerned, was the service between Glasgow and Fort William that Henry Bell operated in the famous *Comet* in 1819. This was a valued aid to travel to the north in its own right and of course anticipated the opening of the Caledonian Canal which was within three years of completion at this time. Bell was given the concession of free passage on the waterway to encourage the trade. The *Comet* established a pattern and unlike the Lowland canals, the Crinan was not directly involved in operating vessels for its passenger traffic. The profitability of the steamers was therefore only of indirect interest to the Crinan management but

their presence contributed significantly to the Crinan traffic.

One year later, the year in which *Comet* was wrecked at the Dorus Mor off the mouth of Loch Craignish, it was recorded that 2,400 passengers had traversed the Crinan. By the time the Caledonian opened in 1822 two steam ships, *Comet II* and *Highlander* were running twice a week from Fort William to Glasgow. As a result in 1823 the number of those in transit had risen to nearly 7,000. Two years later there were four vessels plying twice per week and advertising a three-day passage from Glasgow to Inverness using both canals. In the years from 1830 to 1839 passenger income was 26 per cent of the Crinan's total income and 19,700 travelled in 1839.

A list of ships that passed the Caledonian at Corpach from March to October 1823 survives. It

(Above). 'A Pleasant Sunday Afternoon'
'PSA' Clubs served the social function of organising Sunday afternoon activities, like trips on the canal. Here a group of about 100 are about to embark on a trip on the Monkland. The vessel is an early version of a steam-driven mineral scow of the type illustrated in Chapter 8. Scant regard is paid to safety considerations with the barge very crowded and it being acceptable to stand on the rudder. (NL)

(Opposite). The Sunday School Trip (Union Canal)
Passengers sometimes travelled on the canals purely as a leisure activity. A group of young people in their finest attire await, circa 1912, the arrival of the tracking horses before setting out on an excursion on the Union Canal. (FK)

records that on the 16th of June, the *Douglas* of Aberdeen, 'Wm Kidd, Master, passed from the East to the West Sea with Emigrants to No. America'. William Pitt may have wished that the construction of the canal would staunch the flow of emigration but here, within months of its opening, it was speeding folk from the north-east to a new life overseas.

It is of note that while passenger steam boats in their various manifestations on the Lowland canals did not effectively replace the horse-drawn vessels, passenger traffic on the Highland canals was initiated by steam vessels. But the old problem with 'Locks' Law', the limitation placed on the operation of any canal by the size of its locks, started to come into play on the Crinan. Vessels of more than 88ft in length could not cross from Ardrishaig to Crinan and when the same relatively small ships had to make the passage to Oban or Fort William in all seasons and weathers they were found to be more than a little uncomfortable. Uncomfortable, that is, relative to the bigger and more powerful steamships that were being developed on the Clyde for service in the firth and which could tackle the passage round the Mull of Kintyre. By the mid-1830s there had been a great increase in the number of steamships built on the Clyde and most of the remote parts of the estuary were being serviced by vessels of over 100ft in length. They could travel to Ardrishaig from Glasgow or from Crinan to Oban faster and more comfortably than could the steamers which could pass the Crinan locks. However no-one really wanted to sail the extra miles entailed in avoiding the canal altogether and so the Crinan became a trans-shipment waterway.

Passengers were deposited at Ardrishaig, taken through the canal by horse-drawn passage boats that would have been familiar to a user of the Forth and Clyde, and embarked on a steamer to Oban or Fort William at Crinan. So while the Lowland canals were

desperately trying to introduce steam the Crinan was reverting to horse-power in the original sense. The nine miles took four hours by passage boat which was only half-an-hour longer than the same trip by steamer. The transhipment was introduced in 1839 and by 1840 the system was upgraded to use the swifts familiar elsewhere. They were drawn by two horses, controlled by a postilion and had a top speed between locks of around eight mph.

The hey-day of the Victorians love affair with the Scottish Highlands was on hand and the canal route, known as the Royal Route after Queen Victoria and Prince Albert used the canal in 1847, grew in popularity for leisure and serious travellers alike. The traffic was disrupted when the Caledonian was closed for the best part of three years from 1844 to 1847 but in 1857 over 44,500 passengers were noted as 'crossing the quay at Ardrishaig', mostly in the summer months.

It was only in 1860 that the Caledonian changed its tariff and began a per-capita charge for passengers rather than a toll on the tonnage of the passenger vessels, so we lack records of the numbers using the canal to get to Inverness. But it is a reasonable assumption, given the way that the two canals fed off each other, that as numbers using the Crinan grew, so did those using the Caledonian. In addition, of course, there was internal passenger traffic on the latter.

In the decade from the mid-1850s to mid-1860s around 25 to 30 per cent of the Crinan's income was derived from passenger services. When separate charging for passengers began on this canal, as well as on the Caledonian, the figures recorded for 1862 and 1863 showed totals of 45,059 and 37,356 respectively. However the former is split into 26,236 on the 'quay at Ardrishaig' (presumably landed from the steamers from Glasgow) 13,075 on 'tracking boats', and 5,648 on 'luggage boats' suggesting that only 18,723 of the total

Linnet
The twin-screw steamer *Linnet*, seen here at Cairnbaan, was introduced in 1866 by Hutcheson to replace the track boats which hitherto had taken passengers through the Crinan. She traversed the canal twice per day from May to September and continued in this service until its cessation in 1929. During the high season e.g. the Glasgow Fair, the canal's icebreaker, *Conway*, was often chartered to carry additional passengers. (AB)

actually sailed through the canal.

Eventually the Crinan transit went over to steam when in 1866 the Hutcheson-Macbrayne partnership introduced the famous *Linnet* on the Ardrishaig to Crinan route. Hutcheson had become involved in the Glasgow to Ardrishaig route in the 1850s and used Crinan as the embarkation point for Oban and onward travel to Tobermory and Fort William (he also ran a service from Banavie to Inverness on the Caledonian). Even *Linnet* was to prove to be a bottleneck in the longer term. Clearly not able to carry as many people as the steamers that were feeding passengers into Ardrishaig, (in 1878, *Columba*, capable of carrying 2,000, came on to the route), various ploys, such as hiring the canal's icebreaker, were used to supplement her in the high season. Nevertheless, since it was possible to walk to Crinan as quickly as it took *Linnet*

(Above). Linnet at Crinan Basin
Linnet is at Crinan basin and passengers are transferring to SS *Chevalier* for the passage to Oban. Some would travel onward to Fort William and through the Caledonian, probably on the paddler *Gondolier*, to Inverness. The North British Railway ran sailings from Helensburgh, where they had a rail station, to Ardrishaig to meet the *Linnet*. In 1929 the Crinan to Oban steamer was withdrawn and a bus service was introduced between Ardrishaig and Oban. (GLA)

(Opposite). Gondolier
Built on the Clyde in 1866, and introduced to the Caledonian in that year, the iron-hulled paddler, *Gondolier*, became a popular cruise ship for those wishing to appreciate Highland scenery although the intention of putting her on the Banavie to Inverness run had been to complete the Glasgow to Inverness link. Queen Victoria sailed on her from Banavie to the head of Loch Ness on her way to Balmoral in 1873. Sadly *Gondolier* ended her days as a block ship at Scapa Flow in 1939. (NMM)

to get through the locks, many people did just that.

The railways reached Oban in 1880 and Fort William by 1894 but from the 1860s onward it was possible for the determined traveller to make his or her way north from Glasgow to Inverness by rail. The routes might be circuitous but they were there. In 1863 the Inverness to Aberdeen line added a spur to Dunkeld and Perth which was already connected to Glasgow. All of this must have been more tempting than a three-day and three-boat journey via the Crinan and the Caledonian. There was little the canal authorities could do to combat this. Lowering fares was economically not desirable and in any case would probably not have made an impact on the choice of travel mode. In this watershed year, 15,500 passengers used the Caledonian and as we have already noted perhaps 18,823 made a transit of the Crinan.

In 1873 Hutcheson's brought the *Gondolier* and *Glengarry* to the Caledonian and they sailed daily, one in each direction, from Inverness to Banavie. There was also an internal Fort Augustus to Inverness sailing which stopped at various points on Loch Ness. A new form of the Royal Route became possible after 1894. Passengers could sail from Inverness to Banavie, take the train from Banavie to Fort William and then embark on a steamer for Oban. There was, of course, a connecting Oban to Crinan service.

Passenger numbers through the Crinan inevitably declined in summer as well as winter once the railways offered an alternative. By the 1880s there was only one through service from Glasgow to Inverness operating each week. In the 1890s there was no through service and *Linnet* was operating only between May and September, the months during which the Glasgow to

Ardrishaig and Crinan to Oban/Fort William steamers ran. However, more and more 'passengers' were using their own craft – their yachts, with the steam variety often outnumbering the purely sailing type. There was a considerable increase in the number of yachts registered in the UK between 1880 and the outbreak of World War I and this period is usually considered to be the high-water mark of Victorian yachting on the Clyde when racing became the pastime of rich industrialists and the aristocracy. Yachts could account for up to 25 per cent of the number of transits between May and September and 15 per cent of the annual number.

The *Linnet* service ran until 1915 but was withdrawn thereafter for the duration of hostilities. Apparently yachting continued on an only slightly diminished scale throughout the war although it was restricted in the Clyde. The numbers classified as

yachts fell by about 100 (over 300 per annum being the typical pre-war number), but it is possible that a number of these transits were for serious purposes as many of the larger steam yachts were commandeered by the Admiralty.

By 1920 the *Linnet* was operating only during July, August and part of September, contributing 135 passages to an annual total of 1655 (Appendix XV shows a peak in the number of passages of the Crinan around 1880 with a gradual decline up to and beyond World War I). The MacBrayne services northwards were similarly restricted to the holiday months. As a consequence, by the 1920s the contribution of passenger income to the total had fallen to less than 10

per cent compared with the peak of nearly 30 per cent some 60 years earlier. In 1929 the end finally came. MacBrayne introduced an Ardrishaig to Oban bus service for a trade that had become entirely tourist. The pleasures of three hours on the canal and the views from a cruise through the Dorus Mor or Corryvreckan and through the Firth of Lorne to Mull were forgone for those of the Pass of Melfort and more distant prospects of the sea. It was without doubt more comfortable and a great deal shorter.

In the same year the remaining passenger service, from Fort Augustus to Inverness, was withdrawn from the Caledonian (after 1919 the Inverness to Banavie service had been reduced to one vessel in the summer).

GIPSY QUEEN AT SHIRVA.

But an excursion trade on the canal itself survived for the interval up to 1939 when war intervened. In that decade tourists numbered never less than 9,300 and were as many as 14,800. After a gap this trade revived and grew back again to pre-war numbers, cynics attributing this to the publicity given to the myth of the Loch Ness monster.

While the Monkland and the Forth and Clyde were able to make up for their lost passengers in the 1850s onwards, due to increased industrial cargoes, no such compensation came the way of the Highland canals in the early 20th century.

Their burden on the public purse increased accordingly.

(Opposite). Scot II
Scot II was originally built in 1931 as a tug cum ice-breaker for taking sailing vessels through the Caledonian. She was converted in 1960 to take 65 passengers on summer trips on Loch Ness. (NMM)

(Above). Gipsy Queen
The *Gipsy Queen* of 1905 was perhaps the most famous of the Aitken fleet of pleasure cruisers. 'Shirva' is Shirva Farm, east of Kirkintilloch, at the village of Twechar. Although the Forth and Clyde was closed to through traffic during World War I she operated her cruises throughout hostilities making special trips for members of the armed forces. She was withdrawn in 1939 at the onset of World War II and the company was wound up. (ED)

CHAPTER SIX

SERVICING INDUSTRY

After Watt's transformation of the steam engine the demand for coal from industry became enormous. Luckily, it was there in abundance in Ayrshire, Fife and Lanarkshire. And in Lanarkshire, in particular, it was there with other minerals. The canals were built to move it to the centres of population, where, in addition to industrial requirements, demand for domestic coal also grew. Manufacturing centres were set up on the banks of the canal to have access to the energy supply and the working population came to live on the banks of the canals to be near the manufacturing centres. The Forth and Clyde, and the Union joined Scotland's two main centres of population and the Monkland ran through rich mineral deposits thus connecting them to Glasgow.

Industry needed not only raw materials to make finished goods but also water for their processes and steam engines. For the period that the minutes of the various management committees of the Forth and Clyde and Monkland exist, ie up to the 1860s, they tell a constant story of applications being made by old and new businesses for permission to take water from the canals. This was invariably granted, with conditions, of course. It sometimes led to difficulties. On one occasion when the Monkland was in dispute with the Dundyvan Iron Works, over the latter using too much water to the detriment of other canal users, the Dundyvan branch canal was dammed off from the main waterway on the orders of the canal management. When the branch dried up the canal

committee felt that it had made its point. In 1884 the Monkland indicated to the Summerlee Iron Co that if it did not restart sending its goods by canal rather than by rail, it would consider cutting off its water supply. Hardly a subtle approach but it worked.

The fact that 40 years separated these two disputes may be taken as evidence that few disagreements reached that level of animosity and normally canal and industry co-existed to their mutual benefit. At the peak of canal activity as many as 50 companies were drawing water from the Monkland and the Forth and Clyde to operate their processes. Later on the canals even sold water to their deadly rivals, the railways. Latterly, in the 1950s, when all the commodity transport trade had deserted the canals, it was as suppliers of industrial water that arguments were advanced for keeping the canals open. The three Lowland canals eventually had a combined reservoir capacity of 2,120 million gallons of water – a vital industrial resource.

The range of activity along the line of the Forth and Clyde was extensive. Numbered among the water users were ironworks (using the blackband ironstone from around Coatbridge), distilleries (at Falkirk, Banknock, Port Dundas and Bowling), dyeworks, foundries (at Carron and Falkirk), gas-works, chemical plants, glass makers and seaweed processors. There were large stone quarries at Kilsyth and Possil and a limestone quarry at Wyndford. All used the canal for transport. Wood and timber processors of all types

The Maryhill 'Coat of Arms'
It could be argued that Maryhill would not have existed but for the
Forth and Clyde Canal. Industry was certainly attracted to this
spot. Alexander Thomson, who designed the coat of arms in 1885,
had no doubt about what made Maryhill the place it was. His
design represents the *Charlotte Dundas* crossing over the Kelvin
Aqueduct and the local timber, iron-making and engineering
industries. His design was not registered with the Court of the
Lord Lyon and therefore was not officially recognised.
(Court of the Lord Lyon)

flourished and their raw materials came in from the
Baltic via Grangemouth or North America via
Bowling. Timber basins were built, at various times,
within or adjacent to the canal, at Firhill and
Grangemouth.

But above all it was coal that was moved in
quantity. In 1800 there were 8,000 coal miners in
Scotland and 60 years later, in the decade of the canals'
greatest prosperity, there were 47,000 miners working
in over 400 pits. In 1800 the Forth and Clyde transported 24,400 tons of coal. In 1870 the coal tonnage
through the canal was nearly half of a million. In 1945
it was 8,000 tons (the rise and fall of the canal in three
simple statistics!).

But the users did not just want coal at any price
they wanted cheap coal and throughout there seem to
have been pressures, doubtless from the many coal
masters who were shareholders, to keep the cost of coal
transport low. This certainly was a trend in the
Lowland canals as the following, drawn from the

records of the Forth and Clyde illustrates (see Table 2).

Despite coal accounting for between 25 per cent
and 39 per cent of the tonnage carried it only brought
in around 8 per cent to 15 per cent of total income.
Grain, a valuable cargo, on the other hand could
produce a third of the total tolls earned on less than a
tenth of the weight carried. Coal and grain have a very
similar stowage factor ie the cubic capacity of the hold
of vessel will take much the same tonnage of both, yet,
as shown above, grain earned ten times as much per
ton as coal. The profitability of the canal was therefore
more dependent on what it carried rather than the
number of vessels that passed along it. Yet, the number
of ships passing through determined the canal's water
usage and, for example, wear and tear on the lock gates.

The increase in the grain trade is an indication of
the growing population in Central Scotland. Table 2
also illustrates the development of iron as a
commodity of consequence. Between the 1820s and the
1840s iron making developed as an important industry

TABLE 2. *Forth and Clyde, tonnages/income, 1805–40*

Year	Total		Coal		Grain		Iron	
	Tons	*Tolls*	*Tons*	*Tolls*	*Tons*	*Tolls*	*Tons*	*Tolls*
1805	165.1K	£22.6K	64.5K	£3.4K	9.7K	£4.4K	4.2K	£0.7K
			(39%)	(15%)	(6%)	(19%)	(3%)	(3%)
1825	287.9K	£45.9K	72.4K	£3.8K	10.9K	£16.1K	5.6K	£1.6K
			(25%)	(8 %)	(4%)	(35%)	(2%)	(3%)
1840	707.4k	£68.7k	217.3k	£6.8K	66.2K	£23.4K	127.7K	£14.1K
			(31%)	(10%)	(9%)	(34%)	(18%)	(20%)

in north Lanarkshire, particularly after Neilson's 'hot-blast' method of iron production was adopted. There is a broad correspondence between income and tonnage for this material. Even though the canal continued to carry significant tonnages of coal after the exhaustion of iron-making deposits adjacent to the waterway, its low tariff could not sustain its commercial viability. The Forth and Clyde might well have done better commercially, in the longer term, if it had levied a charge per ship or barge irrespective of the commodity or tonnage carried.

The disparity between earnings and tonnages may be partially explained by the nature of the tariffs levied. The rate for any given commodity was per ton per mile carried. Thereby a cargo carried, say, from Grangemouth to Kirkintilloch would be charged about half the sum for the carriage of the same cargo to Bowling at the other terminus. This cannot account completely for the noticeable differences between coal and grain for there is strong evidence that Glasgow was the destination or origin of most cargoes. The analysis given below of the percentage of tolls earned between various destinations demonstrates this (see Table 3).

Intermediate trade was defined as voyages originating and terminating within the confines of the canal. The Union opened in 1822 and in 1825 6.8 per cent of tolls were earned from goods travelling to and from Port Downie at the junction of the two canals. Not a significant sum and it did not improve as the Union was about to meet its nemesis in the 1840s. The Monkland and Kirkintilloch Railway came into operation in 1826 and was designed to feed the Forth and Clyde with coal (see Chapter 9).

We may fairly conclude that the Forth and Clyde's import to industrial Scotland was as an internal waterway rather than as a coast to coast route. This is not so surprising. After all it had opened from the Forth to Kirkintilloch in 1773 and then stopped at Stockingfield in 1775. It was another 15 years before the canal reached Bowling, and all the time larger ships were being built so making the lock size restrictive. Its main function became that of connecting Glasgow and its surrounds with the Forth and hence to ports in the east and south of England and continental Europe. By

TABLE 3. *Forth and Clyde, tolls, 1805–40*

Year	Percentage of tolls earned					
	Port Dundas/ Grangemouth	Sea to Sea	Port Dundas/ Bowling	Inter-mediate	Union Canal	Kirkintilloch Railway
1805	50.0	31.0	11.5	7.5	0	0
1825	61.0	20.7	3.9	7.6	6.8	0
1840	61.8	7.9	5.8	9.9	4.0	10.6

TABLE 4. *Union Canal, 1840–43*

Year	Total		Coal		Stone		Manure	
	Tons	Tolls	Tons	Tolls	Tons	Tolls	Tons	Tolls
1840	202.8K	£15.0K	83.3K (41%)	£9.1K (61%)	24.8K (12%)	£0.6K (4%)	28.0K (14%)	£1.3K (9%)
1843	160.0K	£ 6.3K	83.1K (52%)	£4.1K (65%)	18.7K (12%)	£0.5K (8%)	18.0K (11%)	£0.9K (14%)

1840 only 8 per cent of its trade was sea to sea. A similar level of earnings came from the Monkland and Kirkintilloch Railway, the traffic of which would almost certainly have been destined for Glasgow directly or for Edinburgh through the Union. The emphasis on internal trading grew after the Monkland and the Forth and Clyde amalgamated. In 1847, the first full year of the canals' amalgamation, the Monkland produced 21 per cent of the earnings and the sea-to-sea tolls were only 6.5 per cent of the £105,000 earned.

A rather different pattern emerges for the Union as is shown above. For 1840, a year in which it reached its highest levels of profitability, coal emerges as the most important source of income. The significant tonnages of stone carried were mostly for the permanent way of the Edinburgh and Glasgow Railway which was to prove to be the canal's undoing (see Table 4).

Several points emerge from this analysis. Coal was the mainstay of the traffic. If a single justification was ever advanced for the building of the Union it would be 'to get coal to Edinburgh cheaply'. It came mostly from the areas around the villages of Redding and Polmont to the west of the capital. Unlike the Forth

(Above). The Canal at Cadder (Forth and Clyde Canal)
A well-loaded barge is drawn along the canal at Cadder around
1900. This area, between Kirkintilloch and Glasgow, was pleasantly
rural and the horses and barge are proceeding at a comfortable
walking pace. Apart from the dress of the people the scene could
easily have been from a century before steam propulsion, in the
form of the puffer, arrived. (ED)

(Opposite). Horse-power on the Union
This photograph dates from about the time when the Union
ceased to be used for commercial traffic in the 1930s and this scene
may be one of the last examples of a horse-drawn barge on that
waterway. (FK)

and Clyde the Union could lay claim to only one
indigenous industry and that was quarrying. Stone
cargoes were produced on its banks at Ratho and
Linlithgow and also in Edinburgh itself at Hailes and
Redhall. There was also St Magdalene distillery at
Linlithgow and another in Edinburgh which required
coal and barley and of course water from the canal
itself. The North British Rubber Company had a large
factory in Edinburgh but the demand placed on the
canal by these facilities was not as significant as the
demand for domestic coal and stone for construction.

Coal, stone and manure accounted for the greater
part of the tolls earned and the tonnage carried. The
trades in these commodities largely ran from terminus
to terminus, and so internal traffic was not as
significant on the Union as it was on the Forth and
Clyde. As can be seen from the above, stone and
manure earned even lower tolls, ton for ton, than coal
so that, in a reversal of the effect seen on the Forth and

Clyde, the coal trade produced around 60 per cent of the tolls for no more than half of the tonnage transported. Through an arrangement with the City of Edinburgh police, a discount on the toll for manure was available in any year in which they, or rather the City's horse-drawn traffic, supplied more than 15,000 tons. We tend to forget how important natural fertiliser was when the horse ruled the roads and the canal towpath and how an important trade developed taking it from source to farmers' fields. A fragrantly named puffer, *Mayflower*, was a frequent canal user. She was owned by the Ulster Manure Company and plied regularly to Northern Ireland.

As shown above there was a drastic drop in income between 1840 and 1843, the first full year of competition from the Edinburgh and Glasgow Railway. The average toll in 1840 was £0.074 per ton and in 1843 it had fallen to £0.039 per ton as the Union management slashed their rates to compete with the railway. We have already seen this philosophy in action on the passenger trade and the effect was the same on the commodity traffic – the canal started to lose money.

From its opening in May 1822 traffic on the Union had built up steadily. Tolls came to one penny short of £999 and 453 passages were made through the waterway in the nine months from March to December 1823. More than half (55 per cent) of the transits were from west to east and they produced 61 per cent of the tolls earned. By 1825 the passages had increased to 1755 and the income to £3134 and a pattern was established of the trade being roughly equally divided as to direction, in numbers of vessels and tolls paid. Appendix XIII shows the trend of the rise and fall of the income earned on the Union from its peak in the early 1840s and its decline as changes in transport technology and railway ownership affected its fortunes. After 1850 there is a remorseless decline in

income throughout the period of its ownership by the railway companies. No doubt it would have declined in any case, but phrases like 'to eliminate competition' from the management of the Edinburgh and Glasgow Railway to justify its acquisition, can be taken as evidence of a policy of letting the Union run down. As a measure of this decline the figures above for 1840 compare well with those for 1921 when tolls amounted to £1,169 (through traffic to the Forth and Clyde had all but ceased in 1909). The tonnage carried, all of which was internal to the canal, was 19,600 tons and 6,700 of this was coal. It is recorded that only 32 vessels used the canal in that year. The Union had an all too short period of 20 years of productive and profitable life.

In 1846, the year in which the Forth and Clyde acquired the ownership of the Monkland, the throughput of the Monkland was 832,000 tons and

that of the Forth and Clyde 537,000 tons. By 1850 the Forth and Clyde had just overtaken the Monkland with 1,148,000 tons to 1,058,000 tons. This total of 2,206,000 tons, for what was essentially a single canal complex, was to rise even higher over the next 20 years. This quantity of raw materials was needed to sustain local industry and it was made efficiently transportable to a large extent through the development of the mechanised canal barge, the puffer (see Chapter 8). A great deal of coal came from around the little towns of Kilsyth and Twechar on the canal banks and of course from Cadder where the Carron Company owned pits and built up its own fleet of puffers to meet its transport requirements.

It would be unjust however to attribute all the improvement in carrying capacity to the puffer. The part played by the decision to install an inclined plane

at Blackhill on the Monkland, at the junction with the Forth and Clyde, must be recognised. This removed the bottleneck of the locks which dropped barges 90ft down from the Monkland. Time and precious water were saved by bringing empty barges up the inclined plane while the full ones went down through the locks to the Forth and Clyde. The inclined plane opened in 1850 and continued to operate until 1884. In 1863 a record number of 16,505 lighters were lifted up. Allowing an average of 60 tons per barge this suggests that 990,000 tons went down from the Monkland to the Forth and Clyde (see Appendix XII).

Appendix XIV illustrates the growth in the tonnage carried by the two canals jointly and individually, from 1810 to 1925. While the throughput in both canals grew significantly from 1830 to 1850, the dramatic increase in the usage of the Monkland from

(Opposite). Arab at Camelon on the Forth and Clyde
Arab was built in 1901 at Port Dundas for Wm Jacks and Co. She is coming out of Lock 15, well-laden and illustrates why such craft were unsafe outside the smooth waters of the canal. One good wave would have swamped her hold, which, in the tradition of these 'inside puffers', is not covered.

(Above). The Carron Iron Company
The Carron Iron Company, which was situated north of the canal at Stenhousemuir, was linked to the Forth and Clyde firstly by a branch canal and latterly by a railway. It maintained its own fleet of puffers to carry its raw materials and finished products. One of this fleet, to which numbers rather than names were given, is seen here on the canal c.1890. (FK)

(Above and right). Summerlee Iron Works
Summerlee, at Coatbridge, had its own branch canal from the
Monkland. It is one of the few parts of the Monkland that is visible
today as a recently taken photograph shows. It was a major user of
coal and ironstone, the transport of which made the Monkland so
profitable. Wm Baird and Co., Summerlee's owners, kept a
fleet of steam-powered mineral scows. (See chapter 8) (NL)

(Below right). Phoenix and Clifton Ironworks
These works on the banks of the Monkland at Coatbridge
illustrate how densely industry crowded onto the banks of the
canal. Coatbridge's main street was just on the other side of these
buildings and it becomes understandable why the town was
known as the 'Iron Burgh'. (NL)

Comparative Statement of the Principal Articles of Revenue on the Forth and Clyde Navigation for Ten Years.

Articles	1806	1807	1808	1809	1810	1811	1812	1813	1814	1815
Grains	4435 . .	4852 12 9	6022 12 3	5677 18 9	7163 13 8	4236 13 3	4674 2 .	6722 9 3	10,903 8 3	9198 16 4
Sugar	2783 15 .	3760 1 7	3005 14 8	5937 15 11	6620 12 6	2890 12 4	4186 15 8	6398 8 6	4943 . .	5513 2 4
Timber Deals & Lath	3719 19 4	4386 4 4	1437 19 10	1817 2 3	4447 4 3	1989 4 2	1986 13 11	1699 15 5	3388 13 1	5177 14 11
Coal	3846 18 .	4201 6 8	4747 10 11	4186 13 3	4728 9 3	3890 4 .	4588 15 9	4014 17 3	3755 3 1	4044 9 5
Goods	2991 1 8	3181 3 5	2655 17 1	2652 17 11	2516 10 8	1628 5 5	1549 15 9	1991 6 5	1869 16 4	2022 10 5
Coffee & Cocoa Nuts	164 1 3	347 . .	344 8 5	1143 . 6	897 11 10	194 15 .	838 7 4	1717 16 6	3372 4 6	2285 9 10
Herrings & Salt	1020 2 10	870 5 8	1181 . 5	1461 11 10	1416 12 3	842 2 11	1002 16 3	2351 6 1	2043 17 4	1842 2 4
Iron, Pig, Bar & Wrought	1669 18 11	1890 6 10	2055 17 2	1515 11 9	1582 8 1	1968 6 8	1519 8 10	1602 . 4	1449 15 .	1432 7 4
Ironstone	391 13 6	313 9 9	612 6 6	555 7 7	694 9 9	502 12 1	391 10 7	526 7 4	450 2 8	281 16 1
Hemp Flax & Tow	302 3 3	323 3 2	265 5 3	251 9 2	870 9 1	507 4 2	659 8 5	1078 6 9	661 2 5	774 12 3
Oznaburgs & Linens	277 6 8	237 5 2	301 2 7	295 9 6	399 6 7	248 18 4	236 4 1	435 14 7	576 5 1	533 18 3
Tallow	242 6 10	433 9 8	229 14 3	247 10 1	257 18 2	324 13 11	322 3 2	182 7 2	243 14 6	530 10 8
Vessels in Ballast	229 10 .	229 2 6	182 . .	280 . .	253 . .	307 19 2	202 17 6	266 17 6	324 19 9	600 15 .

W. Logan

1830 to 1870 was a major factor in the peak throughput of 3,022,600 tons being reached in 1868. Equally it was the fall in the Monkland tonnage that was the more significant feature of the decline in the years from 1880 to 1920.

The route of the Monkland Canal was through a part of Lanarkshire rich in the mineral deposits of coal and ironstone. There were four major pits: Faskine, Dundyvan, Barachnie and Fullerton producing over 100,000 tons of coal annually. The tiny village of Coatbridge grew to be a significant town and became known as the Iron Burgh, as a result of the area's burgeoning iron-making works. By the 1830s there were three smelting works in Coatbridge each of which had its own branch canal to the Monkland. These were the Dundyvan Iron Works, the Langloan Iron Works

Forth and Clyde Commodities, 1806 to 1815
The tolls earned from the transit of various commodities in the decade up to the year of Waterloo shows a pattern of growth. Overall toll income is up 55%. Grain, sugar and timber account for most of the increase. Clearly people were consuming more coffee or chocolate. Coal earnings remain steady as do those of iron and ironstone which were to increase considerably in the middle of the century. (NAS)

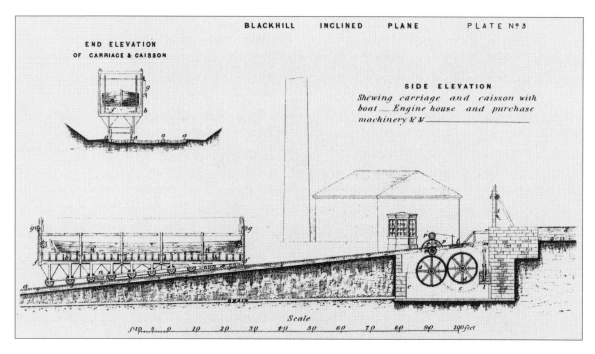

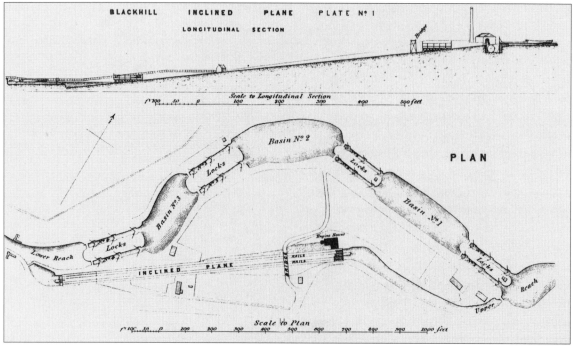

and the largest of the three, Wm Baird and Co of Gartsherrie. There were at least another three of significance, including the Summerlee Iron Works. In 1830 there were seven furnaces producing iron in the Monklands and by 1850 there were 60 and the output rose from 202,000 tons to 1,000,000.

The Baird family had mined coal in the Coatbridge area since 1809 and went into iron-making in 1830. One of the most significant technical innovations in the smelting of iron was the patenting of J. B. Neilson's hot blast method in 1828. Its application had the combined effect of reducing the quantity of coal used in producing iron and speeding up the process. When adopted by the Bairds it raised the output from one of their furnaces from 60 to 250 tons per week. By 1839 Bairds had eight furnaces in production and there were another 24 operating in and around Coatbridge. In 1861, in the period we are examining, Bairds produced 109,000 tons of pig iron. This level of production would have required the delivery by canal to Bairds of approximately 180,000 tons of iron ore,

205,000 tons of coal and 39,000 tons of limestone. This one company therefore needed transport for 533,000 tons of materials to and from its works. What proportion of raw material and finished product was moved by water is not clear but it must be significant that Bairds built up its own fleet of puffers to complement its horse-drawn scows.

Most of the iron ore and limestone would have been moved on the canals because it was coming from local mineral deposits that Bairds owned or leased in areas adjacent to the Monkland. By the 1840s the Bairds were prudently acquiring interests in Ayrshire coalfields against the day when their local supplies would be exhausted. By 1866, ahead of the acquisition of the Forth and Clyde by the Caledonian Railway Company, the canal's chairman, Lord Zetland, was expressing concern to his shareholders at their annual general meeting, about the long term viability of the mineral deposits on the banks of both canals.

It is instructive to compare the source of the raw materials that Bairds consumed in iron-making in 1891

(Opposite). Blackhill Inclined Plane
These diagrams illustrate how the Inclined Plane by-passed the four sets of double locks at Blackhill at the junction of the Monkland and the Forth and Clyde. There was a considerable saving in time and water.

It took 45 minutes for a barge to traverse the locks and only 6 minutes to travel up the plane. Since each barge was estimated to use 11,000 cubic feet of water the reduction in water demand was significant especially in the drier summer months.

The idea of an inclined plane was proposed in the 1840s but it was not until 1850 that it was actually constructed, to a design by James Leslie, at a cost of £13,500. It closed in 1887 by which time it was being rarely used as the traffic on the canal had declined. At its peak, in 1864, it handled about 16,600 barges and probably carried around a million tons of materials. Its main function was to return empty barges from the Forth and Clyde back up to the Monkland. (See Appendix XII).

The plane was 1040ft long and achieved a rise of 96 feet, so the gradient was 1 in 10. Two drums, each driven by a 25 horse-power steam engine, moved in opposite directions pulling wire ropes attached to the caissons, and one caisson descended as the other ascended. The total weight of a caisson, empty barge and water was about 75 tons.

The caissons, into which the barges were floated, moved at two miles or 10,560 feet per hour. It therefore took 1/10 of an hour, or 6 minutes, to raise the caisson from the bottom to the top of the incline. It also took two minutes to load a barge into and two minutes to unload a barge from a caisson. The overall theoretical cycle was therefore 10 minutes. However this was reduced to 8 minutes as a barge could be loaded at the bottom caisson as another barge was being unloaded at the top. Certainly it was reported that as many as 16 barges were being handled in two hours and virtually no water was used.

with that on the eve of the World War I. As Appendix XIV shows the period of tonnage decline on the canals was established by then but the arithmetic of Baird's sources demonstrates that the local fields had run down. In 1891, 28 per cent of Baird's ore usage and 100 per cent of the coal was coming from the company's owned sources. By 1914 these figures had fallen to 13 per cent and zero respectively. By making the very broad assumption that local ore and some coal came by water and all the imported materials by rail, the declining importance of the canals to this important industry in central Scotland is partly explained. In round terms these changes could have meant that at least 100,000 tons less was taken into Gartsherrie by canal in 1914 compared with 20 years earlier. It is still possible that some proportion of the 120,000 tons of the annual production of pig iron went out by canal.

In any case industrial attention turned to steel rather than iron as a fabricating material. The invention in 1856 of the Bessemer converter and a decade later the Siemens open-hearth furnace for steel-making, increased the speed of the process and lowered its cost. The Clyde was demanding steel rather than wrought iron for shipbuilding and as the Scottish steel industry got into its stride from the 1870s it set up

plants further south around Motherwell, and away from the banks of the canals.

Examination of Appendix XIV might lead to the conclusion that for the first 20 years after the railways came on the scene the Forth and Clyde competed well against them as the tonnages it carried increased substantially. One of the factors, as discussed above was the growth of the iron-making industry but the other factor was that they did not compete with them commercially at all. They colluded with them to share the market and to fix the tonnage rates. After the fiasco of the rates war on the passenger traffic from 1842 to 1848 (see Chapter 5) the Forth and Clyde directors sat down on a regular basis with their opposite numbers on the railways and reviewed traffic and rates for their mutual advantage. The railways, the Caledonian, the Edinburgh and Glasgow and the Scottish Central, already had a joint committee in place to eliminate 'wasteful competition'. The Forth and Clyde was invited to join and after it gave up its common carrier status in 1852, it did so. For example, rates were agreed for the traffic between Glasgow and Grangemouth that gave a rough equivalence of cost to the user of either rail or canal. What was more, the tonnage 'allocated' to each carrier was fixed. For example, in an agreement

that was to run for ten years from 1859, it was fixed that the right to carry 40 per cent of all of all tonnages belonged to the canal. If at the end of a financial period it transpired that rail had carried more than its guaranteed 60 per cent it had to pay compensation to the canal at an agreed tonnage rate to make up for the 'loss' it had sustained. Those who would defend the practices of these 'conferences' argue that with no price difference the customer made his choice of carrier on the basis of the quality of the service offered. To a certain extent it was true that if your works sat on the banks of the canal then water transport offered the greater convenience and therefore the better service. This traffic-sharing arrangement lasted until the Caledonian railway took over the Forth and Clyde.

After the Forth and Clyde sold out it lost traffic to the railways as the Caledonian and North British

(Opposite left and right). Fishing vessels on the canals
Fishing vessels used the Caledonian, Crinan and Forth and Clyde canals from the time of their openings to navigation. They still use the Highland waterways to this day. A steam drifter is seen at the entrance lock at Banavie and to the left men and children are using the windlass to open the gate. The Leith registered LH 206 is a 'fifie', an unpowered sailing vessel of the dipping lug-sail type, which, was the craft of the Scottish east-coast fishermen. She is making her way east on the Forth and Clyde towed by crew members who have decided against the expense of hiring a tracking horse. The line (barely visible) is attached to the head of the mizzen mast to allow vessels travelling in the opposite direction to pass under without having to disconnect their tow-rope. The last vessel to transit the Forth and Clyde before it closed in 1962 was a fishing vessel. (FK)

(Above). Rivercloy at Bellanoch on the Crinan
Rivercloy, built in 1910, typifies the 66ft puffer that could transit both the Forth and Clyde and Crinan. She is deep laden here but only too often owners had to restrict the cargo carried when the water depth in the Crinan was reduced by a spell of dry weather. (The Dan McDonald Collection)

Railways fought for market share. As the North British opened more lines in central Scotland the Caledonian Railway decided to counter and in so doing found itself competing with its own canal. Prior to its acquisition of the Edinburgh and Glasgow Railway in 1865 the North British did not run west of Edinburgh but thereafter it offered route alternatives to the Monkland and Forth and Clyde complex.

The Coatbridge to Glasgow line, which was being planned when the Caledonian Railway took over the canals, probably did the most damage. The Glasgow to Helensburgh and Bowling links in the 1850s competed directly. In the 1880s connections to the foundries in the Falkirk area took traffic away; so too did the Larbert to Kilsyth and Glasgow to Clydebank lines. The Grangemouth to Glasgow toll income remained at much the same level but as is shown below all other sections of the canal trade diminished in value (see Table 5).

The strategic decision to close the River Forth to commercial traffic in 1914 had a negative impact on the canal trade. Obviously a great deal of the continental trade for trans-shipment into the Forth and Clyde at Grangemouth was lost (most of the puffer owners, the Leith Hamburg and Hull, Carron, Salvesen etc, laid up part or all of their fleets of lighters). Equally the puffers which had traded extensively on the east coast were penned up in the canal. They had ranged as far north as Aberdeen and Montrose bringing agricultural produce to the industrial central belt through the canal. Puffers, for example, certainly took pig iron to Newcastle via the canal. All this was lost for four years and of course in that period other forms of transport, rail, and even road, filled the need. A great deal of the trade did not come back to the canal after the war.

The following comparison of the tonnages of a range of commodities carried on the canal in 1913 and 1925 illustrates the nature and the dimensions of the change. This is reflected in Appendix XIV (see Table 6).

When added to the fact that the canals' iron trade was in terminal decline (the quantities of ore, coal and limestone moved fell by 320,000 tons between 1913 and 1925), this further reduction of 100,000 tons of general commodities was a mortal blow. The toll income declined to £13,400 in 1925, after a 50 per cent tariff increase had been imposed. It had been £35,100 in 1913.

Little industry fed directly off the Crinan or the Caledonian and so they did not reach the great heights

TABLE 5. *Forth and Clyde, tolls, 1865–1913*

Route	Tolls for 1865	Tolls for 1913
Grangemouth to Glasgow	£22,587	£21,307
Bowling to Glasgow	£5,767	£672
Bowling to Grangemouth	£2,650	£1,364
Intermediate traffic	£17,794	£9,876
Monkland Canal traffic	£35,214	£1,915
Total	£84,012	£35,136

TABLE 6. *Forth and Clyde, tonnages, 1913–25*

Material	1913 (tons)	1925 (tons)
Grain	7,267	3,977
Sugar	46,762	zero
Timber	85,067	53,585
Oil	30,045	11,336
Total	169,141	68,899

or suffer the subsequent lows of the Lowland canals. The two Highland canals had a similar pattern of trade as might have been expected given that they were complementary to each other in linking the Highlands and Islands with Glasgow and the industrial south.

In 1818, the first full year after re-opening and under the management of the Caledonian commissioners, the main cargoes on the Crinan were fish products and slate travelling south and coal, inevitably, going north (see Table 7).

Small craft, or 'boats' as they were designated, were charged on a tonnage rate and steamships were charged a flat rate for each transit to encourage them to use the canal. The steamships were in the main passenger vessels but at this stage the Crinan authorities did not charge per passenger. The important

The Crinan Breached
In February 1859, after heavy rain, the Camloch and Loch Clachaig reservoirs broke their embankments and a mud slide caused great damage for over a mile of the canal. This artist's impression shows the destruction at Lock 9 at Dunardry with Loch a Bharain in the background. Plans to upgrade the whole canal were rejected on cost grounds and HM Government eventually put up £16,000 for the re-instatement. The canal re-opened after 15 months of disruption to passenger and cargo traffic. (GLA)

cargoes of slate (from Easdale for example) and coal typically produced 15 per cent and 10 per cent of income respectively and the steamships 20 per cent. Other income was derived from kelp, general goods, ships in ballast and harbour and wharf dues. A similar analysis of the traffic on the Caledonian in its opening years shows a broadly similar pattern. A direct comparison for the year of 1830 is given below (see Table 8).

While the figures do not provide an exact match, the major commodities and traffics are of the same order on both canals. If there was a discernable trend on the Crinan over the next 40 years it was that income from the fish trade fell away to about 5 per cent of the total and coal increased to the order of 20 per cent (see Table 9).

On the Caledonian the slate and coal cargoes were mostly eastbound ie from Banavie to Inverness, and a good deal of herring came west. Timber movements were important to the Caledonian and there is evidence to suggest that a proportion of this trade was internal to the canal. Indeed it is the internal trade on the Caledonian which distinguishes it from its southern partner where there was virtually none over its nine-mile length.

The most dramatic impact of the opening of the Caledonian was seen in price of coal at Fort Augustus ; it fell from 40/6d (£2.025) to 22/6d (£1.125). In 1822 timber from Glengarry was moving north-east to Wick to make barrels for herring fisheries and barrelled herring began to travel south-west for the Glasgow and Irish markets.

In 1822 there were a total of 1,118 ship movements on the Caledonian of which 526 were internal. In 1825 half of the total of 944 were within the canal. As may be seen in Appendix XVI this pattern of about half of the total passages attributable to internal trade continued for many years. The 60 miles of the Great Glen had

always offered a natural passage from coast to coast even before the arrival of the canal. How much easier travel became for those who lived along its banks when there was a single waterway. It may have been Pitt's vision that the canal would be a great highway across the country and would stimulate new industries but it would seem that the major economic benefit derived by the local population was more mundane. The canal did not stimulate any new industries until the coming of aluminium smelting to Foyers in 1895. It was only from 1864 onwards, when the number of internal movements fell below 300 for the first time, that this pattern changed. No direct causal link can be proven but the arrival of the railways in the Highlands from this time may have had an effect.

On the Crinan the number of vessels moving north (ie from Ardrishaig to Crinan) was usually balanced by the same number moving south (see Appendix XV for totals). Coal and bricks went north and slate, kelp, timber and sand came south. There was an imbalance in tonnage moved as up to 60 per cent of the total cargo carried was northbound coal. Part of this disparity was due to the poor stowage factor of timber and kelp. After the development of the puffer (see Chapter 8) this was partly off-set by the dredging of sand from western sea-lochs which was taken south to Glasgow for the construction industry and other purposes. Coal went in 100 ton lots while 50 to 60 tons filled a puffer full of wood or kelp. When the Kinlochleven smelter opened in 1904 aluminium came south in the puffers in 50 ton parcels.

It is possible to analyse the direction of the sea-to-sea passages of sailing ships on the Caledonian. For many years in their annual reports to the House of Commons the Commissioners recorded not only the internal passages made but also the through voyages from east to west (Inverness to Banavie) and west to

TABLE 7. *Crinan Canal, income, 1818–30*

| Year | Income (£) | | | | | | Total |
	Fish trade	Slate	Coal	Others	Small craft	Steamships	
1818	393	242	124	567	337	0	1663
1821	338	245	125	506	255	187	1656
1825	209	445	189	667	176	456	2142
1830	241	209	197	520	174	465	1806

TABLE 8. *Income comparison, Crinan and Caledonian, 1830*

| Canal | Income (£) | | | | | | Total |
	Fish trade	Slate	Coal	Timber	Passengers	Other	
Caledonian	275 (13%)	143 (7%)	116 (5%)	304 (14%)	632 (29%)	675 (31%)	2145
Crinan	241 (13%)	209 (12%)	197 (11%)	0* 0	465 (26%)	694 (38%)	1806

* Timber was not separately designated in the case of the Crinan and is included in 'other'

TABLE 9. *Crinan Canal income, 1870*

Commodity	Fish	Slate	Coal	Passengers	Other	Total
Income(£)	134 (5%)	404 (14%)	643 (22%)	586 (20%)	1100 (38%)	2866

east. Over a 70 year period, from the time of opening till 1892 there is a slight bias towards east to west passages which tended to be around 55 per cent of the total. No doubt complex trading factors were at work but the intriguing feature of this is that the east to west passage was against the prevailing westerly winds which would be of concern to sailing ships. Better though to face a beat through the relative shelter of the tideless canal, even with its restrictive width for tacking, than face a westerly on the nose and adverse tides in the Pentland Firth. The provision of steam tugs by the Commissioners, after the canal reopened after its major repair in 1847, would have helped the sailing ships but their numbers decreased relatively as the century rolled on. Overall the percentage of sea to sea passages made by sailing ships lay for many years in the region of 40-50 per cent of the total number of all passages. By 1910 this figure was down to 5 per cent, the decline having started around 1880.

The population of the Highlands reached its peak in 1841 and thereafter went into a decline from which it has not recovered. Only in the very Outer Hebrides did population not fall until after World War I. Otherwise the attractions of employment in the growing industrial areas of Scotland and the effects of voluntary emigration and clearances reduced the numbers of inhabitants in regions which were the natural market place of the Crinan and Caledonian Canals. Tourism apart, the basic level of economic activity was falling in the last half of the 19th century and with it the need for the type of transport system offered by the two waterways.

Both the Crinan and the Caledonian, being publicly owned, gave free transit to naval vessels and the latter was particularly busy. There were 326 passages on His Majesty's service in 1915 and a remarkable 1724 in 1919 (the total number of all passages in this year was 5,439 – a record that has not been equalled since). This was due to the establishment of bases at Muirtown and Cromarty for minelayers whose task it was to lay a field from Orkney to Norway to try to prevent German submarines gaining access to the Atlantic (William Pitt's vision of a military use for the canal had been fulfilled 100 years later). An extra 48,000 tons of material went through the canal in support of this activity. In the 1920s the annual tonnage of goods through the canal was in the 22,000–27,000 range much as it had been prior to hostilities. The Crinan, on the other hand, which fed the whole of the western seaboard as well as the Caledonian was, in the same period, carrying 73,000–90,000 tons of which more than half was coal.

World War I was inevitably disruptive for the Scottish canals, particularly for the Forth and Clyde, with Grangemouth docks being closed till 1919, but the future patterns of their trade had been set at the beginning of the 20th century. The Lowland complex had passed its industrial peak and would never recover. The Forth and Clyde, to which we may regard the Monkland and the Union as important tributaries, had not really established itself as a sea-to-sea route but had played an enormous part in the industrial development of the central belt of Scotland for as long as the mineral resources along its banks lasted. By the 1840s even coastal sailing ships were longer than the 66ft of the Forth and Clyde locks. The inconvenience of the size of its locks for a passage to the sea, limiting the cargo size to about 100 tons, was outweighed by the convenience of the proximity to sources. The rapid rate of industrialization in the Forth and Clyde valley from the 1840s onwards was such that the canals prospered. But once this advantage was lost, from the 1880s on, the railways gave speedier access to more distant supplies of raw materials and the canals declined in importance.

Puffers at Crinan Basin
Three 'West Highland Bulk Carriers' lie in the basin at Crinan. G&G Hamilton's *Glenrosa* and *Invercloy* and Scottish Malt Distiller's *Pibroch I* (with her characteristic White Horse at the masthead) would all have had business in Islay. The movement of barley, coal, casks and whisky to and from this island provided important income to the puffer owners and the Crinan was the favoured route of the puffer skippers. (The Dan McDonald Collection)

The 88ft lock size on the Crinan allowed for slightly larger parcels of goods of up to 150 tons and for the Western Highlands and Islands, whose needs were more domestic than industrial, this was often sufficient. Even the whisky industry of the busiest islands, Islay and Jura, was satisfied with the convenience of puffers delivering 150 tons of malt and coal and taking out 50 tons of whisky at a time (this was to change in the 1960s).

The Caledonian, with locks of 170ft x 40ft x 15ft, had been constructed with the larger sea-going frigates

'Pride of Scotland' In 1993 the Royal Mail issued a 39p stamp to commem-orate the bicen-tenery of the passing of the enabling act for the Crinan Canal. The designer has featured the three types of vessels that were the mainstays of the Crinan's traffic – puffers, fishing vessels and yachts. By 1993, of course, puffers had long since ceased to use this canal.

of the day in mind. Until the 1850s when coastal brigs and brigantines were under a 100ft overall and with a beam of 20ft, then the canal was an attractive option as we have seen already. Even an iron-hulled screw steam ship of this era, which might be 150ft overall and have a deadweight of 550 tons, could pass the Caledonian. But in the mid-1860s composite construction (metal frames with wooden planking) was adopted and the sailing ship stretched beyond the length of the locks and soon after iron hulls took lengths up to 200ft and beyond with increased cargo carrying capacity and improved economics. Ocean going sailing ships then bypassed the canal and steam vessels did not fear the tides and winds of the Pentland Firth. By the 1890s

there were as many steamships as sailing ships on the British Register and vessels went into and through the Caledonian for local needs rather than for an easy transit across Scotland. This, of course, did not apply to fishing vessels which became a greater proportion of the total number of passages through the waterway.

The most difficult decision to get right for the longevity of any canal is the size of its locks. The Germans realised they had got it wrong with the Keil Canal when the dreadnoughts arrived on the scene in 1905 and they spent millions of marks enlarging it (see Chapter 10). Nobody was able, or willing, to take such a strategic view of Scotland's sea-to-sea canals.

CHAPTER SEVEN

SERVICING CAPITAL

Everyone who invested in the canals hoped to make a profit when the shares were sold or to have regular dividend for as long as they were retained. The exception was His Majesty's Government when it underwrote the building of the Caledonian Canal. Even when it took over the affairs of the struggling Crinan Canal, through the agency of the Commissioners of the Caledonian Canal, it hoped at least to have its loans repaid.

While government may at times have seemed to be interventionist, to use the modern term, with its direct financing (Caledonian), commissioning surveys (Forth and Clyde), and giving loans by way of the Commissioners of the Forfeited Estates (Forth and Clyde again) it really only rescued the Crinan because the view was taken that to let that canal close would prejudice their investment in the Caledonian. Otherwise the canals' subscribers were expected to stand on their own feet and they preferred it that way too. Their attitude to the servicing of their capital was quite uncompromising and they took every surplus penny they could take. Their view of what was 'surplus' differed somewhat from the modern one.

Of course the poor old shareholders in the Crinan, so seriously did they get into debt with the government, they lost their capital and lost control of their canal. As we have seen previously, their canal opened prematurely in 1801 and suffered technical problems from the very start (the engineer was under great pressure to complete construction as money was running out) and the work done was not of the highest quality. It was 'fully opened' in 1809 ie with nine feet of water, after £141,000 had been spent on it. As only £108,000 had been raised by the subscribers, £50,000 had been borrowed on government mortgages.

It was hardly into its stride when it had to close for major repairs and improvements in 1805 and 1809 and yet again in 1811. Another £5,000 was borrowed for the 1811 repairs after a gale destroyed a reservoir banking. The canal functioned until 1816 when it closed for major renovations recommended by Thomas Telford. It reopened in 1817, under the supervision of the Commissioners of the Caledonian Canal and, as a further £19,000 had been advanced by the Barons of the Exchequer, the company was deeply in debt. In all this time the only income had been the £1730 earned in tolls in 1810. The interest alone on the £55,000 debt, which rose to £74,000 after 1817 repairs had been paid for, was £2,750 per annum.

In the first two full years after the reopening income was £3,694 and expenditure was £2,635 producing a surplus of £1059. As the Barons of the Exchequer had sought 5 per cent on their loans this was not a great return on the £74,000 they had by then invested in the Crinan. The original shareholders, of course, got nothing on their £108,000. Appendix XVII shows the profit ratio of Crinan for the period from 1820–1905 and demonstrates that the canal mostly, but not always, managed to break even without creating worthwhile surpluses.

These financial results are presented in this and following appendices as the income divided by the expenditure. This allows the examination of the financial state of the company over a long period of time without having to make constant adjustments for changing money values, inflation and increases in the rates of tolls charged. When this ratio is 1.0, when income and expenses are equal, then the canal has managed to break even. When the ratio falls below 1.0, as it does in 1860 for example in Appendix XVII, then clearly expenditure is greater than income and a loss is incurred. The average for this ratio for the Crinan over this extended period of time is 0.97 and so the Crinan neither lost or made significant sums. In 1835, when the ratio was 1.35, a high point on the graph, the income had been £1,900 and the running costs of the canal were £1,412.

As in the case of all the canals examined income was largely tolls earned on goods or passengers in transit but there were other sources, such as wharfage dues, rents and feus on canal properties and charges for ships in ballast. Expenditure included running costs such as salaries of officials and wages of lock-keepers, repairs (minor and major), and capital items. There was no depreciation charge and capital expenditure of any form, such as new stables or a passenger boat or an ice-breaker, were treated as revenue items. This was the other side of the 'no depreciation' coin as all such items were taken 'on the nose' in the year that they were incurred and could hit a single year's surplus quite badly. In the cases of the privately owned Forth and Clyde, Monkland and Union interest on outstanding loans, if any, was deducted and the balance made available for the payment of dividends. Quaintly, once the size of the dividend had been determined, the rest was called the 'surplus' and carried forward to the next year. The way most sets of accounts were written made

it quite clear that the dividend was considered as a necessary expense and there was only really a surplus after the dividend had been paid.

There was no question of the payment of dividends in the cases of the public-owned Crinan and Caledonian. Neither was there any expectation of interest on the sums invested and there was no charge for this in the expenses. The taxpayers, for they in effect were the shareholders, did not receive any tangible return on the capital invested in these two canals. Those who used the canals' services benefitted through greater convenience of travel, and goods moved to and from the western seaboard and the Highlands more easily and cheaply. This was all to the advantage of buyer and seller alike. It was to be argued in the 1850s that keeping down the charges on the Crinan and Caledonian Canals brought the costs of visiting the Highlands within the reach of many who otherwise could not afford to travel. To that extent the common weal was served. In an age that may be regarded as a high water mark of Victorian capitalism this was clearly an interventionist attitude and under public ownership it was not intended that these waterways should be profit-making. Many there were though, who complained at the cost to the public purse of maintaining them.

Nor was the repayment of capital in the case of the Crinan realistically likely given the level of the revenue that was being generated. The original subscribers had wished to retake control of the canal and their right to do so was enshrined in an Act of 1848 which formally vested the Crinan to the Commissioners of the Caledonian. All they had to do was repay the public debt with interest and pay the Commissioners any sums expended on repairs to the canal that were in excess of any 'profit' the Commissioners had received. Needless to say these

TABLE 10. *Crinan Canal, surpluses, 1818–58*

Year	Revenue	Expenditure	Surplus
1818	£1,663	£1,132	£531
1828	£1,716	£1,470	£246
1838	£1,903	n/a	n/a
1848	£2,626	£2,270	£356
1858	£2,098	£2,188	£(90)

conditions were never fulfilled. In 1848 the subscribers would have to have put up around £320,000 plus the repair costs over 30 years to clear the money owed. This would have given them the privilege of earning the sums like the £356 surplus made in 1848 (see Table 10). It is not surprising that these clauses in the Act were not invoked and the original £108,000 was consigned to history. A look at a sample of the profits for these first 30 years, after the great repairs of 1817, makes this point quite clearly, and as Appendix XVII clearly shows, the 1830s and 1840s were of the more profitable periods.

This matter of the public purse meeting the cost of repairs when toll income could not is actually disguised to an extent in the global reporting of the figures. Often where the income and expenditure are recorded as being nearly equal and the profitability ratio as 1.0, the income was enhanced by contributions from government to meet all or part of the repairs. The most dramatic example of this is in the financial results for the Caledonian from 1844–1847, a period during which it was closed for substantial renovation. As can be imagined from the length of the closure, the canal had developed serious flaws over the previous decade. So serious were these that permanent closure was contemplated. A Select Committee, appointed by the House of Commons, recommended the canal be kept open and put in order. The income and expenditure of the Caledonian are detailed overleaf for 1842 to 1847 (see Table 11).

The profitability ratio of 0.64 for 1842 was fairly typical of what had been achieved since the opening in 1822, but the repairs needed were mounting by then and money was borrowed from the Bank of Scotland to meet them. The waterway was closed in September 1844 and work begun on an additional flood prevention lock at Gairlochy. Over the next three years the government pumped in £210,150 to meet the expenditure on repairs and alterations. The ratio is shown below as 1.0 for 1845 but this is no adequate measure of profitability in this case as all of the income was a government grant. By 1849 when the dust had settled on this activity, and the canal was getting back to a semblance of normal operations, the income was £5,238 but the costs were £9,724.

Appendix XVIII illustrates the pattern of the financial results for much of the next century. Seldom, apart from the decade 1895 to 1905, was the canal in profit. If Appendix XVI is read in conjunction with XVIII the explanation is to be found in the decline in the numbers of ships using the canal. By the beginning of World War II costs were running at five times

TABLE 11. *Caledonian Canal, profit ratio, 1842–47*

Year	Income (£)	Expenditure (£)	Ratio
1842	2,910	4,578	0.64
1843	2,091	5,767	0.36
1844	925	8,723	0.11
1845	86,359	86,359	1.00
1846	73,402	82,928	0.89
1847	50,389	55,587	0.91

income. Throughout this whole time there were regular injections of public money, usually in grants of £5,000 from the Treasury, to offset the accumulated deficits and overdrafts at the bank produced by negative cash flows from operations.

For many years the subscribers of the Forth and Clyde and Monkland could also have been taken for altruists unconcerned by profit and dividend. The canal was partially opened in 1775 and completed in 1790 but it was 1800 before the shareholders were paid a dividend. In between these dates the Stirling family invested heavily (see Chapter 3), in the completion of the canal. The balance sheet for 1791, after one year of being opened sea-to-sea, gave the assets of the company as £328,920. Of this £200,039 had been spent on the 'old line' of the canal and £79,478 on the 'new line', the extension from Glasgow to Bowling. The Stirlings and the other important coal-masters who had taken up subscriptions were meantime reaping enough benefit getting coal to market, mainly to Glasgow, at a price and in sufficient quantities that kept them from alms-house.

In 1800 the Forth and Clyde earned £21,700 and had expenses of £9,500, a profitability ratio of 2.3. Income had been running at this level since 1797, as

shown in Appendix XIX, which demonstrates how income had risen with the completion of the canal to Bowling and the junction with the Monkland. Encouraged, management loosened the purse strings and declared a dividend. There may also have been shareholder pressure for them to do so, as, although we do not have a balance sheet to make a judgement, it may have been that by then past debts and capital expenditure had been met by operating surpluses. Certainly the £50,000 loan from Forfeited Estates fund was repaid in 1800 (half of this sum was passed on to the subscribers of the Crinan Canal, see Chapter 3).

In 1800 the shareholders' assets in the canal company were worth £421,525, represented largely by the cost of the canal's construction to this date, and the share capital was restructured into 1,297 shares of a nominal value of £325 each. The dividend was declared at £10 per share giving a return of 3.1 per cent on the £325 investment.

Appendices XX and XXI show the trend in canal income and profitability over the 19th century and beyond. An upward movement of revenue and surplus is evident until the 1840s, even through the disruption of the of the trade with Europe of the Napoleonic Wars, with the profit ratio varying between 2.2 and 4.0.

TABLE 12. *Monkland Canal, 1837–45*

	Income	Expenditure	Dividend	Surplus
Aggregate	£150,270	£38,127	£103,172	£8,971
Average per annum	£16,697	£4,236	£ 11,464	£997

In the year after Waterloo shares were valued at £460 each and the dividend of £25 was giving a return of 5.4 per cent. By 1830 the dividend had gone up to £27 but since the shares were fetching £600 the yield was down to 4.5 per cent.

The decade from the mid-1830s to the mid-1840s was one of industrial recession in Lowland Scotland. Some historians refer to the period as the 'hungry forties' (the dominant cotton-spinning trade came under pressure from foreign competition and the iron-making industries were only beginning to emerge). This is to be seen in the downward movement of income and profit of the Forth and Clyde. This trend was to be reversed from 1846 onwards. No doubt the Forth and Clyde would have recovered, as did the state of the economy, but the major factor in the canal's actual recovery was the acquisition of the Monkland.

The turmoil following the opening of the Edinburgh and Glasgow Railway in 1842 and the complex merger negotiations between that railway and the three Lowland canal companies is discussed elsewhere (chapters 3 and 9), but one of the more significant outcomes was the 1846 takeover of the Monkland by the Forth and Clyde.

A few important facts have come down to us about the financial performance of the Monkland over the years preceding the merger (see Table 12).

This was a highly profitable canal with income nearly four times running costs. Their terminology has been used above, with only the residue after dividend payment being described as a 'surplus'. The word profit was not used to describe the difference between income and costs. Annual income had risen from £9,800 in 1837 to £21,000 in 1845 as the iron-making industry around Coatbridge grew. With a share value of £7 and a dividend of £1.875 the subscribers got a return of 27 per cent on their investment, by far the highest of any of the Scottish canals. On average 92 per cent of the profit generated was paid out as dividend. In this respect the shareholders of the Monkland were not unusual. Their counterparts in the Union and Forth and Clyde companies had a similar attitude to getting a return on their investment. No thought of building up a reserve for a rainy day would seem to have entered their collective mind.

Over the years 1830 to 1840 The Forth and Clyde's income had averaged £64,400 per annum and the expenditure had been giving a profit ratio of 2.7. However, whereas the income on the Monkland had risen between 1837 and 1845, as noted above, that of the Forth and Clyde had fallen from £74,700 to £48,500 over the same period. Of all the merger possibilities that were debated in the heated atmosphere of 1845, that of the Monkland was the most tempting. The passenger trades of both canals were under threat from the railway, of course, but the Monkland was less

TABLE 13. *Forth and Clyde Canal, income and expenses, 6 months to 30 September 1846*

	Forth and Clyde	Monkland	Combined
Income	£43,247	£10,872	£54,119
Expenditure	£23,551	£4,028	£27,579
Surplus (before dividend)	£19,696	£6,844	£26,540

dependent on this trade for its profitability than the Forth and Clyde.

A merger was agreed upon and the terms were fixed for a vesting date of 1st of February 1846. The Forth and Clyde was to take over all Monkland's outstanding liabilities (some £77,300) and one Forth and Clyde share was to be issued for three Monkland shares. There were 8080 fully paid up Monkland shares and the Forth and Clyde had to issue 2,693.3 new shares, which ranked equally with its existing shares, to fulfill the bargain. It had on its balance sheet 6,485 shares with a nominal value of £100 each, having sub-divided its 1297 shares in 1842. It paid £346,630 for the Monkland when the £77,300 debt is included. Put another way, the deal meant the original Forth and Clyde shareholders would henceforth receive 71 per cent of the profits of the new combined company as they then owned 6,485 of the total of 9178.3 (6,485 +2,693.3) shares entitled to dividend.

In the first seven months under new ownership the Monkland revenue was £10,872, about average for the preceding four years. Including this sum, the income for the combined canals for the six months to September 1846 was £54,119. The contribution of each company to the surplus is shown on Table 13.

The 71 per cent of the £26,540 due to the old Forth and Clyde shares came to £18,843 so they were sightly worse off as they would have received all of the £19,696 on a stand alone basis. The old Monkland shareholders gained a little but then they had contributed seven months income to the six of the Forth and Clyde. On balance it seems as if the deal was struck on a fair basis for both parties. The new company had a balance sheet value of £1,137,524 and early in 1847 shares were selling for £130 each. The dividend in that year was equivalent to a 5 per cent return on the share price.

As Appendices XX, XXI and XXII demonstrate, the Forth and Clyde entered a period of 20 years, until its takeover by the Caledonian Railway in 1866, of high income, good profitability and the payment of sub-stantial proportions of the profit as dividends. It was a time when capital was well serviced.

The Monkland and the Forth and Clyde had got together having decided, after the breakdown of the negotiations with the Edinburgh and Glasgow Railway, to turn their back on the Union Canal. Their commercial sense could not be faulted for matters were not going at all well there in the mid-1840s. We have commented in Chapters 5 and 6 on the troubles experi-enced after the opening on the Edinburgh and Glasgow Railway and Appendix XIII shows the dramatic decline in its income in the 1840s, largely due to its own price cutting policy. It paid no dividend in 1843, one of £1.25 per share in 1844 and no dividend from then until its acquisition by the Edinburgh and Glasgow in 1848.

The existing Union records tend to report annual profit and dividend. In this case 'profit' is the difference between income and expenses but they do not always give the breakdown of income and costs. However it was reported to the General Assembly of Proprietors that the profit in 1833 was £11,019, the income having been £16,106 and the costs £5,087 (a profitability ratio of 3.2). A dividend was declared which amounted to £11,063 or £2.30 per share. It was not unusual in the Scottish canal business for dividends to exceed profits from time to time but in this case only £7,300 of dividend was disbursed. Only 3,174 of the 4810 authorised shares were fully paid up and they got their cash. The remaining 1636 'burdened' shares, as they were known, got no dividend but the money was credited towards the arrears in the payment of their subscription.

The existence of the burdened shares left the Union with a problem in its financial structure. It was deeply in debt to the Bank of Scotland, in a large part due to the cost of construction over-running the estimate by £200,000. Management had called on its subscribers to make up this gap but about a third of them did not. It is not easy to value the Union's shares as there does not seem to have been an active market in them but, if they are taken at their nominal value of £100, then the 2.3 per cent returned in 1832 was not outstanding compared to the returns available to the Forth and Clyde and Monkland subscribers. The maximum dividend earned was 3.5 per cent in 1840.

In the decade prior to the opening of the competing railway, the Union's profit, from which dividend was paid, rose from £11,800 to a peak of £21,000 in 1841. Dividends paid (with the qualification discussed above) ranged from 66 per cent to 100 per cent of the amounts available for payment. In the year's where smaller percentages were paid, repayments of outstanding loans were made to the bank. The profit fell from £9,700 in 1842 to £4,200 in 1843. It was £4,000 in 1844. No accounts were prepared in 1845 or again in 1847 because of a dispute with the Forth and Clyde over its promised annuity to the Union. The dividend paid in 1844 (£6,000 or £1.25 per share), was justified by the directors on the basis of the combined 1843 and 1844 income and was the last ever declared.

The Forth and Clyde directors had negotiated the takeover of the Union, as part of the tri-partite deal with the Edinburgh and Glasgow which had subsequently collapsed. This had guaranteed the Union shareholders an annuity of £2.5 per share. They took a hard look at the Union's figures in 1845–46 and decided that it could not make enough profit to justify this and withdrew from the agreement.

The Union then went back to the Edinburgh and Glasgow to reopen independent negotiations with it. A take over was agreed which was confirmed in an Act in the spring of 1849. The canal company had debts of £110,000 and assets of £18,214, a gap of £91,786. This would have been considerably reduced, of course, if the burdened shares had been fully paid up. The railway company took over responsibility for the debts, gave a token £5 for each of the burdened shares and £105,800 in total for the 3,174 paid up shares. The total price paid for the canal company was £208,969.

Given the performance of the Union this was not a price easily justified. It had lost its passenger traffic, about 11 per cent of its turnover. Its commodity rates had been lowered to the point of unprofitablitiy and it would be difficult to rebuild them. The Forth and Clyde's judgement was that it would not show enough profit to pay the offered £2.5 per share annuity even if the goods trade did recover. But the Edinburgh and

Glasgow's real motivation for the take over was to restore its own passenger rates, which it had cut in answer to the competition of the canals, to at least double the values then applying. If the Union showed a small profit and the railway passenger trade made money that would be justification enough in their eyes.

We may judge from Appendix XIII that the Union's turnover did not recover over the following years and steadily declined under the management of the Edinburgh and Glasgow and subsequently the North British Railway which acquired both companies in 1865. The take over was accomplished by issuing North British preference shares in exchange for the equity of the Edinburgh and Glasgow. However the Edinburgh and Glasgow shareholders had to wait until 1872 before their dividends were paid up to date as the North British initially defaulted on them. The North British chairman had been cooking the books and falsifying profits to justify the payment of preference and ordinary dividends. He did this to maintain public confidence in the company rather than to enrich himself. When he was found out in 1866 it transpired that the North British had no funds to meet any of these payments! Eleven of the 15 directors, including the chairman, and the company auditors were dismissed by the North British shareholders, and a moritorium put on dividends. In its rush to expand and compete with other railways, principally the Caledonian, the North British had over-stretched itself financially.

There is no great visibility of the financial performance of the Union in the reports of the railway companies but it is safe to argue from the evidence of falling income that it did not prosper. As we shall see in Chapter 11 the canals became pawns in the struggle between the rail companies and very little was done to develop them further.

The North British had gone courting the Forth

and Clyde at the same time as it was talking to the Edinburgh and Glasgow. The courtship became lukewarm, maybe because of the success of the Edinburgh and Glasgow negotiations which were also to give the North British control of the Union Canal. In any case it was the Caledonian Railway that became the successful suitor. After the take over of the Union in 1846, the two railway companies had worked with the Forth and Clyde, through the formality of a joint committee, to regulate business and rates in the central belt of Scotland. Relationships on this committee were fairly amicable, but not always so, and all three parties had a reasonable knowledge of the others' affairs. It was entirely logical that the next development in this process should be the take over of the canal company by one of the railways.

At a meeting of the Board of the Governor and Council of the Forth and Clyde Navigation, on 25th May 1866, the governor, the Earl of Zetland (a descendent of the original Dundas of a century earlier), expressed concern about the exhaustion of the mineral beds along the line of the canal. He proposed, therefore, that powers be sought to extend the Monkland from Sheepford, by means of a lockless cut, 'into the heart of the Wishaw mineral district'. This would cost £130,000 it was estimated and it was agreed to proceed. It was also agreed that the company oppose bills for extensions planned by the North British Railway to Wishaw and to Bo'ness, Grangemouth and South Alloa.

Most importantly of all he proposed that the shareholders be asked to approve the purchase of the whole undertaking of the canal company by the Caledonian Railway. The purchase price had been set at £1,141,333.3, ie the value of the shares in the balance sheet. The shareholders kept the cash in hand, another £215,000, and were to receive a guaranteed payment of

6.25 per cent per annum on the value of their stock in perpetuity. The vesting date was to be 31st March 1866.

The extension of the canal to Wishaw was never built, due in part to the opposition of the North British. However the North British did get the extensions to its lines. The Forth and Clyde subscribers enjoyed their guaranteed income until 1881 when they received 4 per cent preference shares in the railway company and took their chance with the other shareholders. The financial performance of the canal after take over is not readily extracted from the reports of the Caledonian Railway. The evidence we have from analysis of income and tonnages carried indicates that the peak of profitability had passed soon after the take over (appendices XIV and XX) and that Lord Dundas had been justified in the fears that he expressed. Nevertheless, by its purchase of the Forth and Clyde, the Caledonian Railway was able to keep open an alternative form of bulk transport through an area that was dominated by the North British Railway. Most important of all, it acquired Grangemouth Docks … a matter of great concern to the North British which negotiated hard to ensure it was not denied access to this thriving facility.

The subsequent decline in the Forth and Clyde traffic probably did not greatly concern the Caledonian Railway management. To put the matter in context the results of the Caledonian Railway for the half year to July 1867 can be seen on Table 14.

The canal had contributed 6 per cent of the

TABLE 14. *Caledonian Railway, half year to July 1867*

	Railway	Canal	Combined
Income	£847,657	£54,884	£902,541
Expenditure	£397,051	£13,286	£410,337
Surplus	£450,606	£41,598	£492,204

turnover even if it produced 8.5 per cent of the surplus of the combined enterprise. The canal was a minor activity in the totality of the operations. What was important was that the £41,598 that the canal produced was enough to pay the guarantee of £37,093 due to the old Forth and Clyde shareholders and leave a bit over. How long this state of affairs continued is not clear but the fact that the Caledonian Railway negotiated itself out of the guarantee in 1881, and replaced it with a more modest preference share, is probably significant. The profit ratio (see Appendix XXI) was certainly falling by then and the canal approached breakeven in the 1890s.

In the nineteenth century those who invested in the three Lowland canals did not do at all badly, and those with shares in Forth and Clyde, and particularly the Monkland, had handsome returns. Was this cash spent in the support of lavish life styles or cannily reinvested – in the booming railway companies for example?

CHAPTER EIGHT

'THE GREAT CANAL'

The line of the Forth and Clyde Canal that we know today was settled by John Smeaton in preference to other competing routes and a narrower and less deep channel. He referred to 'his' waterway as 'The Great Canal' to distinguish it from what were in his eyes less worthy projects. If there was one sense in which the Forth and Clyde justified Smeaton's description of 'great' it was as a location for the constant search after technical improvement in the water-borne carriage of goods and passengers.

The *Charlotte Dundas* experiments on the canal, and their place in the history of marine propulsion, has been well documented but less notice has been paid to an earlier experiment before the Forth and Clyde was open from sea to sea.

Patrick Miller was a shareholder in the Carron Company which was at that time possibly the most important single commercial user of the canal. It is possible that his interest in marine propulsion, apart from intellectual curiosity, was stimulated by the thought of faster and cheaper transportation of his company's goods. In 1788 he had financed the fitting of one William Symington's engines to a twin-hulled paddle boat that he was experimenting with on Dalswinton Loch near Dumfries. Encouraged by the modest success of this trial another Symington engine, (parts supplied by the Carron Company), was fitted to a larger vessel and with the patronage of Lord Dundas, Governor of the Council of the Forth and Clyde Navigation, it was tried on the canal in December 1789.

A speed of seven miles per hour was claimed for this vessel. But at this speed the paddles started to fall apart. Miller would seem to have decided that he had spent enough on steam navigation and moved on to other interests.

Why Dundas waited another 10 years before taking up the cause of steam propulsion again is not clear. Perhaps the scarcity of horses or the means to feed them during the war with Revolutionary France was a factor. What is clear is that he approached Symington in 1800 to provide an engine for a new boat. In June that year he had a model made of a boat, designed by a Captain John Schank, and had it presented to a Council meeting in London for their approval. The vessel was to be engined, he suggested, by Mr Symington and used for tracking vessels on the canal. The Council ordered that this combination be built 'under the inspection of the Governor', who was to be allowed to draw down cash to pay for it.

In July 1801 this vessel, constructed in Grangemouth by Alexander Hart, was tried out on the canal. In the opinion of the Management Committee, which unlike the Council met in Glasgow, she would 'by no means answer the purpose of tracking vessels'. What is more she had cost a staggering £858. They were not sure that this was the total cost for they demanded of Symington that he account fully for all expenses so that a final settlement could be made and ordered that 'steps be taken to turn the boat and its apparatus to the best use'. This was a damning judgement and was the

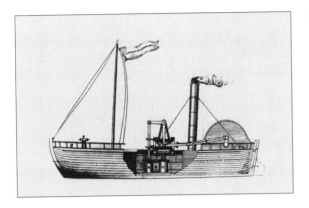

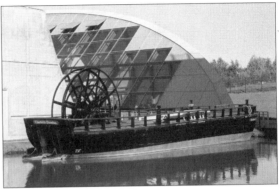

Charlotte Dundas
This line drawing gives an impression of the general lay-out of the successful version of 1803 of the world's first practical steam-driven tug boat. She was 56ft in overall length and 18ft in the beam. A trust has been formed to build a three-quarter scale replica of the *Charlotte Dundas*, to sail on the Forth and Clyde. The picture of the partially completed work, taken at the basin of the Falkirk Wheel, perhaps gives a clearer impression of her single stern paddle wheel and double rudders.

end of the matter as far as the Committee of Management was concerned. Symington's requests for payment were resisted, somewhat pedantically, and referred to London for approval.

In 1802 the Management Committee criticised Symington for his care of the vessel, complaining that she was lying in the canal half-submerged and instructed him to look after it properly until the Governor decided how to dispose of it. They were shocked, therefore, to learn that a second steamship was on the stocks at Grangemouth and was reputedly for the canal's account. The superintendent was instructed to write to London and ask who had ordered this second vessel.

Lord Dundas had. He had been persuaded that if the engine *and* the hull were designed by Symington success would attend the venture. The second vessel, with engine parts again supplied by the Carron

Company, appeared in 1803. On her second trial in late March, the *Charlotte Dundas*, named after his lord-ship's third daughter, successfully pulled two loaded scows over the 17 miles of the summit reach from Lock 20 (Castlecary) to Port Dundas. The average speed achieved was two or three miles per hour, (depending on which of the various reports of the trial is accepted), and into a strong headwind at that. Not only could Symington's total design move herself but she could also tow other craft. This was a genuine breakthrough in marine propulsion. She was the first steam tug to operate successfully in British waters.

However the doubters remained unconvinced and the *Charlotte Dundas* was consigned to be tied up at Rosebank. She was not used again. The official reason was the fear that her paddle wash would erode the banks of the canal. There would, of course, have been a highly visible wash from her large single stern

CANAL CART BOAT.

Canal Cart Boat
While the principal attraction of the concept of the canal 'cart boat' was that it was for the carriage of coal carts, it is notable that half the cargo space is given over to cattle and sheep. It is not clear from this drawing how they were loaded but presumably this was done over the bow. (ED)

wheel, compared with that from the relatively smooth and slower passage of a horse-drawn scow, but the one trial would not have proved that damage would result. Nor in those days was there any scientific knowledge of turbulence in water to substantiate that opinion. When Henry Bell's *Comet* started to make regular passages through the Crinan Canal in 1819 the proprietors of *that* canal seemed unconcerned about the effects of paddle wash. Then there was the politics of the relationship between London and Glasgow and there is evidence of personal friction between Symington and Baird, the local superintendent. There would also have been those who would have been happy to ensure that their tracking horses would not lack future employment.

For some reason, Lord Dundas, to whom the

Committee of Management were generally most deferential, did not press the local management to continue to use his daughter's ship (the fact that Symington ended up out of pocket when all the dust had settled suggests that Dundas turned his back on the project for some reason). He would probably have got his way on the matter had he insisted but the fact is the new vessel was not tested further.

Having speculated thus, at this distance in time, it has to be said the *Charlotte Dundas* really was not the complete answer to increasing the speed of transit over the whole length of the canal. The *Charlotte Dundas* only really came into her own on that section of the canal where the trial had been conducted – the lockless stretch of the summit reach. But the Forth and Clyde had 39 locks over its length and the passage of these would have brought the average speed achieved from sea to sea to not much better than that of horse traction. The tug herself at 56ft overall with a beam of 18ft almost filled a lock and so would have had to be disengaged from her towed scow(s) while she passed through. The barges would then have had to be warped through individually in some fashion – perhaps even by a horse! As was later to be proved steam tugs were most effective when tracking on lockless canals, like the 32 mile stretch of the Edinburgh and Glasgow Union Canal. What a canal like the Forth and Clyde really needed to shorten the transit time was a *self-propelled* barge and preferably one that did not use those space-consuming paddles.

The boiler and machinery of the *Charlotte Dundas* had occupied practically the whole of the hull space so there was no way she could have carried cargo. This problem was to frustrate all of the Forth and Clyde's attempts to speed up the transit of the canal whenever an external towing agency was used to move the scows. High speed could be achieved between

locks, and most beneficially over the length of the summit reach, but the passage of the locks brought the average tumbling down again.

As far back as 1787 an iron barge had been built for use on the canal at Coalbrookdale so that ordering an iron-hulled passage boat for the Forth and Clyde was not exactly a revolutionary concept. There was an abundance of iron being produced in and around Coatbridge on the Monkland Canal so that when the Committee of Management took the step of ordering a fourth passage boat for the growing passenger trade they decided not to have her built in wood. Passage boats had been introduced in 1809 and after the example had been set by the *Comet* and others on the Clyde, steamships had come into operation, sailing from Grangemouth to Leith, to speed travellers from Glasgow on to Edinburgh. The growing popularity of this service increased the demand for passage boats from Port Dundas to Grangemouth.

The new iron boat was ordered in October 1818 for delivery in March the next year. In fact the *Vulcan*, as she was known, did not come into service until September of 1819. The successful bidders for the contract were Thomas Wilson, a carpenter from Faskine on the banks of the Monkland, and the brothers Thomas and John Smellie, who described themselves as smiths and boilermakers. She was made to the plan of a Mr Crichton and was the first Scottish example of the successful commercial use of what was then a new material for boat-building. Considering that it was not until 1834 that the first all iron ship was built on the Clyde some credit must go the Forth and Clyde for its enterprise (today a replica of her 61ft x 11ft x 4.5ft hull may be found at the Summerlee Industrial Heritage Park in Coatbridge). She had a long career of half a century as a horse-drawn passenger boat. Unwittingly perhaps, with this rigid hull, the

Committee, although it hoped that the expense of the iron would be justified by greater durability, were putting in place the first part of the of the package of technical improvements that was to lead towards the development of steam lighters for the canal. And from 1824 onwards when new scows were needed the Forth and Clyde built them in iron, often at their own yard at Tophill (adjacent to Lock 10) under the supervision of the same Thomas Wilson.

The Forth and Clyde did not turn its back completely on steam propulsion after the ill-fated *Charlotte Dundas* experiment. It could hardly ignore the example of the *Comet* and the many others that followed swiftly on her heels. In 1816 *Comet* was providing a service to the canal's passage boats by running from Newhaven to Grangemouth. Henry Bell was well known to the Forth and Clyde directors with whom he cooperated in running a feeder service up and down the River Carron to Grangemouth. It was evident in the late 1820s that the emerging railway companies could be able to offer much higher speed of delivery than the canals and potentially would be a threat to their passenger traffic in particular. Steam propulsion could mean higher transit speeds on the canal and was seen as a way to combat the railways. This competition with the railways was the great spur which drove the innovations on the canal for the next 30 years.

Between 1828 and 1831 there were three attempts, with the vessels *Cupid*, *Manchester*, and *Lord Dundas* to introduce steam to the Forth an Clyde but none of them had really significant impact on the trade of the canal.

In a sense the trial of the *Cupid* was a repeat of the *Charlotte Dundas* project another generation later. It was almost as if the lessons of 25 years earlier had been forgotten. *Cupid* was owned by David Napier who

operated her on the Clyde. She was hired for trials on the canal because with a length of 58ft and a beam of only 11ft this side-paddler fitted comfortably into the locks. She achieved six mph towing a loaded scow but again objections to wash were raised against her. Towing, as already observed, had its limitations on the canal and she really was so tiny that she could not carry an economic number of passengers or weight of cargo.

The *Cupid* trial did move opinion enough for the Committee of the Forth and Clyde to approve of the introduction of steam propulsion to the canal in principle. An advertisement was placed in the newspapers in 1829 to that effect and steamship owners were invited to trade on the canal. It was made clear at the same time that the Committee did not intend to fit out a steam ship at their own expense and it drew up a set of regulations for the conduct of steamers on the canal. Speed was to be limited to five mph and steamers were to slow down when passing sail or horse-drawn vessels and go offside of them. No steamship owner took up the invitation.

So the committee had to fit up a steamer after all. A narrow track-boat owned by the canal company was converted at a cost of £2,000 and named *Cyclops* (perhaps because the Committee were one-eyed about the benefits of steam?). In 1830 she plied from Alloa on the north bank of the River Forth to Port Dundas carrying around 40 tons of cargo. She was given a 15 horsepower engine and stern paddles. She accomplished the voyage of forty miles from Port Dundas to Alloa faster than a horse-drawn vessel went from Port Dundas to Grangemouth. *Cyclops* was later to be found running between Stirling and Glasgow. So at least the avowed objective of connecting Port Dundas with the ports on the east and west coasts was being achieved.

Encouraged somewhat by the *Cyclops* an improved version of her, the *Manchester*, built by

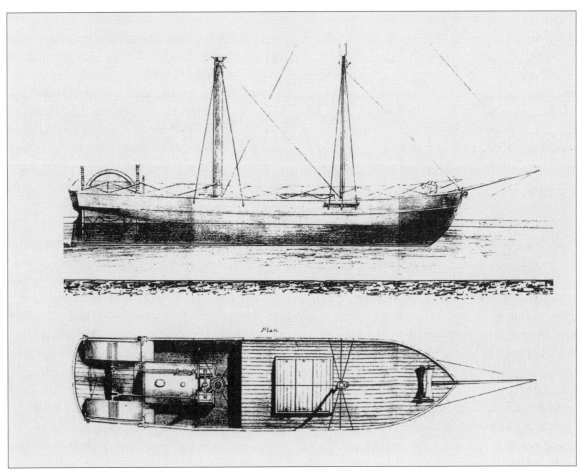

Fairbairn and Lillie of Manchester, was brought onto the Alloa run. She was also fitted with two stern paddle wheels and they and the engine took up nearly half of her overall length. She was later joined by the *Edinburgh*, which had been built for the London Leith Edinburgh and Glasgow Shipping Company by the Forth and Clyde and hired to them for use on the Union Canal. Reputedly she could carry six tons of cargo and up to 40 passengers. They were not successful with her either as a goods or passenger boat and she was given back after being damaged in a collision with a bridge. She was fitted with new steam

PS Manchester
To save space in the locks the stern-wheel design of a paddle steamer always recommended itself for the canal. On *Manchester* there were two wheels. As part of the Forth and Clyde management experimenting with speed to combat the perceived threat from the railways, she was brought into service between Port Dundas and Alloa on the Forth in 1832.

engines and redeployed by the Forth and Clyde between Port Dundas and Lock 16. She eventually ended up with side paddles working as a tug in Grangemouth harbour. By 1831 the Forth and Clyde had spent £6,000 on steamships and they regularly lost money operating them, admittedly after they had charged themselves the tolls on the goods and passengers carried. No more of these types of craft were built. Of greater curiosity was the experiment with a form of catamaran that led to the introduction of the *Lord Dundas*.

An experiment, initiated by management committee member Thomas Graham, in lashing two hulls together to form a passage boat had met with approval of those looking for higher speed. Horses were still used at this stage but the intention was that an engine would be fitted to the configuration. As all were happy with the performance of the twin hulls and the higher speed achieved (around seven hours for the 56 mile trip from Port Dundas to Port Hopetoun), a twin hulled steam boat was ordered from Fairbairn and Lillie. *Lord Dundas*, as she was named, had the edge on her ancestress *Charlotte* as she actually went into service and was expected to maintain an average speed of six mph dragging a passage boat or carrying passengers. Her engine and single paddle lay amidships and athwartships and the intention was that water would be drawn to the paddle through the gap between the hulls for greater efficiency of propulsion. This curious arrangement meant that she had two separate passenger cabins, one ahead and one astern of the engine. She was withdrawn around 1836, as she did not give a return on the investment of £1,675 that had been made in her.

Over the period from 1833 to 1835 attention moved to the matter of aiding the transfer of cargo from rail to canal. As we will see the first railway in the area was built to feed the canal rather than compete with it. This was the Monkland and Kirkintilloch which by 1831 had introduced steam locomotives to replace its earlier horse-drawn waggons. Significant tonnages of coal (around 26,000 tons pa at this time), were coming to the canal from this railway. It all had to be double-handled – unloaded from carts and wagons and then reloaded into the canal scows. Now double-handling has been anathema to the shipper from time immemorial so it was perhaps inevitable that they, practical men of the canal and the railway, would get together to provide a solution.

It is not clear who gets the credit for coming up with the idea of 'cart boats' and 'waggon boats', though the name of Thomas Graham has been associated with the concept, but they made their appearance in 1833 and 1835 respectively. The cart boats, which the Forth and Clyde had built in iron at a cost about of £300 each, were loaded up by driving the horses and carts onto the deck of the scow which had a turntable in the middle. The horses were then unharnessed and taken off. In this manner up to 18 carts, each of which could carry three tons, could be accommodated. With the wagon boats it was possible to take the wagons directly on deck from the tracks of the Monkland and Kirkintilloch Railway. About 40 tons of coal in 14 wagons were thus loaded. It was a popular and successful method and the Forth and Clyde derived a regular profit from hiring out these boats to third parties as well as earning tolls on the coal carried. It must be supposed that the speed and convenience of the operation outweighed the disadvantage of carrying relatively smaller tonnages than the conventional scow. The sacrifice of dead-weight capacity due to the weight of the carts or wagons was significant on vessels otherwise capable of loading upwards of 60 tons.

These special cart and wagon boats were a very

early manifestation of the 'roll-on-roll-off' principle so commonly seen today on deep-sea, coastal and river ferries, around Scotland's coast. This may well be another first for the Forth and Clyde to rank alongside the *Charlotte Dundas* trials.

Attention now turned, at least temporarily, to steam traction on land to improve canal transit speed. In 1837 the Committee considered a proposal, put forward by the consulting engineer John McNeill, to experiment to drag scows by means of a steam locomotive operating from a canal-side track. By July 1839 a half mile long of straight track had been laid on the west side of Lock 16 near Falkirk for the trials to take place. A second hand locomotive had been acquired and rails borrowed from the Wishaw and Coltness Railway. The superintendent reported enthusiastically to the committee that all had worked well but that it was important to see how the configuration coped with the curves in the canal. To this end it was suggested that a four mile stretch of track should be laid between Locks 16 and 17. A month later the committee, attended by representatives from the Monkland and Kirkintilloch, Ballochney and the Wishaw and Coltness Railways, went to see for itself. A maximum speed of 17 mph towing a single loaded barge was accomplished. Later a single passage boat was towed at 19 mph and combinations of two, four and six passage boats were dragged 'with various degrees of velocity'. Six vessels and two scows with 360 tons of cargo between them were moved at 2.5 mph.

It is not clear from the reports if this was the speed of the locomotive or the barge but it would have taken about 1 minute 45 seconds to travel the length of the half mile track at 17 mph and it is equally unclear how the engine and the barge were stopped after they got up to that speed! However the committee was highly pleased and ordered cost estimates for a four

mile test track between Locks 16 and 17, and for a track between Port Dundas and Grangemouth with engines 'necessary for the same' with a rail track on one side of the canal and a towpath on the other. All of these were to be compared with the then known costs of the horse-drawn day and night passage and tracking boats. By April 1840 McNeill's report was available and the superintendent was asked to review this and report ' as to the advantages both now and as will be likely after the opening of the Edinburgh and Glasgow Railway.' And nothing more was heard of the proposal to track vessels by steam locomotive on the Forth and Clyde Navigation.

The clue may be in the words, 'opening of the Edinburgh and Glasgow Railway.' This railway was under construction and would open in two years time. The Slamannan Railway was in operation in 1840 and it appeared to be adversely affecting passenger numbers on the Union and the Forth and Clyde. So the superintendent would have had difficulty in predicting a rosy future for the passage boats and perhaps even for the goods traffic. Again the steam locomotive was another form of towage and it presented the usual problems at locks and the added one of getting the rail line round each lock for it surely could not cope with the steep inclines where the towpath rose 10ft in a very short distance. It made sense to consider laying rails between Port Dundas and Grangemouth for that was the route which had the heaviest traffic but it would have been a costly exercise. Did it make sense for the Canal Company to compete with railways by building a railway for itself?

Later in that year of 1840 the committee had to consider a letter from an irate shareholder who could not credit that the company was still using horses for tracking when surely steam tugs were the future. The superintendent was delegated to explain the difficulties

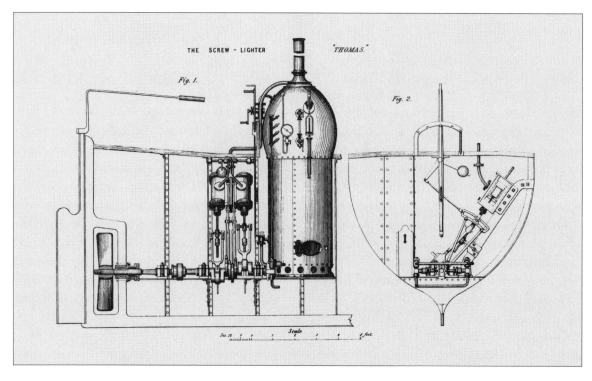

THE SCREW - LIGHTER "THOMAS."

Fig. 1.

Fig. 2.

Scale

and he volunteered that as there were to be experiments on the Union Canal and the Lancaster with screw propellers the committee would keep that situation under constant review. The committee was about to take another small step towards the development of the puffer.

The supremacy of the paddle had come under threat in 1836 when F.P. Smith patented his screw propeller and over the next decade the concept was experimented with in many ways. After a series of trials, when a screw ship pulled her sister paddle ship astern in a tug-of-war, the Royal Navy came to accept the propeller. However the most convincing demonstration of all was when SS *Great Britain* became the first British screw steamship to cross the Atlantic in 1845. The Birmingham and Liverpool Junction Canal had experimented with a somewhat complex screw system and this was observed by representatives of the Union who bought two steam tugs, which operated well on their lockless system, prior to their being taken over by the Edinburgh and Glasgow Railway in 1846. Both Union and Forth and Clyde representatives had witnessed the trials on the Paisley Canal of Kibble's patented 'propeller' and repeated them on their own canals. Claiming to be superior to the screw, this somewhat complicated system rather like an early form of the tracks on a tank which was fitted to the sides of the hull, was never really widely adopted. One

steamboat using this system, *Firefly*, did operate on the Forth and Clyde in 1844 towing passage boats but by this time the passenger trade was being lost to rail. If steam had any part to play in the future of canal transport it would be in the movement of materials rather than people.

All the elements were now in place for the Forth and Clyde to develop a self propelled barge uniquely suitable to its own requirements. It was experienced in the use of iron hulls which provided the necessary hull rigidity for the proper alignment of shaft and propeller. It was experienced in the construction and operation of steam engines and of modifying hulls to accept them. It now had the example of the successful operation of the screw propeller which had none of the space disadvantages of paddles, side or stern, for operation in narrow locks.

And so it was to be. In 1856 a boiler and engine, costing £320, and a propeller were fitted to one of the Forth and Clyde's 80 ton lighters, the *Thomas*, and the first puffer was born. She was a success and recognised as such by all parties, including Thomas Dundas, second Earl of Zetland. On trial in September 1856 a speed of five mph was achieved, and given the relative absence of wash, was considered acceptable. This was a comfortable two mph faster than the horse-drawn scow. Her three tons of machinery and water and a space for coal bunkers was accommodated in five

(Opposite top). Thomas
This drawing shows the layout of the stern of the *Thomas*, the converted scow that became the first 'puffer'. It was first published in the transactions of the Institute of Engineers in Scotland in 1857. The propeller had a pitch of four ft and 130 revs per minute gave a speed of five mph. At a pressure of 35 pounds per square inch the power produced was 'sufficient for propelling the lighter with a full cargo of 70 to 80 tons.' When the pressure was raised to 85 pounds the vessel became a very effective ice-breaker. (GLA)

(Opposite below). Horse power on the Monkland
This is the system that the puffer replaced. It may be assumed that the boys are not part of the scow's crew but three of the adults would have been involved in the operation. Normally two boatmen, a horse-man, and of course, a horse, was the complement. Four-legged horse-power only achieved about two-thirds of the speed of steam horse-power. (NL)

frame spaces at the aft end in an area not given over to cargo in the traditional scows. As a result her carrying capacity was scarcely impaired.

The simple two cylinder engine of the *Thomas* exhausted steam directly to atmosphere. In other words it puffed – much in the same way that we are familiar today with the puffing of vintage steam locomotives. It is not known who gave the breed the nickname 'puffers' but it stuck. And they continued to puff until the introduction of condensers which were pretty much universal from the 1870s. After this puffers no longer puffed but they could not shake off the name.

Three types of puffer evolved. The simple canal boat had no bulwarks, no cargo handling gear and minimal accommodation, if any, for her three man crew. The 'outside boat' was meant to travel further afield to the Western Isles and the northeast coast of Scotland. For this type the Board of Trade took a serious interest in freeboard, bulwarks, hatch boards, load lines and insisted on a complement of four men. A third variation, the 'shorehead boat' was meant for Clyde estuary trading and was a compromise between the two other types. Overall length was around 66ft with a beam of 18ft. Puffers on the Monkland had to be shallower drafted, as the canal was only 4ft deep, than their Forth and Clyde alternatives and they usually had a deadweight of 60 tons. On the Forth and Clyde, where the water depth was 8ft, puffers were nearer 80 tons in capacity. Outside boats could take up to 110 tons of cargo.

After the trial the *Thomas* worked for over a year between Port Dundas and Bowling and averaged three to four return trips per week compared with the two of the horse-powered scow. She made three mph over the whole 12 mile voyage including the time taken in passing the locks. She could travel 100 miles on one ton of coal. At first the converted *Thomas* had a crew of two

but a third was later added to tend the engine. As a scow it had needed two boatmen, a horse and a horseman. As a result the economics of barging were transformed.

A cost comparison, taken from data from the 1860s (appendix VI), illustrates the benefits of steam, the cost per ton for which was around 80 per cent of that for pure horse-power.

Below are the comparative costs for a journey from Gartsherrie Iron Works on the Monkland to its connection with the Forth and Clyde at Blackhill and thence to Bowling on the Clyde – a journey of some 24 miles (see table 15).

The engine and boat costs per journey took into account, depreciation, interest on the capital outlay, consumables and repairs. The puffer consumed on average 0.2 tons of coal per journey. Horse expenses included stabling and fodder but no depreciation! The capital cost of the horse was not brought into consid-

TABLE 15. *Barge and puffer cost comparison*

	Steam lighter	Horse-drawn scow
Capital costs	£907.85	£207.90
Cargo deadweight	67 tons	56 tons
Cost per journey		
Engine	£0.61	£0.0
Boat	£0.51	£0.40
Horse	£0.0	£1.06
Crew wages	£1.14	£0.96
Total	£2.26	£2.42
Cost per ton	£0.34	£0.43

(Above). Mineral Scows
The smaller width and depth of the Monkland meant that a smaller version of the Forth and Clyde's puffer had to be produced for it. The 'mineral scow' here was designed for the 14ft width of the Monkland and was a version of the 'inside' puffer. The name *Gartsherrie* suggests an association with Baird's iron works on the banks of the Monkland.

(Right). Kelpie
Built in 1868 on the Clyde, *Kelpie* was one of the first generation of puffers and illustrates the type. Her dimensions were 66ft x 14.7ft x 6ft and she has the raised bulwarks, mast and derrick and sail of an 'outside' puffer. She has the sophistication of a wheel (rather than a tiller) but there was no protection from the weather for the helmsman. The sail was not just for decoration – at least one puffer is recorded as making it back to the Forth and Clyde by wind power after an engine failure.

eration. Crew wages were paid on tonnage delivered which partly explains the higher costs in this category for the steamer.

The capital cost of the puffer at £908 is over four times more than that of the scow. The fact that the capital journey costs of the steamer (£1.12) is only 2.8 times that of the horse-drawn barge (£0.4) gives the clue to the speed differential of the two configurations. The steamer was achieving speeds of 55 per cent more than that of the scow. The combination of the higher tonnage capacity and greater speed of the steam lighter brought the transportation cost down. Not only that but it increased the carrying capacity of the canal itself. This was to be vital to meet the great surge in demand for the transportation of raw materials and finished product which followed the growth of the iron-making industry.

Thereafter there was an explosion of interest in steam propulsion on the Forth and Clyde. The Canal Company itself put in hand the further conversion of existing scows in March 1857. Meanwhile it had been approached in November 1856, by two local firms, J.W. Salvesen and Wm Burrell, for loans to allow them to build eight new steam lighters between them. Fifty per cent of the costs were advanced to these companies on suitable interest rates and appropriate securities and repayments terms.

The motive of the Forth and Clyde management was simple. The more tonnage that was moved on the canal the higher was the income from dues. Yet it was a remarkable business strategy. The risk of financing the *Thomas* trial had been accepted and once the concept was proved it stood aside and said to the world at large, 'There it is. It works. Now you get on with it.' It did not seek to exploit its innovation except indirectly through the potential for greater tonnages being carried on the canal.

Other hauliers asked permission to introduce their own steamers to the canal and were encouraged subject to their vessels being inspected by the Canal's superintendent. Another company, McConnell and Laird, wished to purchase one of the Forth and Clyde scows to convert it specifically for the trade between the canal and Kirkcaldy on the Fife coast. So evidence is there from the earliest that the puffer was intended to go to sea. The same company was loaned £1,000 in 1858 to purchase the *Glasgow*, the first purpose built puffer (as distinct from a converted scow), which had been launched from Swan's yard at Kelvindock on the canal in 1857.

Some indication of the rate of development of the puffer trade may be found in Appendix VII. This is based on an analysis of a list of some 300 new buildings that the author has researched. It is not claimed that this list is exhaustive as it does not include all those early conversions of existing barges that took place in the period 1857–66. The rise in the number of vessels built reflects the increasing demand for the movement of commodities through the Forth, and Clyde and Monkland complex in the second half of the 19th century (some of those built in 1890–1900 would have been the replacement of older craft of 1860/80 vintage). Much of this was directly related to the flourishing Lanarkshire iron-making industry of the period. The decline in numbers during and after the 1914–18 war reflects the closure of the eastern end of the Forth and Clyde during the hostilities and the exhaustion of those same Lanarkshire ironstone and coal deposits. It has been reported that by 1867, 10 years after the *Thomas* experiment, there were 70 puffers employed regularly on the canals.

The Carron Company Ltd, which prosaically gave its vessels numbers rather than names had built *No. 9* by 1871. The Leith, Hull and Hamburg Steam Packet

Kype
Kirkintilloch was not the only place on the Forth and Clyde where puffers were built. From 1857 until 1921 vessels were built at Maryhill in Glasgow. Swan & Co. leased the dock there from the Canal company for the purpose. Cumming and Swan had a yard at Blackhill and Burrel & Son built for their own use at Hamiltonhill. Like *Kype*, seen here, all puffers were launched sideways because of the restricted width of the canal. Built in 1921 at Kelvindock, *Kype*, was the yard's last ship. (ED)

Company Ltd., which was engaged mainly in transshipments from the Forth to Port Dundas, used letters for names. They began with *A* in 1873 and had reached *Z* by 1889.

The development of the puffer brought more than the mechanisation of transport to the canal. It also brought an active shipbuilding industry. J & J Hay established a yard at Kirkintilloch on the canal and launched the first puffer for their own account in 1869. They had 16 vessels 20 years later and at their peak had a fleet of 24 puffers. A second yard, P McGregor & Sons, also based at Kirkintilloch, constructed a variety of small vessels but produced puffers including the

Hay's Yard at Kirkintilloch
This is a late-19th century view of Hay's shipbuilding ship repair
yard on the banks of Forth and Clyde. The ship on the slip, Hay's
own *Delta*, one of their earliest 'outside' puffers, was launched
in 1881. The slipway was installed in 1889. Next door in the
canal basin was the yard of P McGregor & Sons. (ED)

famous 1912–13 series of eight motor driven lighters for
the Coasting Motor Shipping Co.

This fleet was dispersed during the First World
War and as their internal combustion engines had a
poor reputation for reliability, the steam engine
remained the puffer owner's first choice for another 40
years. Puffers were occasionally built at Blackhill (by
Cumming & Swan), on the Monkland and in greater
numbers at Kelvindock (by Swan & Co.), Hamiltonhill
(by Wm Burrell & Son) and Port Dundas (by Wm Jack
& Co.) up to the 1920s.

McGregor operated from 1902 to 1921 and Hay
kept going until the Forth and Clyde closed to
navigation. The McGregors were timber merchants
and they had operated as such for many years from the
Canal Basin in Kirkintilloch, adjacent to Hay's yard.

They were very successful in attracting orders from Scotland and further afield over nearly 20 years of activity during which they produced more than 100 ships. Overall about a fifth of their buildings were puffers or puffer types and they constructed the one really successful motor puffer. She was *Perfection* launched in 1916 for the Anglo-American Oil Co. She was a miniature oil-tanker and plied the canal success-fully for many years. Ironically their last deliveries in 1921 were three steam lighters of an enlarged puffer type. McGregors gained a considerable reputation for specialised small ships, particularly tugs and they did not let the limitations of the canal locks restrict their offers to build. They frequently transported their product out by rail in sections for reassembly elsewhere. They only took five orders from 1915–1921 and the general recession in shipping of the 1920s possibly persuaded them to get out of the business. Nevertheless they contributed to the economic well-being of the canal area and to the unique reputation of Kirkintilloch as an inland shipbuilding town.

The Hay family were established farmers in the Kirkintilloch area and owned scows for their own purposes – largely the transport of manure from one part of their holdings to another. At some time in the 1850s or 1860s they made the transition from scow-owning farmers to farm owning barge-masters. In an attempt to correct the severe local unemployment left by the troubles of the weaving industry, a ship-building co-operative had been set up at Kirkintilloch in 1867 under the name of Crawford and Co and when this did not succeed financially the Hays took it over. They were everything that the McGregors were not. They only built puffers and with two exceptions, in the 76 years they were in the construction business, they built only for their own use. Their main activity was ship repair for their own fleet and while new puffers were always

on the slip these tended only to be finished in lulls in the repair cycles.

Their first production was the iron screw lighter *Helena* in 1869 and the last was the steel puffer *Chindit* in 1945. With the launch of Briton in 1893 they began to adopt 'tribal' names (like *Gael, Tartar, Dane*) as their fleet tradition.

After about 1896, in line with the changes that were occurring in the levels of internal traffic on the Forth and Clyde and the Monkland, the Hays built no more inside boats and decided to put their emphasis on the coastal trade. Of course the outside boats could still trade on the Forth and Clyde as required, but from that date no Hay new puffer earned its living exclu-sively on the canal.

It could be argued that, in an empirical way, the Hays refined and developed the design of the puffer more than any other organisation. Their 1939 design for *Anzac* and *Lascar*, which were not constructed at Kirkintilloch but at Scotts yard at Bowling, was adopted by the Admiralty for its wartime lighter, the Victualling Inshore Craft (VIC). Over a hundred of these were launched, mostly from English yards, and they served widely in World War II.

When the time came to close the yard, the decision having been made that the Forth and Clyde would itself close, the Hays made the announcement with great reluctance. It could be argued that had been loyal to the canal and its restrictions too long for their own good. Their operating base had been a feature of Kirkintilloch for over ninety years and it had drawn its workforce mainly from the town. So the contribution of the puffer to the local economy came to an end.

In 1846, the year in which the Forth and Clyde acquired the ownership of the Monkland, the throughput of the Monkland was 832,000 tons and that of the Forth and Clyde 537,000 tons. By 1850 the

Gael on the Forth and Clyde
The puffer, *Gael*, built at Hay's yard at Kirkintilloch in 1931, is seen
approaching a bascule bridge which is opening to let her pass.
It can be judged how closely she will fit the gap, illustrating how
these ships were designed to an optimum size to pass through
locks and bridges with a minimum of space to spare. (ED)

Forth and Clyde had just overtaken the Monkland with
1,148,000 tons to 1,058,000 tons. This total of 2,206,000
tons, for what was essentially a single canal complex,
was to rise even higher, to over 3,000,000 tons, over the
next twenty years. This quantity of raw materials was
needed to sustain local industry and it was made trans-

portable to a large extent through the 'invention' of the
puffer. Wm Baird and Co., the major iron producer,
based on the banks of the Monkland, and which
typically moved 500,000 tons of materials per annum,
quickly developed its own fleet of steam lighters.

The strategic decision to close the River Forth to

commercial traffic in 1914 had a dramatic effect on the canal trade. Obviously a great deal of the continental trade for trans-shipment into the puffers was lost. Equally the puffers which had traded extensively on the east coast were penned up in the canal. These trades were lost for the duration of the war and beyond (See Chapter 6).

Puffer numbers declined with the loss of these trades. However for many years they had had another string to their bow. As McConnell and Laird had planned in 1857, the puffer could go to sea. And over on the west coast of Scotland it had virtually banished the sailing gabbert from the seas. In the service of the outer Clyde estuary, the Highlands and the Hebridean islands it had provided a unique service to those area's isolated communities.

The great days of the puffers, despite today's somewhat romanticised view of their role in sustaining the Highlands and Islands, were those of the late 19th century when they plied the canals and fed the industries of Central Scotland. It is often said that 'Glasgow made the Clyde and the Clyde made Glasgow'. With equal justification it could be said that the Forth and Clyde made the puffer and the puffer made the Forth and Clyde.

CHAPTER NINE

'RAILWAY MANIA'

'Railway Mania', the term usually applied to the explosion in the number of railway companies that were formed in the mid-19th century, followed on where 'canal mania' left off. In truth there was about 50 years between the peaks of these activities but canals were still being built as the age of rail began.

The opening of the Stockton to Darlington Railway in 1825, using Stephenson's 'Active' as a locomotive, began the excitement but even more so the Liverpool-Manchester line in 1830, employing his even more famous 'Rocket', woke businessmen up to the possibilities of steam driven rail transport.

Between 1820 and 1900 nearly 200 enabling Acts of Parliament were passed for the formation of railway companies in Scotland. Each was specific to a company to build and operate a line between two named destinations. One hundred and fourteen of these company Acts passed through the legislative process between 1840 and the end of the 1860s at a rate of nearly four per year. If not a sort of madness, it certainly was a considerable enthusiasm and in its nature as speculative as any stock-market boom experienced since. In August 1845 alone, three separate railway companies were being promoted to join Glasgow to the Airdrie-Coatbridge district in addition to those that already existed. 'The country is become an asylum of railway lunatics', said Lord Justice Cockburn. It could not but have an impact on the operation of Scotland's canal systems. By 1850 the capital invested in Scottish railways stood at over £20 million and this had doubled 20 years later. The capital costs of the five canals which are our subject had been £1.96 million. There was no comparable re-investment in canal improvements after the railways arrived. The Forth and Clyde actively supported the incorporation of two of the early railways in the Monklands area, the Monkland and Kirkintilloch Railway and the Ballochney Railway, which were intended as feeder systems for the canal.

The earliest lines, built to the 4ft 6in 'Scottish gauge', used horse-drawn wagons and were usually single track. They served very local needs, often a single colliery or factory, and were seldom more than 10–15 miles long. Progressively in the 1840s, the new lines had locomotives and the old lines converted to steam too. On successful routes, when traffic grew, a second track would be added. As the lines started to link up with each other or new lines were built as spurs of an existing line, the gauge became standardised at 4ft 8½in (1.44 metres).

The high rate of expansion could not last of course and many of the local railways linked up, firstly in a physical and then in a commercial sense, to form more meaningful lines for longer distance traffic. In the 1860s the number of Acts for amalgamations and take overs almost matched that for new lines. By the end of the century there were really only five railway companies of any significance left in Scotland. Two of these, the North British and the Caledonian, had become owners of major canals (see Appendix V on the Glasgow, Paisley and Johnstone Canal).

'George Stephenson'
Named after the inventor of the famous 'Rocket', this early engine was used on the Garnkirk and Glasgow Railway after it opened in 1831. Since its route was from Gartsherrie to Port Dundas it provided direct competition to the Monkland. (NL)

Jessop's Kilmarnock and Troon Railway was, in 1811, Scotland's first railway – as distinct from a wagonway. Wagonways, with wooden rails, had been used for a century, usually for private transport purposes, within a mine or harbour. For example temporary railways were used for earth moving in the construction of the Caledonian Canal. Jessop used the more durable cast iron for the flanged rails. Wagons and carriages were horse-drawn and if your axle span fitted the rails you could pay a toll to take your wagon on the railway. In 1817 it is recorded that passengers were carried on the Kilmarnock and Troon – possibly the first instance in Scotland. This was five years before the Union and the Caledonian were opened.

The first railway in the central belt was the Monkland and Kirkintilloch which was built to service the Forth and Clyde Canal and not to compete with it. The M&K was the first, in 1831, to switch to steam locomotives, having begun life as a horse-drawn system. As ever in late 18th century west of Scotland, the price of coal was the motivator. The new railway, with its terminus at Kirkintilloch, offered an alternative to the monopoly the Monkland Canal held on shipments of coal from the Coatbridge area to Glasgow. It also opened up markets for Lanarkshire coal, in the east of Scotland through Grangemouth and the Union Canal. The enabling Act was passed in 1824 and the line opened in 1826. A wharf was built on the canal for the convenience of the M&K by the proprietors of the Forth and Clyde and in the 1830s a basin was constructed. Typically a single horse pulled half a dozen wagons carrying around twenty tons of coal at a speed of three miles per hour. A single horse-drawn barge on the canal conveyed 50 tons at much the same speed.

In 1829 the Monkland Canal opened a branch cutting to the Gartsherrie Colliery. Gartsherrie coal for Edinburgh went first west to Port Dundas before travelling east on the Forth and Clyde and Union. That same year an extension to the M&K, the Wishaw and Coltness Railway, brought the Motherwell district into the system. In 1831 the Monkland Canal was carrying 200,000 tons of coal to Glasgow compared with 24,000 that went by rail on the M&K.

The next railway planned, was however, a more direct attack on the Monkland Canal. The M&K and Forth and Clyde route to Glasgow was 17 miles compared with only seven on the direct Monkland waterway. The Garnkirk and Glasgow Railway ran directly to Glasgow, starting just north of Coatbridge as a branch from the M&K, and heading for a terminus at the Cut of Junction between the Monkland and the Forth and Clyde at Blackhill. As such it did not affect the M&K's traffic on the Forth and Clyde, as sea-going ships were too deep-drafted to use the Cut. It was however a direct challenge to the Monkland Canal as it ran virtually parallel with it. The G&G officially opened in September 1831, using a Stephenson locomotive, and the line carried not only coal but passengers as well!

In 1828 the Ballochney Railway was opened to connect the Monkland Canal, via the M&K, to the coal pits further east, such as the Ballochney and Rawyards North collieries, in the environs of Airdrie. It was anticipated that around 60,000 tons of coal and 6,000 tons of ironstone, would move annually along the proposed line. Most of the railway lay above the level of the M&K and gravity brought the loaded wagons down (a horse rode down in a special wagon, a 'dandy' cart, to drag the empties back up the incline). Locomotives from the M&K were employed from 1832 onwards to work below the incline, and, if necessary, take the coal to Kirkintilloch. In 1828 the Ballochney also ran a horse-drawn coach for passengers to the head of the M&K at the Forth and Clyde, where it connected with the canal's passage boats.

With the opening of the Ballochney Railway lines had moved east and ever closer to the Union Canal. Local interests resolved to complete the link to exploit the mineral fields in the Slamannan area. The new railroad passed by the village of Slamannan to Causewayend on the canal, just west of the Avon Aqueduct, a distance of just over 12 miles. Both the

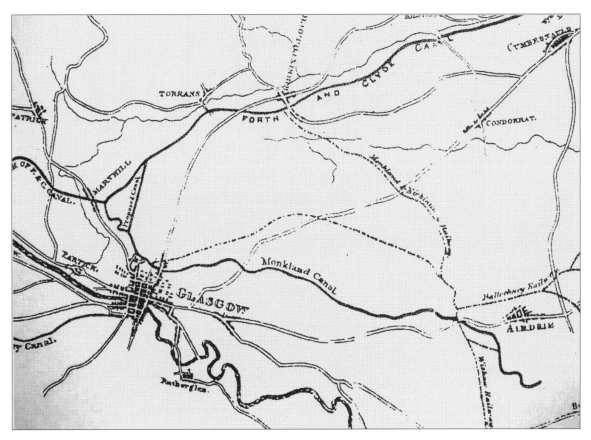

Ballochney Railway and the Union Canal companies gave financial support to piloting the Slamannan Railway Bill thorough Parliament, seeing it as complementary to their businesses. Yet in 1830 the Union Canal committee of management declined to support a proposed railway from the west end of the Union to Glasgow, not wishing to undermine its trade with the Forth and Clyde.

When The Slamannan Railway opened in 1840, using locomotives, it provided a link from Glasgow via the Garnkirk and Glasgow, the Monkland and Kirkintilloch, and the Ballochney to Causewayend and thence by the canal to Edinburgh. This effectively cut out the Forth and Clyde. The distance was shorter than

The 'Coatbridge' Railways
Although Coatbridge is not shown on this map of 1835 it is in fact at the junction of the Monkland and Kirkintilloch and the Ballochney Railways. The line branching westwards from the Monkland and Kirkintilloch is the Garnkirk and Glasgow although it is not named as such. As can be seen it duplicates the route of the Monkland Canal.

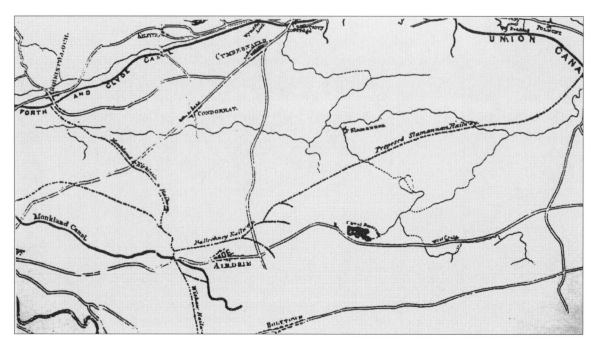

The Slamannan Railway
In 1840 a branch to the Ballochney Railway was extended east to join directly to the Union. A basin was built at the junction at Causewayend, just west of the Avon aqueduct. Apart from the carriage of minerals from the areas around the village of Slamannan it also carried passengers from Glasgow. They could by-pass the Forth and Clyde altogether and pick up a passage boat for Edinburgh at Causewayend.

using the two-canal route and saved the trouble of negotiating 15 locks as Causewayend is on the summit reach of the Union. It also provided a useful route to both Falkirk and Linlithgow. In July 1840 on an inaugural passenger service, the eastward trip took four hours including over two hours by passage boat on the canal.

The Slamannan's attraction for passengers was to be short-lived. When the Edinburgh and Glasgow Railway opened in 1842, with a two hour journey time between its termini at Haymarket and Queen Street, the circuitous rail-canal link was quickly abandoned by the public in favour of the more direct all rail route. The opening of the Edinburgh and Glasgow Railway was the greatest threat that had materialised to that point to the prosperity of the Forth and Clyde and the Union Canals. In the early 1830s there had been three attempts to get Acts for a Glasgow–Edinburgh railroad through Parliament but all had fallen (the Union proprietors spent a lot of money on opposing the Bills). However in 1838 the railway lobby triumphed.

It has been claimed that within a week of the rail service opening all but one of the stage coaches between the two cities had gone out of business. The Union and the Forth and Clyde agreed to act jointly to oppose the Edinburgh and Glasgow and under no circumstances to deal separately with the railway company. The canals cut their rates for goods and passengers more than once and the railway responded in kind to each of their reductions. In 1843 the canals were charging cabin passengers just under half of the five shillings they had been paying in 1840. By 1844 this rate was down to one shilling and four pence and until 1848 the canals managed to keep some of their passenger traffic. In 1843 the Union bought two steam tugs to pull its passage boats and shorten the journey but the canal could not compete for speed. By 1845 it was losing the battle for passengers. Negotiations opened with the intention that the Edinburgh and Glasgow should acquire both the Forth and Clyde and the Union. They did not mince their words over the battle with canals for passengers. They regretted the continuation of the competition and desired 'to put a stop to it'.

The proprietors of the Edinburgh and Glasgow Railway were ambitiously and aggressively expansionist. In 1844 they had built spurs to both the M&K and the Slamannan and they formulated a strategy to take control of the growing transport market in central Scotland. They were also concerned about the Caledonian Railway's possible plans for coast to coast lines. By 1846 they were in negotiations to take over the Monkland and Kirkintilloch, the Wishaw and Coltness, the Ballochney, the Slamannan and the Scottish Central Railway's links to Perth, Falkirk and Castlecary. The also wished to acquire the Forth and

Clyde, the Monkland and the Union Canals. The objections of traders in Glasgow and Edinburgh to a monopoly of water and rail transport between the cities could have been met. By incorporating a scale of maximum charges in the amalgamation legislation abuse could have been prevented. However, there was no mollifying those of the Edinburgh and Glasgow shareholders, mostly English, who thought that the Scottish directors were offering to pay too much for the acquisition of the three canals.

A new board was appointed and they dropped the amalgamation schemes. They hoped to raise traffic rates by negotiation with the competing canals rather than by buying them out. One result was the amalgamation of the M&K, the Ballochney and the Slamannan, which had shared a management structure, into the Monkland Railways in 1848 (ironically the Monklands was to become part of the Edinburgh and Glasgow just prior to it being taken over in 1865 by the North British Railway).

Part of the Edinburgh and Glasgow's grand scheme had been that the Forth and Clyde would take the leading role in the amalgamation of the three canals into one organization. When the railway deal fell apart in September 1846 the Forth and Clyde decided, after a serious investigation, not to proceed with its joining with the Union even though a draft bill had been negotiated and the Forth and Clyde had made a payment to the Union in anticipation of the arrangement being completed. Apart from the fact that the Forth and Clyde would have had to meet the whole purchase price itself, it is not difficult to see why. The Union was losing its passenger traffic, had substantial debts to service and had had to close for four months in 1846 because of leaks at the Avon Aqueduct. It had ruthlessly cut its rates (to half in some cases), to combat the railway opposition and yet had lost tonnage and passengers and gone into the red (see Appendix XXIV). A substantial increase in turnover would have been necessary to get back into profit. On the other hand amalgamating with the Monkland was a much more attractive proposition for the Forth and Clyde.

The two canal companies had worked together for their mutual benefit over the years, in fact since 1793, in making improvements to water supply and to the facilities around Port Dundas and the Cut of Junction. Further the Monkland had combatted the railway threat by building cuts to four important iron works in and around Coatbridge and the demand for iron for shipbuilding had grown and was likely to grow further (in 1834 Tod and McGregor had built the first all iron sea-going ship on the Clyde). There was also a regular demand for iron for railway lines! The take over price went to arbitration and the deal was agreed on the basis of three Monkland shares being valued as equal to one Forth and Clyde share and the Forth and Clyde assuming all of the Monkland's debts and liabilities. Parliamentary approval for the amalgamation was given in July 1846.

Today, when we are used to aggressive takeovers or willing-buyer-willing-seller negotiations, the Victorian arbitration process seems quaint. Both parties agreed on a group of three arbiters (the famous engineer, Robert Napier, was one of the appointees in this case), and then they argued their case on price and conditions to them. Eventually the three wise men handed down their judgement with high Victorian religiosity having, as they said, '… repeatedly heard the parties and being well and ripely advised in the said matter and having God and a good conscience before our eyes to give forth and pronounce our final sentence and decreet arbitral as follows …' Apart from possibly incurring the wrath of the Almighty, the parties faced

a fine of £10,000 each if they defaulted on the terms laid down!

On the other hand discussions with the Union (and with the new Edinburgh and Glasgow directors), over goods rates had continued through 1847 but no agreement was reached. Amalgamation of the two canals was always on the agenda and the Forth and Clyde offered the Union a discharge its debts, up to a limit of £116,000, and one Forth and Clyde share for five of the Union. This was a reasonably generous offer, taking into consideration the parlous state of the Union that the shares were in the newly combined Forth and Clyde and Monkland company. The offer was not accepted. The Forth and Clyde made it clear it would not continue to pay the annuity to the Union. Throughout 1848 the Union kept pressing for at least a tri-partite agreement on rates and the Edinburgh and Glasgow was keen on a deal for 'the avoidance of loss by competition'. But again no agreement emerged and, in some spirit of defiance or an attempt to break the deadlock, the Union unilaterally reduced its rates on coal, iron and cotton.

In truth the Union was in the weakest position of the three. Since the opening of the railway in 1842 and the subsequent fare cutting fight for passenger traffic, the Union profits had slumped. A deal with the railway company seemed to be the best way out of the dilemma. There was little possibility of the situation improving as the Caledonian Railway was constructing another Glasgow to Edinburgh line and competition for passengers could only get worse. Negotiations for a takeover by the Edinburgh and Glasgow were completed in August 1848 (meanwhile the Edinburgh and Glasgow scooped up the Monkland Railways). As discussed earlier a handsome offer was made to the Union shareholders. The formalities of the takeover were completed in 1849. Sixteen years later, the

Edinburgh and Glasgow itself was to be absorbed by the North British Railway. It was the first in a number of acquisitions that NB, which itself had been launched at the height of the 'mania' in 1844, was to make over 50 years. It became part of the London & North Eastern Railway in the great post-war rationalisation of the UK railroad system in 1923.

The decision of the Forth and Clyde proprietors to go it alone was fully justified by events for it enjoyed another 20 years of profitable independence as the coal and iron trades in and around the Coatbridge area expanded. During this time it continued to make technical improvements in the canals and developed the basin at Grangemouth into a full-fledged dock system. It acquired, and subsequently extended, the Drumpellier Railway in 1851. This line, incorporated in 1843, was something of a curiosity, being only 2,000 yards long. (It had an inclined plane with a static steam engine at one end to haul the coal wagons. It had opened originally to feed the Monkland Canal from the coalfields at Calder.) At various times in the 1850s and 1860s it reached accommodations on rates with the competing railway companies such as the Caledonian and the Edinburgh and Glasgow. It was responsible for the introduction of steam and screw propulsion (the 'puffers') on the Forth and Clyde. It took over the Forth and Cart Canal in 1855 (this tiny half-mile-long waterway, joining the Forth and Clyde to the Clyde opposite the mouth of the River Cart, had been opened in 1840 to get Lanarkshire coal to Paisley). It built its own railway line from Grangemouth docks to Grahamston (Falkirk) to provide a speedier link to the canal.

But the railways were crowding in. The Glasgow, Dumbarton and Helensburgh Railway, which opened in 1859 and was acquired by the Edinburgh and Glasgow in 1862, started to attract traffic to the west of Glasgow, that would otherwise have gone by canal. The Edinburgh and Glasgow opened a branch from Grangemouth to their main line in 1860. The Caledonian Railway opened a line between Coatbridge and Rutherglen in 1865. The Forth and Clyde failed to get parliamentary approval in 1866 to extend the Monkland 10 miles south to the Wishaw coalfields largely because of the opposition of the North British Railway who were planning a direct Glasgow to Coatbridge branch. This opened in 1870 and was a direct challenge to the Monkland. There were signs that the mineral seams through which the Monkland passed were becoming worked out and not being allowed to extend south to the Wishaw coalfields was a severe blow to the Monkland, and was fully intended as such by the North British.

In 1867 the proprietors of the Forth and Clyde Navigation sold their undertaking to the Caledonian Railway Company, after being courted by the North British, and did rather well out of it. Their judgement was sound. They could see decline ahead for the Monkland and within a few years the more gradual decline in the Forth and Clyde's tonnages would begin. The opposition of the North British to the takeover was bought off by giving it equality of charges with the Caledonian Railway at the Grangemouth docks, and the right to use the line from there to Grahamston.

The Caledonian (incorporated in 1845 as a Carlisle to Glasgow route), had bought the Scottish Central two years earlier to add to a portfolio which contained the Glasgow, Paisley and Greenock and the Glasgow, Garnkirk and Coatbridge railways. So its interests in the industrial central belt was not new. The Caledonian survived as an independent unit until the great 1923 upheaval when it became part of London Midland and Scottish Railway.

The railways came later to the Highlands but the

competition with the Highland canals was not so directly intense. In general terms the opening of cross-country rail routes in central Scotland and in England, such as the Newcastle and Carlisle Railway which opened in 1838, must have had an effect. They must have encouraged merchants to move goods from say the Humber to the Mersey for onward movement to Ireland rather than to ship them through the Caledonian. In the same way the Baltic and continental Europe was 'nearer' for the Glasgow trader if he used rail to take his commodities to the Forth before shipping them onwards.

For a traveller Glasgow to Inverness was a three day and three ship journey using the Crinan and the Caledonian. A railroad from Glasgow to Oban or Fort William should in all logic have diverted travellers away from the Crinan at least. Any direct line from the Lowlands to Inverness was going to affect the numbers who would potentially use both canals.

By 1850 rail travel was possible between Glasgow and Aberdeen. Four railway companies were involved; a different one for each of the Glasgow to Castlecary, Castlecary to Perth, Perth to Forfar and Forfar to Aberdeen sections. Since the Caledonian Railway had linked London to Glasgow in 1848 an Aberdeen to London journey was possible. By 1856 two companies had achieved a link from Aberdeen to Keith and Inverness to Nairn but it was 1861 before the gap from Keith to Nairn was closed. This was hardly a direct line from Glasgow to Inverness. It was slow, circuitous and not very popular. A slightly more direct line was opened in 1863 by branching south from the Inverness to Aberdeen route at Forres to Dunkeld and Perth. The amalgamation of these Aberdeen and Inverness lines in 1865, named the Highland Railway, started to build a line from Inverness to Aviemore in 1883 and the long Forres detour was avoided. Any or all of these was

more convenient than the three ship trip through the two canals or even a one ship voyage round the Mull of Kintyre. Unless of course the traveller was on holiday and wanted to enjoy the scenery in a leisurely manner.

The Highland Railway was promised support for opposition to the proposal to create a line, to be called the Glasgow and Northwestern Railway, alongside the canal all the way up the Great Glen, if it built a link to Aviemore. The opposition was successful as this project failed to get Parliamentary approval. It may be conjectured that both railways would have struggled to make a profit from the relatively small number of passengers wishing to travel from Glasgow to Inverness. It is not difficult however to imagine that on a less than warm summer day more tourists might have preferred to enjoy the views from the comfort of a carriage rather than from the deck of a steamer.

The Callander and Oban Railway was essentially an extension northwards of the Dunblane, Doune and Callander Railway, and when it opened in 1880 it was operated by Caledonian Railway. This line did not seem to unduly concern the commissioners of the Caledonian Canal who did not oppose its building. However in 1883 they thought it 'in the public interest' to oppose the Glasgow and Northwestern railway bill which clearly was much more of a threat.

It was 1894 before a railway reached the Caledonian Canal at Fort William when the North British opened the West Highland Railway from Cardross via Crianlarich. The Commissioners at the Caledonian Canal did not oppose the bill for this railway and it appeared that when they opened their branch line to Banavie a year later it actually stimulated tourist trade for cruising on the canal. Nor did they object during the Parliamentary procedures for the Inveregarry to Fort William Railway Bill of 1896 or, two years later, the Highland Railway Bill for a line from

Inverness to Fort Augustus. They took the view that certain clauses in the proposals protected the canal's interests.

The coming of the railways to the Highlands may be said therefore to have an influence on the traffic on the Highland canals from the 1860s onward. And while they almost certainly took traffic away they can hardly be said to have contributed to their decline in the same dramatic way that was witnessed in the Lowlands. Of course nothing like the mass movement of people and materials was involved in those remote, rural and sparsely populated areas. Not having been taken into the ownership of any railway company the Crinan and the Caledonian avoided being swept up in the great rail reorganisation of 1923. Before then, of course, in 1919 their control had been vested in the Ministry of Transport.

CHAPTER TEN

THE MID-SCOTLAND CANAL
THE CANAL THAT NEVER WAS

In October 2002 there was a press announcement, after the publication of the Scottish Executive paper, 'Scotland's Canals – an asset for the future' that a canal to link Loch Lomond with the Clyde along the course of the River Leven was under consideration. It was certainly 'news' but it was not a new idea. John Smeaton, the 18th century builder of the Forth and Clyde Canal, certainly investigated using the Leven valley when he was surveying routes for the Forth and Clyde. The last manifestation of a proposed canal along the course of the River Leven was more than a century ago when the great debate about the project to build a 'Mid-Scotland Canal' was occupying many minds.

As the Forth and Clyde approached the centenary of its opening there was much comment about its limitations, namely, its inability to take the sea-going ships of the day. Construction of the Manchester Ship Canal had begun (It opened in 1894), and the initiative of the city of Manchester in promoting and partially funding the new waterway, which gave the city access to the sea, was much applauded. Was Scotland to be left behind? Surely, the Clyde and the Forth, Glasgow and Edinburgh, could be linked by a new canal capable of taking the largest naval and commercial ships?

Admittedly the Leven canal was a side issue to the main controversy, which reached peaks both before and after the First World War, about the course and nature of new canal across Scotland which would allow the nation's battleships to cross from the Atlantic Ocean to the North Sea. A passage of a few hours (say, about five), rather than a sail northabout of hundreds of miles through the Pentland Firth (taking about two days), it was argued, was going to be of considerable strategic advantage to the nation.

To allow the passage of battleships a canal would have to be around 26ft deep and 100ft wide at the bottom. The existing Forth and Clyde Canal, catered for vessels with a draft of 8ft and a beam of 18ft. Enlarging it was not considered by the proponents of a new canal and they referred to it somewhat disparagingly as the 'barge canal'.

Essentially there were two possible routes, both of which had their fervent advocates:

– The 'Direct Route', which began at Yoker on the Clyde and more or less followed the line of the Forth and Clyde Canal, north of Milngavie and Kirkintilloch to Grangemouth.

– The 'Loch Lomond Route' came through Loch Lomond, which is only 22ft above sea level. It exited at its south-east corner, using the course of the Water of Endrick, and drove east across the Carse of Stirling to the Forth.

There were three possible routes into Loch Lomond from the Clyde. One was a cutting of four miles from Ardmorehead, south-east of Helensburgh, to Arden on the Loch. A second was to use the valley of the Leven from Balloch south to Dumbarton. The

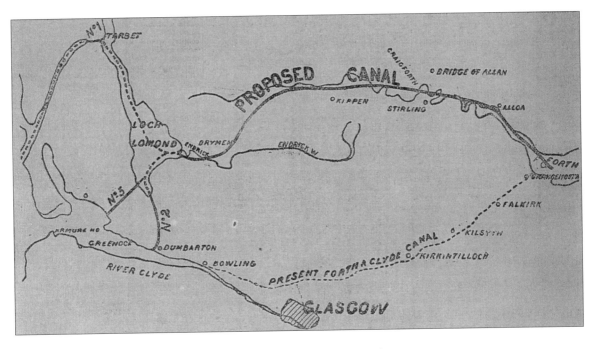

third, and the one which became favoured and which featured in most discussions entered Loch Lomond at its north-western corner by a channel cut through from Loch Long, from Arrochar to Tarbet.

Further stimulation may have come from Germany in 1887 when the construction of the Kiel Canal, to link the Baltic with the North Sea, began. In 1889 the civil engineering partnership of D&T Stevenson, (the 'Lighthouse' Stevensons), in the person of D A Stevenson published a report, at the behest of Edinburgh interests, advocating the merits of the Loch Lomond route, based on the Arrochar-Tarbet link. J Law Crawford, secretary of the Committee of the Forth and Clyde Ship Canal Association, went in to print, in the *Glasgow Herald*, in defence of the Direct Route on the basis of a study commissioned from the civil engineers Crouch and Hogg. So what was to be a protracted battle was joined.

The 1889 Proposal
In November 1889, D A Stevenson, of the established firm of engineering consultants and builders of many of Scotland's light-houses, proposed a scheme for a ship canal across Scotland. A choice of three routes from the Forth to the Clyde were set out as shown. Glasgow and the line of the Forth and Clyde were avoided due to engineering problems associated with the high ground of this route. (GLA)

TABLE 16. *The 1890s proposals*

	Lomond Route (via Tarbet)	Direct Route (to Yoker)
Length of the canal	51 miles	29 miles
Distance to the Cloch	66 miles	49 miles
Passage time to Cloch	9 hours	6 hours
Canal dimensions (bottom width x depth)	120 x 26 feet	100 x 26 feet
Locks	2 at each end	1 at each end
Cost estimate	£8 million	£5 million

The protagonists were agreed on the need for the canal and deployed very similar arguments – the strategic benefit to a Royal Navy that would be hard pressed to defend the Empire in time of war, the advantage to commercial shipping from a short east to west passage and the development of towns and industries, from ease of access to a cost-effective transport facility.

They were in accord, also, in specifying that their canals would be large enough for the biggest naval and commercial ships and open for passage at all states of the tide. Table 16 compares and summarises the two sets of proposals as they evolved in the 1890s as each party responded to criticism from the other. Table 17 will show how the specifications had changed by 1917 (battleships had got bigger for one thing), after the debate had rumbled on for more than twenty years.

The Stevenson proposals seem to have been the better-researched technically and sharp criticism was levelled at the other project. The cost estimate of the Direct Route, which had been based on a somewhat simplistic comparison with the Manchester Ship Canal, was accused of being too low. The Direct Route,

a 'no-locks-sea-level' concept, passed through ground as high as 150ft above sea-level for about 17 miles and would, it was pointed out, require the excavation of 280 million cubic yards of soil. At 12 pence (£0.05) per cubic yard this put the cost at £14 million not £5 million! If the Direct Route was to be open at both ends how were ships to cope with the currents in the canal caused by the fact that high tide in the Forth occurred at different times and over a different range from high tide on the Clyde? (The high water range on the Forth was 18ft and 11ft on the Clyde). These problems, and the relative shallowness of the Clyde, were in fact the main reasons why the Stevensons had come out in favour of the Lomond Route.

So the Direct Route proposal was modified to have a lock at each end. The excavation costs could be reduced, it was argued, by introducing hydraulic lifts at the summit, and the 'Direct Routers' stuck to their £5 million estimate. But what about dredging the Clyde from Yoker to Greenock? (In 1890 there was only 21ft of water in the Clyde at high tide and there would be 26ft in the canal). Should that not be included in the cost of the Direct Route?

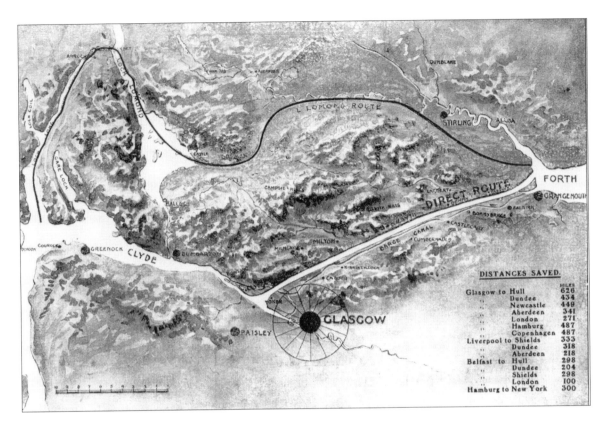

DISTANCES SAVED.	
	MILES
Glasgow to Hull	626
" Dundee	434
" Newcastle	449
" Aberdeen	341
" London	271
" Hamburg	487
" Copenhagen	487
Liverpool to Shields	333
" Dundee	318
" Aberdeen	218
Belfast to Hull	298
" Dundee	204
" Shields	298
" London	100
Hamburg to New York	300

The Direct Route was planned to go through high ground, but not any higher than the Lomond Route does at Arrochar, it was noted. 'And if the route is also longer so it seems doubtful that a canal can be made for only £8 million. In any case the Direct Route is a sea-level, sea water canal and will be less likely to freeze than the fresh water Lomond Route.' And so the argument waxed and waned.

The Convention of Royal Burghs of Scotland had discussed the concept in 1891 and approved of it. So too had a special conference held in Edinburgh in April 1894 attended by 60 delegates from towns all over Scotland. But neither party had made much progress by the turn of the century in raising private capital or government support for their particular route.

The Glasgow, or 'Direct' Route
Taken from a pamphlet entitled 'Glasgow's Danger!', this map shows the alternative to what was called the 'Loch Lomond 'route. At 29 miles the Direct Route was only half the length of the alternative based on the Stevenson design and could have been traversed in five hours. It was suggested that some of the government's income from its Suez Canal shares could pay for the interest on the capital of £23,000,000 that it was estimated it would cost. (GLA)

However the European arms race of the early 1900s gave new impetus to the strategic arguments for a trans-Scotland canal.

When in 1906 Admiral Sir John Fisher, First Sea Lord, had HMS *Dreadnought* launched he made every other battleship in the world redundant. She was the first 'all big gun' ship and was superior in fire power, speed, (she was turbine powered), and armour to any other capital ship then afloat. She gave her name to the type; the 'Dreadnought'. Every other maritime power responded by scrapping its existing battleship fleet and building its own version of the *Dreadnought*. Germany certainly did and in consequence enlarged the Kiel Canal for its new battleships.

The Kiel Canal, or Kaiser-Wilhelm Kanal, had opened in 1895 and had cost £8 million. It had allowed ready access from the Baltic to the North Sea for the German fleet. From 1907 onwards, as well as building its new battleships, Germany spent an additional £12 million widening the canal and deepening it to 37ft. The German government was known to subsidise its operation. If Germany could invest in a canal and subvent its operation for her Navy why could not Great Britain take a similar strategic view?

As fortune would have it the future of Britain's canals were being considered by the government and a Royal Commission on Canals and Waterways sat from 1906 to 1909. This gave the opportunity for the two parties advocating the trans-Scotland canal to present their cases anew and the Royal Commission took evidence from both. By this time the two cases had been refined to take into account the cost of over 20 road and rail bridges that would have to cross the canal and the fact that a depth of 36ft was now wanted for the Dreadnoughts. The cost of the Lomond Route was then put at £20 million and the Direct Route some £3 million more (Much the same cost as the enlarged Kiel

Canal it was later pointed out).

WT Douglas, acting for the Public Work Loans Commissioners, argued for the Direct Route and proposed that it should be a high level construction (ie not a sea level canal), with six locks, three up and three down. Admiral Sir Charles Campbell, secretary of the Forth and Clyde Canal National Association, advocated the Lomond Route. He added that it was better to spend £20 million on the canal than much more building a Royal Naval Depot at Rosyth, the contracts for which were being let at that time. If battleships could get from the Clyde to the Forth in a few hours there would be no need for a depot in the east. Stevenson added a financial case for the Lomond Route based on 11 million gross tons per annum of shipping using the waterway and producing a return of 3.8 per cent on the £20 million investment (It has to be said that nobody else talked of the commercial success of the canal with anything like the same certainty as Stevenson).

Reporting in 1909, the Royal Commission came down on the side of the Lomond Route, possibly because the Admiralty seemed to prefer it, but rather sat on the fence saying that a wider canal of 148ft at the bottom '… would unquestionably possess some strategical value.' But not so great a value, it said, as to justify large scale government expenditure on the project or a state guarantee of interest on the total estimated cost of construction. The Royal Commission further suggested that government aid might be forthcoming if the Lomond route was followed and the canal's dimensions met Admiralty requirements.

Throughout 1908 Glasgow Corporation had been considering its attitude to a ship canal. Its findings were pro-canal and it said as much to the Royal Commission. It stopped short, however, of agreeing to subscribe to a canal company as some members of the

Corporation doubted that it would be a profitable concern. In 1909 Glasgow was asked formally by the Royal Commission if it would put up cash or guarantee of the interest on the capital cost (The precedent of the City of Manchester investing £5 million in the construction of the Manchester Ship Canal was referred to). Glasgow's response was to set up a special committee to investigate the matter. However it reacted with more urgency after the Royal Commission came out in favour of the Lomond Route as it feared that Glasgow would be severely disadvantaged through being by-passed.

In March 1911, a meeting of the executive committee of the Mid-Scotland Canal National Association heard debate on the merits of the two routes and decided that in future its policy would be to advocate the Direct Route, recognising that Glasgow would not give financial support to the Lomond Route as it would get no advantage from it. Seven months later the Corporation of Glasgow adopted as policy, by a majority of two to one, to support a canal by the Direct Route. Yet it was described during the debate as 'the most wild, harum-scarum, hair-brained scheme' by one irate councillor.

By 1913 Glasgow's Special Committee had reached its verdict. It recommended the Direct Route to the government if it thought the canal was of sufficient strategic importance but it doubted if the canal could be justified for commercial reasons alone. It thought that no private capital would be forthcoming to build it. When in February that year McKinnon Wood, the Secretary of State for Scotland, came to Glasgow, in part in response to a publicity campaign for a canal run by the *Daily Record and Daily Mail*, and part in response to pressure from Scottish MPs, he was advised of Glasgow's views. However the government took no action.

But the Lomond Route devotees had not gone away. They had continued to lobby and a sub-committee of the Committee of Imperial Defence had found the Lomond Route to be preferable to the Direct Route and of enough strategic value for the government to 'aid' a commercial canal. It stopped short of recommending that it be paid for by public money. Its view was endorsed by the Royal Commission and passed to Prime Minister Asquith in 1913.

The Convention of Royal Burghs again debated the subject. But a motion to memorialise government for a sea level canal by the Direct Route from Yoker to Grangemouth, proposed by Falkirk and seconded by Glasgow, lost to an amendment to have the words 'Yoker' and 'Grangemouth' removed. 'They should go forward in an united manner for Scotland as a whole and not for the interests of one part of the country against the interests of another part', was the consensus of the meeting. The Provost of Inverness had suggested that if the government wanted a battleship canal it should enlarge what it already owned – the Caledonian Canal (By no means was this an impractical suggestion. By making Loch Ness the summit and making a deep cut through to Loch Lochy all the locks from Fort Augustus to Banavie would be eliminated. Loch Lochy would have become some 40ft shallower but it would still have been deep enough for battleships).

The mood of the Convention was the mood of many others who were calling for unity on the principle of building the canal and leaving the decision on the route to government. Is it a Scottish characteristic that enthusiasm for the dispute over the detail detracts from the pursuit of the larger vision?

The government decided it could not give any guarantees of the interest on any capital that might be subscribed for a commercial canal and, with the country plunged into the First World War, the matter of raising equity for a canal across Scotland faded into the background.

During the war British battleships sailed to the Battle of Jutland from Scapa Flow. They sailed east, but could just as easily have sailed west if the confrontation with the German fleet had taken place in the Atlantic. Perhaps this made the point that the traditional Orkney anchorage allowed the fleet to cover both east and west coasts with equal facility.

However, even in time of war, the Admiralty worked away at refining the proposals and commissioned Armstrong Whitworth & Co. to prepare plans for a trans-Scotland canal. A summary of their proposals is shown in Table 17.

To meet the Royal Navy's needs the proposed canal was enlarged to a width of 150ft on the bottom with a depth of 45ft. Armstrong Whitworth's estimate of £53 million for the Direct Route included £10 million for the necessary dredging of channels in the Forth and the Clyde.

The locks, with a length of over 1400ft, definitely had battleships in mind. Such a canal would have accommodated, Cunard's ocean liners like *Aquitania*, and the future *Queen Mary* and *Queen Elizabeth*. It is intriguing to imagine these great ships cruising through the suburbs of Stirling or the islands of Loch Lomond. The cruise ship potential in the present day is obvious, whether it be from central Scotland to Loch Lomond or by ocean-going liners passing from the North Sea to the Western Isles. A century ago liners did not 'cruise'; that was to be a market that was developed in the second half of the 20th century when the jet aircraft ousted the liner from its purely passenger carrying role.

Government attitude was clear. It had to be a commercial canal financed by private enterprise. This

was a clear lead. The shipping community showed no enthusiasm for the project in the decade after World War I in what was a period of deepest recession for the industry.

Alleviating the high unemployment of the late 1920s was a stated motive for reconsidering the possible construction of the Mid-Scotland Ship Canal. A committee, chaired by Sir Sydney Chapman, was asked to report into 'the advantages which might be obtained from such a canal and the probable economic results of its construction.' The Mid-Scotland Ship Canal National Association was still in existence and manfully advanced its usual arguments in favour of the canal by the Direct Route. There was nobody to advance the case of the Lomond Route, the Defence Departments having reconsidered their views on the strategic worth of such a canal. Little support was forthcoming from the Corporation of Glasgow, the Chamber of Shipping or the Corporation of Edinburgh.

By 1930 the Committee had reached the conclusions that the likely cost of a sea-level Direct Route canal would be of the order of £50 million, that no private investment would be forthcoming, that the return on the capital would be negligible and that the effects on reducing unemployment during construction would not be felt for at least four years after planning started. The Mid-Scotland Ship Canal was not to be.

However, there was to be one last throw of the dice. Again the high level of unemployment was one of the drivers of the post-World War II enquiry, conducted by the Scottish Council for Development and Industry in 1947.

The strategic argument had gone. The battleship was obsolete. Pearl Harbour and the sinking of *Prince of Wales* and *Repulse* by bombers off Singapore had

TABLE 17. *The 1917 Proposals*

	Lomond Route (via Tarbert)	Direct Route (via Yoker)
Distance to deep Water	71.3 miles	50.0 miles
Artificial works	44.7 miles	47.8 miles
River Dredging (Forth & Clyde combined)	4.0 miles	18.7 miles
Length at 50 feet above sea level	12.0 miles	22.5 miles
Length at 100 feet above sea level	9.0 miles	20.3 miles
Dimensions (bottom width x depth, in feet)	150 x 45	150 x 45
Air draft (in feet)	120	120
Number of locks	2 at each end	2 at each end
Max. lock dimensions (length X breadth x depth in feet)	1440 x 130 x 45	1440 x 130 x 45
Number of road & rail crossings	14	28
Cost estimate	£33.5 million	£53 million
Estimated construction time	7 to 12 years	10 to 16 years

demonstrated the battleships' vulnerability to air power. HMS *Vanguard*, laid down in 1944, had been delivered in 1946. She was to be Britain's last battleship.

A Direct Route canal of 40ft depth, a base 150ft wide and locks 1200ft long was priced at £125 million. A cost benefit analysis was carried out taking into account savings in unemployment payments and income tax recovered but it was demonstrated that the savings would be less than 3 per cent interest on the £125 million capital cost. The principle of a new waterway got support from shipping interests but they doubted if a canal would 'pay'. The SCDI report saw no need to change the view taken in 1930.

Probably the best chance for the Mid-Scotland Canal had been before World War I and especially around 1909 at the time of the Royal Commission's report. The promise of government financial support at that time would have made all the difference. But the Royal Commission was hopelessly split on the principle of the government investing in the transport infra-structure. Having said that, the divisions over the route and the hesitancy of the business community to invest in the project were equally at fault.

The Forth and Clyde Canal, the 'barge canal', was, as we shall discuss later, rejoined to the Edinburgh and Glasgow Union Canal and reopened for leisure traffic in 2002 after many years of closure. The final cost was £84.5 million. This was funded by the Millennium Commission, Scottish Enterprise, the European Union, Scottish Local Authorities and British Waterways. In other words it was funded by a great deal of public money. The justification for the expenditure was the economic, leisure and amenity benefits of the project. 'Leisure' and 'amenity' were not words that were heard in the debate on canals a century ago.

The Canal Route through Loch Lomond
The Lomond Route, according to the 1917 proposal, would have
brought the canal into the Loch at the south-east corner near the
Endrick. It would have continued north through a dredged channel
between the islands of Inchmoan and Inchcruin and south-west of
Inchlonaig. (GLA)

CHAPTER ELEVEN

THE WATERSHED
THE ROYAL COMMISSION ON CANALS
AND WATERWAYS OF 1909

By the turn of the 20th century a great number of Britain's canals had passed their centenary and what is more had faced about 50 years of serious competition from the developing and expanding railway systems.

Concerns over the balance of legislative restrictions between the two modes had led to a raft of legislation from the 1840s onwards most of which had tried to free up the waterways to allow them to attempt to compete more effectively with the railways. To quote one example, an Act of 1845 gave the canals the right to act as 'carriers'. They were allowed to ply for hire as barge owners and to charge freight for the carriage of goods. Previously they had powers just to charge dues on cargoes carried in other owners' craft. This put them on the same footing as the railroads. Two years later they were given powers to borrow money to allow them to develop their carrying trade if they so desired.

Further in the 1840s approximately one third of canal mileage had come under the ownership or control of railway companies. This had raised fears about the elimination of competition for inland traffic and the consequent upward manipulation of charges.

Unfavourable comparisons were drawn between the United Kingdom and continental Europe where, under governmental guidance, the canal systems had been improved at the end of the 19th century to balance the expansion of rail traffic. It was claimed that considerable growth in the tonnage canals carried and benefits in the reduction of internal transport costs,

had resulted. The British experience was simply stated. From 1888–1905 the tonnage carried by rail had grown from 281.7 million to 461.1 million while that moved by waterway had fallen slightly from 35.3 million to 34.1 million. Of this 34 million, 62 per cent had been carried on canals which accounted for only a fifth of the nation's mileage of waterways. In the 60 years from the start of the 'railway age' the canals had been overtaken in tonnage and marginalised in use. Many had simply ceased to function as carriers of goods.

There had been a Railway and Canal Act of 1888 and a Board of Trade enquiry into the condition of the canals in 1892 to 1895 but these had little effect. Pressure to address the situation really grew after 1902. A number of disparate bills, to try to improve the situation of the canals, was introduced to Parliament in 1904, 1905 and 1906 by Sir William Holland and others, and the demand for a Royal Commission to examine the state of the waterways grew. The government bowed to this and set up a 19-man commission which sat from 1906. It travelled widely in the United Kingdom and Europe, took a great deal of evidence and reported in 1909.

The Royal Commission understandably concerned itself mostly with the waterways of England and Wales (after all of the 4670 miles of canal in Britain only 150 were still operating in Scotland in 1905). Nevertheless serious proposals for the future of the Scottish canals were explored. No recommendations were to be made in respect of the canals owned by railway companies ie the Forth and Clyde, the Monkland and the Union. But their condition and performance were analysed.

The trends in the United Kingdom as a whole were mirrored in Scotland. In 1849 the Union had been absorbed by the Edinburgh and Glasgow Railway which in turn was acquired in 1865 by the North British Railway. Two years later, when the Forth and Clyde and Monklands configuration was taken over by the Caledonian Railway Company, the tonnage of goods carried on the system had been in excess of three million. By the time the Commission sat this had fallen to 931,500 tons. Little more than 250,000 tons in total was being transported over the other three Scottish canals.

The Royal Commission was much exercised by the frequently expressed view that it had been unhealthy for the railways to buy out canals as it had been done for the devious purpose of eliminating competition and keeping rail freight rates high. 'Traders require more speed and punctuality in delivery of goods than transport by inland waterway can ever give' and, 'How is it possible to ensure that an enterprise competes with itself?' were typical of the defences offered by the railway lobby. Nevertheless the commission concluded that if the balance between railway and waterway transport was to be *rectified*, (its choice of word), then reconstruction of the carrying capacity of the canals was necessary. 'This is the remedy which has been successfully applied in other countries,' it pointed out. But who was to pay for this reconstruction? The commission was in no doubt that 'private enterprise cannot be expected to take the improvement of the canals in hand.'

The matter of the competition between the Scottish railways and their canals was given an interesting explanation in the evidence submitted.

The first Scottish canal to lose its independence was the Union and it may have been a coincidence that it was the first to go into decline. As we have seen, when the Edinburgh and Glasgow Railway opened in 1842 its effects were immediately felt in the competition for passengers. The Union and the Forth and Clyde managed to maintain their goods traffic by rate reductions but by 1845 a complex tri-partite agreement was being negotiated.

However the Edinburgh and Glasgow withdrew from their agreement with the Forth and Clyde in 1846 due to internal and external opposition and the whole deal collapsed. Shareholders balked at the expense of buying both canals to secure the passenger traffic between the two cities. In fact the canal was already losing the passenger rates war. The Union canal company withdrew from the passenger trade, in 1848, during renewed negotiations in with the Edinburgh and Glasgow and by June 1849 an Act had been steered through Parliament vesting the Union Canal in the ownership of the railway company. The railway could now set passenger rates with freedom. By 1865 the Edinburgh and Glasgow had been acquired by the North British Railway, which company claimed that it did try, unsuccessfully, to stimulate the coal trade on the canal.

The Forth and Clyde continued to be independent and prosperous for another 20 years but it and the railways in central Scotland undoubtedly fixed rates between them to protect themselves against all out competition. But the Caledonian Railway Company had its eye on the well-developed and busy Grangemouth Docks. Attractive terms were offered to the Forth and Clyde proprietors and in 1867 the vesting act was passed.

The Lowland canals were therefore outwith the terms of reference of the Royal Commission. But did their experiences under railway ownership offer any evidence for the enquiry of the need to 'rectify the balance'. The evidence offered by the Caledonian Railway Co was instructive, but no mention was made of the rate-fixing that had gone on 40 years before. It was conveniently or genuinely forgotten about.

Usually the vesting acts had required the railways to maintain the condition of the canals as they found them on acquisition. Generally they had discharged this responsibility by a policy of maintenance rather than one of improvement. By the beginning of the 20th century the best that could be said for railway owned canals was that they were in the same state of technical development as they had been in the middle of the 19th century. The Caledonian Railway claimed that it regarded its Forth and Clyde Canal as its main artery for competing with the North British Railway and had kept it in a 'high state of efficiency' and done all they could to encourage traffic. When canal traffic fell, partly due to a natural decline in mineral workings on the line of the canal and partly due to competition for coal traffic from the North British, the Caledonian felt obliged to build railway lines in the district served by the canal to compete with the rival railway and thereby with the canal and itself.

It is difficult to take exception to the view, given in evidence, that 'If enormous sums had been spent in developing canals – you must have a more efficient canal than you have today – but the canal would not have been an effective competitor with the railway.' With some prescience more than one observer suggested that, in any case, there were signs that railways would lose out to transport by motor vehicles for heavy goods carried over short distances!

For all that Smeaton's canal lay outside the Royal Commission's remit it was to spend most of the time that it devoted to Scottish matters on the question of

providing a new link between the Clyde and the Forth. The 'Battleship Canal', the 'Mid-Scotland Ship Canal' as the concept was variously called is discussed in Chapter 10. In this, as in many other matters, the Royal Commission managed to sit on the fence.

The Highland Canals were of course under public ownership and the commission, in reporting to government, was speaking directly to those who had the power and the means, if they had the will, to make changes.

When submissions were made on the Crinan Canal the commission found itself being lobbied on the building of a canal on Loch Fyne from Tarbert to west Loch Tarbert. A three-mile-long, 21ft-deep, waterway was costed at £301,000 by Hall-Blyth although this figure was disputed by some. Crouch and Hogg, put a price of £800,000 on modifying and enlarging the existing Crinan route. The Tarbert transit would have taken less time, it was accepted. But once through and having sailed nearly 10 miles further down the Loch from Ardrishaig, the westerly exit of the canal was 22 miles further away from Oban than Crinan was. Access to Gigha and the Sound of Islay were better from Loch Tarbert although opponents of the scheme attempted to make much of its exposure to gales from the south-west.

Common ground was found by all parties in criticising the state of the Crinan. 'The Crinan is worn out and in need of extensive repairs and alterations if it is to continue in its present form.' was the conclusion reached by the Royal Commission which visited the canal in 1907. Better, it was suggested, to spend capital making the canal modern and fit for the future rather than to continually make up income shortfalls to effect stop-gap repairs. Nobody seemed to question the need for a canal across Kintyre.

The £800,000 proposal was for an eight mile 20ft

deep by 80ft wide channel, with two new locks, instead of nine of the originals, capable of taking the sea-going steamers of the day. The locks were to be at Dunardry and Badden, just north of Oakfield.

However the Crinan had to be closed for four years while the alterations were to be made. A 'new' Crinan on a different and slightly longer route was not given much support even though the 'old' Crinan could have continued in operation throughout the construction phase. This would have met the main objection by David Macbrayne, who opposed the enlargement of the Crinan, and who, short-sightedly, was overly concerned with the short term disruption to his tourist trade from the Clyde to Oban. His passengers could have been bussed across the peninsula, for a period, at the end of which his largest steamers could have made direct transits to the Western Isles. Generally the local town and county councils supported the idea as did British Aluminium who wanted a deeper canal to improve the link from Glasgow to their smelters at Foyers on the Caledonian and at Kinlochleven. No one doubted that the Crinan was a vital link for the west Highlands.

Would the commission come down on the side of the cheaper Tarbert alternative and thereby possibly condemn the century-old route, and all that it had cost the public purse, to a slow death? If it favoured the Crinan route, would it be brave enough to recommend tackling its inadequacies once and for all and modernising it at double the estimated cost of the new Tarbert proposal? Surely continuing the unsatisfactory policy of piecemeal repairs of what was recognised to be an inadequate facility was not an option?

Between the two rival options the Commission would '… not attempt to decide as that would be better left to those in the west of Scotland who would be most interested …' They were not convinced that either

project would generate enough traffic to give a return on the capital outlay. It did suggest that government make it a condition of its advancing capital for either Tarbert or Crinan, that local trade and tourist trade interests should contribute as well or give guarantees of interest on the capital. As we know the 1801 canal continues in existence to this day and continues to be repaired and maintained to meet today's requirements – from the public purse.

Inverness Town and County Councils, Inverness Harbour Trustees and British Aluminium all wanted to see the Caledonian enlarged and improved. Again we hear the complaints of a canal being 'antiquated'. In places the channel only provided fifteen feet of water and there was frequently so little water in Loch Oich that the result was canal closure. The Caledonian was losing out to the coastal trades by only offering passage to ships of around 500 tons deadweight while enlargement to a depth of 30ft with locks of 600ft x 80ft would make the canal competitive and allow the passage of ships of war 'of a smaller kind'. What is more it would encourage industry, of which British Aluminium was a prime example, to locate near the canal to the general benefit of the Highlands.

At this time the Admiralty was specifying locks of 850ft x 110ft x 36ft for its 'battleship' canal so these proposals were some way short of that. Nevertheless the Provost of Inverness was later to advance the idea that the Caledonian should be enlarged rather than build the Mid-Scotland Ship Canal. His concept was that all locks between Inverness and Banavie should be eliminated was a perfectly feasible one and a variation on this had been advanced by the canal's resident engineer, Davidson, to the Royal Commission. He suggested the elimination of the summit between Lochs Oich and Lochy with the removal of three locks at a cost of £100,000. This proposal was not aimed at enlarging the canal but rather at the worthwhile but limited objective of easing the passage of vessels.

It seem strange, at this distance in time that Davidson, who had also served as engineer on the Crinan, should, in opposition to most local opinion, argue against the enlargement of the Caledonian. But he did. It was his view that enlargement would not divert larger ships from continuing to use the Pentland Firth. Was he farsighted and public spirited in his thinking? We shall never know. It is difficult to conceive that he took this public stance without the tacit approval of his employers, the Commissioners of the Caledonian Canal, who were in effect Parliamentary appointees. The Royal Commission also took this stance and said it did not believe there would be any material increase in traffic from the proposed enlargement.

Consequently it was unable to recommend '… that there should be any expenditure of public money in making the considerable enlargements of the Caledonian Canal suggested …' It was much more sympathetic to Davidson's Loch Oich project, and given that government had been known to advance grants for improvements of up to £20,000 per annum, it felt brave enough to recommend the resident engineer's limited improvements. As we know there is still a summit today between the two lochs in question.

We must wonder at the double standards applied by the commission. Its main recommendation was for the development, by upgrading existing waterways, of 'The Cross' a system of canals centred on Birmingham at an estimated cost of some £15 million to the public purse. In advocating this policy it had concluded that '… private enterprise cannot be expected to take the improvements of the canals in hand.' Having done its sums on the value of likely increases in income accruing from the development two further conclusions make interesting reading:

'Therefore we do not think that it would be right to make a confident statement that there will be a direct return on the probable cost'

'In any case there would be the reward which we anticipate of an indirect return in the shape of benefit to the trade of the country – which is the only return on the expenditure that was looked for in those foreign countries where no tolls were imposed on new or improved waterways.'

Could this thinking and these arguments not have applied equally to the improvement of the Crinan and the Caledonian? The cost would have been a fraction of the £15 million.

The Cross was to be administered by a new body, a 'Waterways Board' whose duties would be to raise capital by issuing bonds, guaranteed by the government, and then to acquire and modernise the canals of The Cross. But nothing happened before the First World War. Between the wars canal trade contracted further, partly due to the growing popularity of road transport, and even though another Royal Commission in 1930 advanced the idea of developing The Cross the idea was shelved.

The Waterways Board, if and when it was formed, was to take over the responsibility of the management of the Crinan and Caledonian from the commissioners of the Caledonian Canal. This august, unpaid, body was praised for its work but it was stated that they would be happy to hand over responsibility. In 1919 the Ministry of Transport did indeed relieve the commissioners of their burden.

The real problem, from the point of view of getting government action, was that the Royal Commission was hopelessly split on what to do. Of the 19 commissioners who served, three did not sign the final report and five submitted minority reports, dissenting from the main conclusions to a greater or lesser degree. With the commission almost equally divided it was not difficult for the government to avoid taking any initiative.

The underlying principle which divided the commission was whether or not public money should be used to 'interfere' in the transport market. One dissenter began his minority report with the words ' But as a Free Trader …' and concluded, 'I can only look upon any suggestion of State aid to particular individuals or traders as a most dangerous precedent.'

No action was taken on the report. The Royal Commission's investigation of 1906-9 was a missed opportunity. It was a watershed in the history of the Scottish canals. Nothing was done. So the Scottish canals went into the 20th century much as they had been planned in the 18th century. There was no injection of private or public money to take them forward into the 20th century. Those canals in private control withered and died because the owners' interest essentially lay elsewhere. The public-owned canals were denied any major capital improvement by their owner. Not for nearly a century would the public money be used to reinvest in the Scottish canal systems.

CHAPTER TWELVE

DECLINE AND CLOSURE

The tale of the Scottish canals in the inter-war period is swiftly told. The Lowland canals, the small unimportant subsidiaries of the ever larger railway conglomerations, fell into disuse. There was political pressure to infill them and as they were not profit-making there was little commercial defense for their retention. The Highland canals too suffered from changing transport technology and even if the railways did not spread further into the glens, improved road transport facilities opened up many areas in the Highlands and Islands, hitherto the province of the cargo ship.

So inconsequential was the traffic on the Union, that in 1912 Ports Hopetoun and Hamilton were effectively closed for traffic. A year later the Caledonian and North British Railways were in discussions with Edinburgh Corporation about abandoning and infilling sections of the canal within the city to construct new rail lines. However the First World War broke out and these ideas were not developed.

The Ministry of Transport had taken over the running of the railways from 1914–1918 to co-ordinate the war effort and the control of the two nationalised Scottish canals remained vested with them by the Ministry of Transport Act of 1919. As we have seen the Forth and Clyde (and Monkland) had become part of the Caledonian Railway group and the Union had fallen into the hands of the North British after its acquisition of the Edinburgh and Glasgow Railway. Neither of these companies reported their traffic infor-

mation to their shareholders during the hostilities presumably lest it would somehow be of use to the enemy. We do get a picture of these railway companies being paid compensation for their services by the government but we learn little of their commercial affairs and even less about those of the canals. By the 1919 Act the Ministry retained a loose control over the railways until 1921 but it allowed them the freedom to set fares and traffic rates.

Government experience of a single controlling authority for rail during the war had convinced it of the benefits of a less fragmented approach to national rail management. The Railways Act of 1921 received royal assent in August of that year and the new scheme had a vesting date of 1st of July 1923. Under the terms of this Act the Caledonian Railway became part of the group known as the London, Midland and Scottish Railway Company. At the same time the North British Railway was subsumed into the London and North-Eastern Railway Company. The scale of importance of the canals to these two new extended companies was now very small indeed.

In the last period of its independence, the year ending in February 1922, the Caledonian Railway had a turnover of £11.65 million and the turnover of the Forth and Clyde was £20,000. The canal had carried 157,200 tons but produced a loss of £39,800 which hardly made a dent in the railway's surplus of £4.27 million. In 1922 the Union carried 13,700 tons but this was a decrease of over 11,000 tons on the figure for

Bus and Bascule
This 1930s picture illustrates some of the frustrations felt by those
who had to maintain and operate transport links across the Forth
and Clyde. Only one vehicle, and at that a light one, could cross at
a time. The road had to close and traffic was disrupted when the
bridge opened to let a vessel through. As road transport grew and
canal traffic declined the waterway was considered more and
more of a nuisance. (ED)

1920. The existence of the canals in these large
companies was an historical accident and in the scale
of their operations they did not merit serious consideration. The minimum expense necessary to keep
them open was incurred and no development capital
was employed on what were seen, in transport terms,
as anachronisms.

But it was not just the diversion of traffic to rail,
or indifference of the railways to their waterways, that
were alone responsible for the decline of the canals.
The industries that had flocked to their banks lived out
their allotted time spans and were not replaced by new
ones when they closed. Their closure caused economic
distress to the populations in their immediate vicinities
and their derelict premises created an air of decay and
were barriers to the development of the land for other

TABLE 18. *Forth and Clyde, income and tonnages, 1925–45*

Year	Income	Expenses	Loss	Tons carried
1925	£23,500*	£37,200	£13,700	170,400
1935	£16,400	£25,600	£ 9,200	128,900
1945	£15,700	£29,600	£13,900	23,400

* A mere £351 of this total had come from earnings on the Monkland

purposes. For the same reasons, new workforces no longer gathered on the canal banks. If anything the enterprising ones fled the area. The closed canals were blights on their neighbourhoods and the question of their regeneration, for social and economic reasons, was not addressed till the end of the century when the movement that led to the building of the Millennium Link gathered momentum.

The continued decline of the Forth and Clyde is illustrated in Table 18.

Traffic had ceased on the Union in 1933 and a year later the locks joining the Union and the Forth and Clyde at Falkirk, and the Port Downie basin, were being filled in. The basins at Port Hopetoun and Port Hamilton had been sold to the City of Edinburgh in 1921 (when the tonnage carried had been 20,000), and the land reclaimed from them was used for building. The Union was closed at both ends by 1933 and was then an isolated stretch of waterway.

The Monkland was not carrying anything by 1935 and it was formally abandoned, using an obscure section of the Railways and Canal Traffic Act of 1881 for the purpose. After nearly 20 years of dereliction it was piped in at Blackhill from 1954 on. The Monkland became the second stretch of waterway that was not going anywhere even though its water was judged to be an essential supply for running of the Forth and Clyde.

It may be deduced, from data reported by the British Transport Commission for all the Scottish canals and figures available individually for the Crinan and the Caledonian, that traffic in goods on the Forth and Clyde had dwindled to nothing by 1955. The main activities were the occasional puffer going to Hay's yard at Kirkintilloch and fishing boats making seasonal changes in fishing grounds, from east coast to west and vice versa.

With the nationalisation of Britain's railways in 1946 all Scotland's canals came into public ownership and as a result of the Transport Act of 1947 the canals became the responsibility of the British Transport Commission (BTC) from 1948 to 1962. The Crinan and the Caledonian were taken away from the Ministry of Transport and put under the same management as the other Scottish canals for the first time. Within the BTC the canals were the responsibility of the Waterways Sub-commission to whom the Scottish canal managers, one for each of the Crinan and the Caledonian and one for the three Lowland canals, reported. Appendix XXV shows the decline in the total tonnages carried on the Scottish canals from around 118,000 to 44,000 under its stewardship. No particular blame should be attached to the BTC for this state of affairs as economic factors outwith its control were at work. The Forth and Clyde was in terminal decline, the

(Above). Kelvin Dock, Maryhill
This picture was taken in the 1960s and it is easy to understand why unused canals were regarded as eyesores, nuisances and dangers to the public. This was once the location of a thriving shipbuilding and repair business. The first custom built puffer, the *Glasgow*, had been launched here. (JRH)

(Right). 'Culverting'
When bridges on the canals became fixed and closed to waterborne traffic the canal was piped underneath a new bridge to maintain the water flow. This picture shows this type of work in progress on the Forth and Clyde at Kirkintilloch in the 1960s. Even when closed to navigation both the Forth and Clyde and the Monkland continued to be important sources of water to industry. (ED)

Caledonian had little commercial activity in its hinterland and only the Crinan was continuing steadily as a feeder route from the Clyde estuary to the west Highlands (this was soon to change however).

The Highland canals had continued much as before up to and beyond the Second World War. The Caledonian experienced an increase in traffic to as much as 60 to 70,000 tons per annum during the war. This soon fell back to the 10 to 20,000 ton range which had typified the 1930s after peace was restored. The earnings of around £4,500 to £7,000 per annum in the post-war decade were a fraction of the operating costs. The passenger trade, or rather the excursions on Loch Ness, had a post-war revival, after ceasing during hostilities, with over 3,500 being recorded as enjoying time on the water in 1950 (the pre-war peak had been over 14,000 in 1937). A replacement tug and icebreaker, named *Scot II*, was purchased in 1931 and nearly 30 years later she was converted into a passenger excursion boat with some success.

The number of vessels using the Crinan were 1,600 to 1,800 prior to the 1930s with as many as a third of them being yachts but around half of them were still commercial vessels. The number of passages through the waterway fell during hostilities as the yachts disappeared and the increased naval activity failed to compensate. In 1951, 2,366 passages were made, those by commercial vessels, fishing boats and yachts being 41 per cent, 30 per cent and 29 per cent respectively of the total. Income was £9,600 and expenses £20,900. Just over 66,000 tons of goods went through and 35,000 tons of this was northbound coal. In the 1950s the Crinan emerged as the most important commercial canal in Scotland.

By the mid-1950s the puffer owners, the principal coal-carriers, were looking hard at their own economics and decided that they did not want their

ships restricted to the 88ft length limit that the Crinan locks imposed upon them. They were disenchanted with the canal as the design depth of water, of 9½ft, was seldom achieved. Consequently they reduced their ships' drafts to pass the canal and had to charge higher freights to compensate for the reduced cargoes. The first diesel driven puffer had made its appearance in 1953 and while Hamilton and McPhail's *Glenshira* was a Crinan boat in length and beam she pointed the way to further developments of the puffer being a complete departure from the traditional design (ideally she needed 10½ft of water in the canal). By stretching the *Glenshira* concept to over a 100ft in length a faster, larger deadweight, more sea-worthy vessel evolved and by the 1960s the puffer owners were by-passing the Crinan with the greater part of their west coast cargoes. The smaller older ships still used the canal but in the late 1960s the roll-on-roll-off ferries made an appearance on the routes from Kintyre to Islay. In less than a decade the puffers lost 90 per cent of their distillery trade of that island as Western Ferries and Caledonian MacBrayne battled for dominance. The canal sized puffers, being older and smaller, found themselves confined to the Clyde estuary and the numbers of them using the Crinan declined accordingly.

The 1950s were a bleak time for Scotland's Lowland canals. The Monkland and the Union were lying unused, weeding over and being used as dumping sites for the detritus of modern living. They looked unattractive and became the focus of populist political campaigns to have them infilled or somehow removed from sight. Much was made of their being a safety hazard for the young to whom they were all too easily accessible. A series of unfortunate accidents caused a petition to be raised in 1948 to fill in the Monkland locks at Blackhill and there were similar popular

(Above left). The Infilling of the Monkland
Apart from the Summerlee Branch, the Monkland was almost completely filled in and most of it now lies under the M8 motorway east of Glasgow. But it was important as a water feed to the Forth and Clyde and so it was piped. This view is taken from the centre of Coatbridge looking east towards Sheepford and shows piping lying alongside the soon-to-disappear canal. (NL)

(Above right and opposite). Coat's Bridge
This spot where the Monkland canal was originally crossed by a bridge was known as 'Coat's Bridge'. Here, where the railway bridge crossed the canal line, we see the piping and filling work going on in the early 1960s. Today the same view, looking east, presents a short stretch of water beside a grassy bank. The Gartsherrie Branch runs under the small bridge on the left of the picture. Facing west from the same spot the line of the canal is now a pleasant tree-lined area adjacent to Coatbridge's main street.

moves, led by local and national politicians, to close the Forth and Clyde and the Union in the 1950s. Sadly people, lock-keepers, boat crews and the public, had always drowned in the canals from the time that they opened but by this time no defence on the grounds of their utility could be advanced and they had become a noisome nuisance in the eye of the public.

The Clyde Valley Regional Plan of 1946 had advocated the filling in of both the Monkland and the Forth and Clyde describing them as barriers to the development of modern transport systems. The Edinburgh Development Plan (1953), in the face of opposition from the North British Rubber Co., which wished to defend its water supply, proposed the closure of the Union. Legally 'closure' meant no longer maintaining the waterway for navigation but closure in the popular imagination meant elimination, a far from

simple task. The cost of piping the Monkland within Coatbridge was put at £750,000 and Coatbridge Town Council took the realistic stance that it could not afford such a sum. Nevertheless the infilling of the Monkland's Castle Street basin in Glasgow began in 1954 followed by the piping of the Blackhill locks.

The BTC had appointed a Board of Survey to examine its canal responsibilities and in 1954 it categorised the United Kingdom's canals in three ways. The Forth and Clyde, Union and Monkland fell into Category III, the little used or disused group for which they recommended discontinuance. A stay of execution was granted to the Caledonian and the Crinan (Category II) for the meantime, because they still carried important traffic. No Scottish canal, therefore, was given the favoured Category I status (only 16 per cent of the length of the nation's canals qualified), which conferred the promise of continuance and development. From the viewpoint of commercial significance at that time it is difficult to argue with the Survey's findings. In 1958 the Committee of Inquiry into Inland Waterways, commissioned by a government alarmed at BTC's annual losses, produced its findings. It took a refreshingly different view of the waterways.

Perhaps, it suggested, it was important to consider more than the transport of goods and examine such matters as water supply, land drainage, effluent control and *leisure uses*. For the first time in an official report we see the seeds of an idea that was to find full bloom at the end of the century — that weight should be given to leisure and amenity considerations (on the other hand the committee could not countenance trying to put the clock back and making all the canals viable again). It worth quoting from the report in this regard as it makes refreshing reading against a background of petitions for closure:

'... they (canals) often traverse attractive country bringing water and associated vegetation and wildlife to otherwise unwatered areas.'

'... some canals were the works of engineers of acknowledged genius ... works which are of considerable interest as examples of the mechanical achievement of the early industrial revolution. Avoidable destruction of such things would be deplorable.'

'... rejecting indiscriminate restoration, therefore, we recommend selective treatment.'

'But if canals do not pay their way we will not abandon them. Other uses may justify their retention ... but they will need a strong "social and economic" case.'

For the most part we may regard these quotations as looking forward to the attitudes of today and perhaps we commend the committee for them. However the Forth and Clyde, Union and Monkland clearly did 'not pay their way' and in the committee's view did not justify the investment to keep them in existence as they did not see that their situation was likely to improve. In 1956, the last year the committee was able to analyse, the three Lowland canals earned £51,000 and cost £120,000 to operate and maintain. Neither did the Caledonian and Crinan pay their way (a combined loss of £64,000 in 1956) but they were to be retained, in the committee's opinion, as part of the national transport system, and put into the care of the Secretary of State for Scotland. They were to be regarded, the committee said, as a 'social service'. The other three canals should be 'eliminated'. They took this not to mean abandonment but to mean a breaking up and redevelopment of the entity.

The committee further recommended that the

closure of the Monkland, the Union and the Glasgow Branch of the Forth and Clyde should be done in such a way as to protect the water flow to their adjacent industries. As to the Forth and Clyde itself a 'prima facie case for closure and redevelopment exists'. Keeping it open was a hidden subsidy to the fishing industry (up to 180 passages per annum) and 'the cost outweighs what is derived.' the committee concluded. It was encouraged in this view by Glasgow City Council and by Falkirk Town Council both of whom argued against having to bear the cost of operating and maintaining the bridges in their areas and who pointed out the severe restrictions to road development that the presence of the bridges presented.

In June 1961 the Secretary of State for Scotland announced the closure of the Forth and Clyde canal. It was the issue of the cost of a bridge that decided the matter. The main Glasgow to Stirling road, the A80, was being redeveloped to dual carriage status and the cost of building a high level bridge to carry the new road over the canal at Castlecary was put at £160,000. The decision to take the road over the waterway by culverting it effectively closed the canal to navigation. The Act to extinguish the navigation rights was passed in March 1962 and the canal was to close at the end of that year.

While the members of the Committee of Inquiry into Inland Waterways did not agree on the details they were of a single mind that a body should be created with the sole responsibility for the governance of the nation's canals. Canals in the BTC's portfolio were the poor relations in transport terms and really required a body specifically to concentrate on their unique strengths and problems. Another rethink on government's part created the British Waterways Board in 1962 with the specific remit to concentrate on the management all of the nation's inland waterways. Hailed as 'a new charter for the Waterways' by the then Minister of Transport, the people of Britain were urged to see the move as an opportunity to renew their canals.

Ironically the British Waterways Board came into existence on the 1st of January 1963 ... the date on which the Forth and Clyde Navigation was closed.

CHAPTER THIRTEEN

REVIVAL

It is no simple matter to eliminate a canal physically. The new British Waterways Board (BWB) very quickly reached this conclusion. It had set itself the objective, in its first year of life, of devising a broad strategy for the future of the canals. The difficulties inherent in elimination were thrust upon it very early in its deliberations.

The main advantage of elimination was that it involved a once off cost. There would be no maintenance and repair costs stretching interminably into the future if the waterway was simply obliterated. However many argued that the costs of elimination were just too high ever to be contemplated.

A list, by no means exhaustive, of what had to be done to eliminate a typical canal gives some feel for the complexity of the process. It would be necessary to:

– demolish and or infill locks
– demolish aqueducts or transfer ownership
  for an alternative use
– de-water the canal and as a consequence
  – divert incoming water-flows
  – provide alternative water out-flows
– demolish access bridges
– negotiate the transfer of ownership of bridges
  carrying public roads or railways
– infill the canal by grading towpaths and
  embankments or using other infill material
– make reclaimed land suitable for alternative use
– fence as appropriate to define land boundaries
  and rights of way

– extinguish navigation rights, towpath rights of way,
  and fishing rights

Such processes were bound to be lengthy and costly and the idea began to emerge that they need not be undertaken if sustainable uses for the waterways could be found.

While it was wrestling with these types of problems the BWB was under pressure in Scotland to carry out the previously declared, and partly implemented, policy of closing the Lowland canals and removing them as obstacles to redevelopment.

It complied with the culverting of the Forth and Clyde for the new A80 road and in a short period of years this canal was cut in a major way at six sites, mostly within Glasgow's boundaries, but also at Kirkintilloch. With the canal closed to navigation local engineers and planners took the easy options when they had to cross it. A pipeline would be put across the canal at water level as the cheapest and most practical way of achieving a crossing. A culvert was the easier and cheaper option than a bridge which allowed headroom for the passage of even a small vessel. Under pressure from local authorities, BWB relieved itself of the obligation of keeping the Union open for navigation from Edinburgh to Falkirk. Its application for a Scottish Provisional Order to accomplish this in 1964, was 'not opposed'. Water supplies to industry were safeguarded.

Also in 1964 the board was in discussions with the

City of Glasgow and the Burgh of Coatbridge about the piping of the Forth and Clyde and Monkland. The piping of the two canals at Blackhill began in order to provide for a new road development, the Townhead Interchange. Work also started on over a mile of the Monkland between Sheepford Locks and Coatbridge Cross to the west to release land for development.

Both of these schemes were completed in 1966 and another section of piping of the Monkland, from Coatbridge Cross to Blair Bridge, was agreed. The Burgh of Coatbridge got a grant of 90 per cent of the cost of these works from the Scottish Office. Road plans affecting the canal were approved for Falkirk and Kirkintilloch. In Grangemouth over a mile of the Forth and Clyde at Dalgrain Road (which was to be filled in), and the canal basins were transferred to the ownership of the Burgh.

In 1968 BWB agreed to surrender four miles of the Monkland from Blackhill to the Glasgow City boundary to be infilled for the proposed Monkland Motorway, the M8, work on which was due to begin in 1972. The water was to be piped on a line parallel to the line of the canal. At the same time West Lothian Council wanted to build two culverts at Preston Road and at Broxburn for the eastern section of this Glasgow to Edinburgh motorway. Edinburgh also submitted plans, for the piping of one and a half miles of the Union at Wester Hailes, for a housing development to be built.

In summary, by the mid-1970s, the Union was filled in at both ends, cut by culverts in two places and ran in pipes under a housing estate. The Monkland had virtually disappeared under a motorway. The Forth and Clyde had lost its eastern exit to the sea and was impassable at many points. In particular it was cut at Castlecary and the summit reach was broken at Kirkintilloch. However the way in which the public viewed its canals was beginning to change.

Even while it was supervising the fragmentation of the Lowland canals BWB was seeking to find what it described as the 'best use' for the waterways under its control. Indeed it was charged to do so by the Act which set it up. Its view, set out in its Interim Report, published in 1964 as a policy document, was that it would examine the canals, not only from a commercial aspect but 'in the light of all the other varied purposes inland waterways could serve.' It had taken over a British canal system which was in serious decline and which had accumulated losses, before capital and debt charges, of £5.9 million between 1954 and 1962. The operating loss in 1956 had been £483,000 to which the five Scottish canals had contributed the disproportionate amount of £133,000. It was charged to make canals pay their way. It aimed to reduce the annual deficit and it did so. Part of its plan was to optimise income from sources other than goods traffic.

BWB saw itself faced with three choices. One was a deliberate run-down with progressive closure of waterways. A second was to concentrate on canals with the potential for a viable commercial future and to hive off the others. A third choice, of keeping all canals under a unified management for transport and other uses with the aim of optimising income from all available sources, was the one for which BWB opted. The canals were to be multi-user facilities and every business, economic or social purpose to which the canals could be put, should be developed as fully as possible. For the first time in the pronouncement of an official body concerned with the nation's waterways 'social purpose' was recognised. In stating that the waterways could not be '… neatly and separately arranged as those usable and those not usable for transport; nor in fact can they be separately labelled as particular waterways usable for single particular

The Bridge Inn at Ratho
Activity at this spot kept the flame alive on the Union for many
years before the Millennium Link was dreamt of. The Seagull Trust
was born here and successful 'sail and dine excursions' gave many
their first taste of the pleasures of canal cruising.

purposes.' BWB in effect turned its back on the findings
and the categorization of the 1958 Committee of
Inquiry into Inland Waterways.

Nevertheless they opted to concentrate their
'transport only' policy on maintaining about 400 miles
of canals of the 2,000 under their control (these
waterways carried about nine tenths of the total traffic),
and included the Caledonian and Crinan in this group.
Unlike most of the English canals in this category the
Crinan and the Caledonian were losing money. Their
Lowland canals were of course in the process of
dismemberment. They fully realised that in exploring
the pleasure craft, angling (75 per cent of the canal
mileage was suitable for fishing) and general recreation
and amenity markets that they were facing balance

sheet versus social policy issues. The BWB reinforced its argument for an amenity policy in its 1967 report *British Waterways, Recreation and Amenity*. General acceptance of this report in government circles found its expression in the formation of the Inland Waterway Amenity Advisory Council in the Transport Act of 1968. The IWAAC was to act as an independent body to give advice to BWB. The IWAAC was the body that later was to tell the Minister of State for Sport and Recreation that a study of the Scottish Lowland waterways was needed urgently and that nothing should be done to compromise the future of the Forth and Clyde in the meantime.

One of the most significant events in the revival of the Scottish canals was perhaps the refusal of a Public Enquiry to let Stirling County Council fill in a section of the Union. The Council had wanted to use a section of the canal at Glen Village, on the southern outskirts of Falkirk, for road developments and found the concept became the subject of an Inquiry in 1970. In the same year BWB had consultations with those local authorities through which the Monkland and the Forth and Clyde passed on the future of these canals. Some still favoured infilling but others came out for retention for amenity use and out of the consultation process a Joint Working Party was set up. With the impetus given by the rejection of the Stirling plan this body began to work with the Scottish Development Department and the Countryside Commission for Scotland on the future of the Lowland canals. The only black spot in 1970 was a study which advocated filling in the Forth and Clyde to recover derelict land for recreational purposes. It did at least suggest that Maryhill Locks and the Kelvin Aqueduct be retained as a heritage site.

After Scottish local government reorganization in 1976, BWB convened a meeting of interested local authorities which produced a broad strategy statement for the Forth and Clyde. Inter alia it said that:

– sea to sea restoration of the canal was too expensive to be adopted as policy – the canal was to be retained and no further restrictions on its use were to be allowed
– the locks were to be maintained and any new bridges should allow for navigation
– the leisure boating potential was to be developed
– a working party was to be established to prepare a Local (Subject) Plan.

As a result, late in 1977, a study group was set up comprising the Planning and the Leisure and Recreation Departments of all the local authorities along the Forth and Clyde and in July 1979 they produced a Survey Report. This was essentially a consultation document but, significantly, it posed a range of questions, the positive answers to which, could only lead to the restoration of the canal in some form.

The Survey Report was a comprehensive investigation of the problems and opportunities that the Forth and Clyde presented. It documented its sites of industrial archaeological significance and the listed buildings. It found 69 obstructions to navigation and surveyed the state of the locks, aqueducts, weirs and bridges. It sought the opinions of twenty recreational bodies with an interest in the waterway. The potential for the use of the canal in the areas of education, tourism, tourist accommodation, boating, angling, towpath use and picnicking was examined. It sought to prioritise areas for development, to establish design guidelines, to estimate the costs of change and to find methods of financing them.

Having received answers to the questions it posed the study group presented the Forth and Clyde Local

(Opposite). Leisure Pursuits
Lady rowers practising at Harrison Park, about a mile from the
present Edinburgh terminus of the Union. The canoeists are
competing at Temple (near Lock 27) on the Forth and Clyde. (Both
JRH) Even though the canals had fallen into disuse as links for
commercial traffic they still served minor social purposes such as
these. Had it not been for such activities which continued and
flourished after the closure of the canals the case for the restoration
of the waterways as leisure amenity would have been weakened.

(Above). 'An act of faith'
The Scott Russell Aqueduct was built in 1989 to take the Union over
the Edinburgh City Bypass (A720). Considering that at that time
the canal was cut for a mile at the Wester Hailes housing development the decision to build this new aqueduct over this major
roadway could only be described as an act of faith that one day the
canal would be reopened. John Scott Russell (1808–82) was
appointed in 1834 to advise the Union canal management on the
possibility of introducing steam navigation to the canal. He used
the canal as an early type of test tank to experiment on hydro-
dynamics. Near this spot, Bridge No. 9, he formulated the Solitary
Wave Theory, for which he is best known.

(Subject) Plan in its final form in 1980. The responses had been positive and the canal was to be restored. The Plan was adopted and supported by BWB, the Scottish Development Agency, the Countryside Commission for Scotland, and all eight of the Regional or District Councils through whose lands the canal ran. Strathclyde Regional Council and Falkirk District Council undertook to take the lead in having the Plan made a Statutory Instrument. The Forth and Clyde Canal Society, formed in 1980, owed its existence to the Plan.

Activity in saving the canal was by no means limited to the local authorities and government departments. Almost from the moment that the canal closed to navigation enthusiastic volunteer bodies took an interest in it. The Scottish Inland Waterways Association was formed and it took a lead, with BWB support, in the 1970s in cleaning up the canal, removing dumped rubbish from locks and channel, clearing weeds and restoring footpaths. In 1971 a Joint Working Party was established for the Union as well which developed into Union Canal Development Group in 1975, the year in which the Linlithgow Union Canal Society was formed. Again BWB, the Scottish Office, Countryside Commission and local authorities were members. The Seagull Trust was established in 1979 at Kirkintilloch on the Forth and Clyde and Ratho on the Union to own vessels to give the handicapped the opportunity to sail on the canals. The Forth and Clyde Canal Society put an excursion vessel, the Ferry Queen, into operation in 1982. (The name was the combination of a deference to the turn-of-the-century excursion fleet and to the fact that the craft was a converted river Clyde passenger ferry). With a helping

hand from BWB the Edinburgh Canal Society, which mirrored the Forth and Clyde, organization was established in 1986. It is important to recite these events as evidence of the genuine groundswell of public support which existed for the canals. The statutory bodies may well have had the powers to plan and implement change but the popular support proved that there was indeed a market for the outcome of the social and amenity agenda.

Under the Transport Act of 1968, BWB was given powers to spend on recreational developments as and when finance became available. Local authorities could make grants and help in kind for recreational projects as could the Countryside Commission, the Scottish Tourist Board and the Scottish Sports Council. The Scottish Development Agency had the authority to make grants for clearing derelict land – a description that could be applied to certain urban areas of the canals. So gradually projects were put together, using these types of facility, for the purposes of restoration.

In 1986 BWB was able to announce that £2.6 million would be spent on reopening the Forth and Clyde from Kirkintilloch to Temple and that substantial repairs were to be carried out on the Union, west of Linlithgow at a cost of £1.75 million. This was indeed real progress but restoring the canal for navigation from Clyde to Forth had been priced at £20 million 10 years before. What would it cost now? If the dream of reopening the Forth and Clyde from sea to sea and to rejoin it to a fully restored Union was to be realised, how was the enormous sum of money to be raised? The answer was to lie in the government's determination to tap the nation's propensity for gambling.

CHAPTER FOURTEEN

THE MILLENNIUM LINK

The Lottery Act of 1993 not only provided the opportunity for members of the British public to become millionaires overnight, at the attractive odds of 14 million to 1, but it diverted some of the proceeds of the sale of lottery tickets to 'good causes'. For the modest investment of one pound it became possible to win millions once or twice per week. The public responded enthusiastically to this novelty and was soon spending over £3 billion per annum on lottery tickets.

After it had allowed half of the income from ticket sales to be set aside for prizes, the government diverted 28p from every 100p to aid what it called 'good causes'. The arts, sport, heritage and charities were all to be the beneficiaries of the British having a flutter and one further category of recipient was created, a Millennium Commission. These five were to share the good causes income equally. The Millennium Commission, which invited applications in 1996 after enough funds had accumulated, had the rather loosely defined remit to 'do anything they thought desirable … to support worthwhile causes which would mark the year 2000 and the start of the third millennium.'

The Millennium Commission indicated that it was prepared to consider projects which '… show public support and celebrate our heritage while taking us forward into the future and creating a lasting legacy.' No more than half of the cost of any project would be granted by the Commission and the project's sponsors were required to find the balance of funds themselves.

Could the restoration of the Forth and Clyde and

Union canals qualify, under these broad terms of reference, for financial aid? Could public support for the idea be generated? Where was the balance of the money, almost certainly more than half of the restoration cost, going to come from? British Waterways did not see these as intractable problems – after all the Local (Subject) Plan had covered a lot of this ground.

The Local (Subject) Plan had been drawn up with the full participation and co-operation of every local authority through which the canals ran. The likely social and economic benefits of restoration had been fully discussed and their potential was well understood. The physical barriers to re-opening had been enumerated and the associated costs had been evaluated. However the various parties involved had stopped short, when the Plan was drawn up, of advocating full sea to sea reopening and the financial implications of re-linking the two canals had not been explored. BWB now tackled these outstanding matters. In 1994 it announced its plan for the Millennium Link and in 1995 it formally submitted a bid for funding, on behalf of the Millennium Link Partnership. The comprehensive nature of the Partnership, BWB, local authorities and public and voluntary bodies is detailed in Appendix XXVI.

Nothing less than reopening the Forth and Clyde from Grangemouth to Bowling and the rejoining of the Union to the Forth and Clyde at Falkirk was contemplated. The canals would be restored to their

(Above). The Dalmuir Drop Lock. (Forth and Clyde)
The changes wrought by the Millennium Project are many and
varied and start in the west at Dalmuir. As can be seen the road,
(the A814), passes over the Forth and Clyde a few feet above water-
level. Throughout the project only four opening bridges were
restored (see Appendix XXVI); otherwise road traffic had to be
raised up on fixed bridges to go over the canal at a height to allow
sufficient headroom for vessels to pass. Uniquely, at this spot, the
decision was taken to drop vessels down into a lock to let them pass
below the road and be raised up on the other side. This was a cost-
effective solution and traffic disruption was minimised.

(Opposite). The A80 Bridge at Castlecary (Forth and Clyde)
It was the decision to cross the Forth and Clyde at near water-level
that forced the closure of the canal in 1962. It was considered that a
cost of £160,000 for the alternative of bridging the seldom-used
waterway to allow the passage of vessels was not justified. Today the
four lanes of the A80 cross the canal on a new bridge. The cost of
achieving this was £2.5 million.

original operating dimensions and the only restraint
would be a three metre air draft. This would be more
than adequate for leisure craft and had the great merit
of not requiring opening bridges. The project had a
budget cost of £78 million (Appendix XXVI details the
major components and these correspond broadly to
the construction contracts that were bid for and let).

It was argued that, apart from creating employment in the construction phase, the fully re-opened
and linked canals would, inter alia:

– create 4,000 new jobs by enabling commercial
  developments
– improve the environment by restoring and/or
  reclaiming sites on the canal banks

- provide access to the canals for tourism, leisure and recreation
- restore and preserve unique industrial heritage sites

in what had become some of the most socially and economically disadvantaged areas in Scotland's two great cities and in its central belt.

The first bid for funds was referred back for adjustment and it was then resubmitted. On St Valentine's Day in 1997, the Millennium Commission announced that it would support the Millennium Link with a grant of £32 million or 41 per cent of the budget cost of the whole project. To put this figure in context, it should be noted that the Commission's support for all canal restoration schemes in the UK was to amount to

£61 million. So the lion's share went to the two Scottish canals. Alternatively, of a figure in excess of £2,000 million that the Commission disbursed, up to August 2001, when it ceased to make any more grants, the Forth and Clyde and Union received 1.6 per cent of the total.

The Commission's press statement announcing the grant was effusive:

- 'This is an excellent example of a water-based regeneration scheme which will create a broad green corridor, providing a natural focus for leisure and cultural activities and supporting a chain of amenities and visitor attractions right across Scotland.'
- 'This project is truly millennial in its scale and vision.'

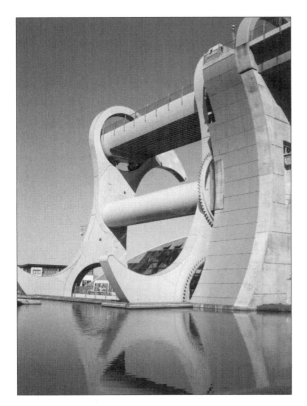

How 'millennial' was its scale? The truly imaginative focus of the project was the link itself; the Falkirk Wheel, the world's first rotating boat-lift. Conceived as an alternative to the replacement of the eleven locks that had once joined the Union to the Forth and Clyde, the proposed rotating boat lift was a master-stroke. Not only did it solve the technical problem of moving vessels up and down from the Forth and Clyde to the Union, but it was a visually stunning and sophisticated piece of modern engineering. Situated on the site of a disused open-cast mine, it also provided a focal point for a visitor centre that would bring the public to the canals.

The Wheel and its associated basin, aqueduct, locks and new canal channel was costed at £17 million, more than a fifth of the total budget. It was to lift a cassion of 300 tons weight, of water and/or eight boats, 115ft in fifteen minutes while another counter-balancing cassion was lowered. It was the key to the whole project.

The separate reopening of the Forth and Clyde from sea to sea was to be a great canal revival but the renewal of the link between the two canals at Falkirk symbolically united Scotland's two largest cities.

The design of the Wheel emerged from a consid-erable co-operative effort between BWB, engineering consultants Ove Arup, manufacturers Butterley Engineering and Scottish-based architects with a worldwide reputation, Robert Matthew Johnson-Marshall (RMJM Concept). Various designs were considered and rejected before the unique wheel was decided upon. The outcome a steel structure measuring 115ft x 115ft x 100ft, was considered by the Royal Fine Art Commission for Scotland to be 'a form of contemporary sculpture.' It was recognised by the American Society of Civil Engineers as an Inter-national Historic Civil Engineering Landmark.

The Millennium Commission had offered £32 million towards the costs and another £46 million of matching funds had to be raised before the project could proceed. For the next two years BWB was busy fund-raising and co-ordinating the efforts of the Partnership, an extremely complex, but worthwhile, task. After Scottish Enterprise, BWB, seven local Councils and the private and voluntary sector had contributed as far as their means and authority would allow, a gap of £8.6 million remained. Ministers at the then Scottish Office supported approaches made to the European Regional Development Fund for this balancing sum and they were instrumental in the success of this application. By the beginning of 1999 all the funding guarantees were in place and the project could begin. The Secretary of State for Scotland cut the first sod in March 1999 to let construction begin at Lock 31 on the Forth and Clyde.

The supervision of the building phase by BWB, as lead client, was a considerable task and it is to their and the constructors' credit that the various contracts, that made the whole, were completed largely on time and within budget. There was a shortfall in the matching funds and the Waterways Trust Scotland was formed in 2000 to close the gap and once that was done to continue to seek financial support for projects to help local communities benefit from the canals. We have

(Opposite). The Falkirk Wheel
(Forth and Clyde and Union Junction)
The striking appearance of the structure of the Falkirk Wheel is much praised. It raises vessels a hundred feet or so from the Forth and Clyde to the Union, a task that had been originally achieved by a set of 11 locks at Camelon. This modern example of a rotating boat lift has won many design awards and has proved to be a major tourist attraction in its own right. These photographs show the wheel at the beginning and the end of a cycle with the lower caisson, with a vessel within, about to 'touch down' in the basin.

examined earlier how the two canals were blocked to navigation in a variety of ways and it is perhaps sufficient merely to highlight below, by way of illustration, a few of the major works which re-opened and re-joined the two canals.

The Grangemouth Link – Since the Forth and Clyde had lost its eastern entrance at Grangemouth docks a new half mile cut was made to the river Carron and two new locks one which was the entrance to the tidal river were made.

Leamington Lift Bridge – This bridge was restored to a lifting pedestrian bridge over the Union at the Lochrin Basin in Edinburgh having previously been fixed in place at road level.

Wester Hailes – A major work was undertaken to renew the canal through the housing estate at Wester Hailes at the west of Edinburgh where it had been in-filled. A major new road bridge, one of seven in total, had to be constructed.

M8 Motorway – The Union was realigned at Broxburn and a new bridge built to carry the motorway over the waterway that it had blocked since the 1970s.

The Falkirk Wheel – The original eleven locks joining the two canals having been filled in a new junction was needed. The junction between the Union, apart from the Wheel itself, involved extending the Union west by three-quarters of a mile, building two

Roughcastle Tunnel and Locks (Union)
At the top of the wheel a 475-ft tunnel takes the Union under a railway line and the Roman Antonine Wall (a nearby fort on the Wall is known as Rough Castle). An excursion boat is shown returning to the wheel on the north side of the tunnel. On the south side of the tunnel, also shown, there is a basin leading to two new locks which finally raise boats up to the Union level. (JRH) To make this junction the Union was extended west by almost a mile from its original 1822 terminus at the top of the Junction Locks.

locks, an aqueduct south of the Antonine Wall, a 475ft tunnel under the Antonine Wall, a 115ft high aqueduct to connect to the boat lift, a holding basin at the foot of the lift and a lock to connect it to the Forth and Clyde. A visitor centre was constructed on the east side of the basin.

Castlecary – The notorious crossing of the A80, the cause of the Forth and Clyde's closure in 1962, was raised by a new bridge to create the required air draft.

Kirkintilloch – the 1930s swing bridge over the Forth and Clyde in the town centre was restored as an opening bridge.

Glasgow – Infilled Locks 31 and 32 were opened up and a new road bridge made to take a western road artery over the canal together with a new 900 yard section of waterway.

Clydebank – Because of the complications of rebuilding the bridge at Dumbarton Road, which blocked the Forth and Clyde, the unusual step was taken of making a 'drop-lock' to take the canal under the road with adequate headroom for vessels. The headroom is nominally 1.5ft when the gates are open. When the lock is closed and pumped out the air draft becomes 10ft.

Most of these works were completed between 2000 and 2001 and as each section of the canals became free to sail upon the fact was duly celebrated by local festivities involving the local communities and voluntary bodies. Sadly the opening of the Wheel was delayed after vandalism of a lock on the Union flooded the system through to the basin, emphasising that a task remained for the Partnership to convince some of the benefits that the reopened canals could bring to their communities. There were however three major celebrations:
– on 26th May 2001, the Forth and Clyde was
  officially reopened from sea to sea by HRH The

(Above). Leamington Lift Bridge (Union)
A view from the east of the restored Leamington Lift Bridge in
Edinburgh which originally lifted the roadway vertically to allow
vessels to pass. A hundred yards east of here is the present terminus
of the Union at Edinburgh Quays.

(Right). Wester Hailes (Union)
On the western outskirts of Edinburgh the Union had been filled in
and a modern housing estate created. As a result 1.1 miles of canal
had to be re-instated at Wester Hailes. Nine fixed bridges were
built, like Number 6, shown here, to accommodate roads and paths
and pleasant urban walkways were created. Around £9.5 million
was spent on this part of the re-opening project.

(Opposite). Edinburgh Quays (Union)
Edinburgh Quay is a new office, retail and housing complex at the
eastern end of the Union and is a demonstration of the type of
regenerative investment that is following in the wake of the canal's
re-opening. It is a short walk to Tollcross and to the former sites of
Port Hamilton and Port Hopetoun. 'Port Hamilton' lives on in the
name given to a nearby modern housing development.

Prince of Wales who, in a reversal of the 1790 opening ceremony, emptied a barrel of Clyde water into the Forth. A passage was made from Grangemouth to Bowling, in three days, by a flotilla of small craft.

– on 25th August 2001, the Union was reopened through Wester Hailes.
– on 24th May 2002, the Falkirk Wheel, which had first turned in December 2001, was formally opened by HM the Queen and the link between the two canals was re-made after a gap of nearly 70 years.

The four extant canals, the Caledonian, the Crinan, the Forth and Clyde and the Union, have been scheduled as Ancient Monuments by Historic Scotland. Scheduling of certain features of the waterways had begun with the Falkirk Tunnel (1973) and the Moy Swing bridge (1974) but the full lengths of the canals themselves were scheduled between 1996 (Caledonian and Crinan), 1997 (Forth and Clyde) and 2003 (Union). They should now be safe from the type of depredation that almost saw the Lowland canals disappear in the 1960s and 1970s. The designation of a number of areas adjacent to the canals as Sites of Special Scientific Interest should similarly protect their environment.

With the exception of the forlorn remains of the Monkland, (at Coatbridge Cross and the wharf at Summerlee) also scheduled as an Ancient Monument , the Lowland canals had been restored for navigation, and Edinburgh and Glasgow were once again linked by waterway as they had first been in 1822.

The final project cost of the Millennium Link was £6.1 million over the original budget at £84.5 million. Nevertheless it was a considerable technical, financial and organizational feat on the part of British Water-ways (Scotland), and a praiseworthy one.

The Eastern Entrance (Forth and Clyde)
As an alternative to restoring the old eastern entrance to the Forth
and Clyde through the modern docks at Grangemouth, a new link
was made from the canal to the River Carron. This link and the two
new locks involved a cost of £4.5 million. Vessels from the Forth
now have to enter the Carron at Grangemouth docks, pass under
the M9 Motorway and use the new 'sea' lock. There are tidal
restrictions, as this picture taken at low tide, shows.

CHAPTER FIFTEEN

THE FUTURE
THE DEVOLVED CANALS

From April 2001 the funding of the five Scottish canals was devolved to the Scottish Executive, under powers granted to it by the Scotland Act of 1998. There was no escaping the implication: the Scottish Executive intended to accept the responsibility of supporting and developing the canals.

Although it operates within the milieu of the British Waterways Board, which remains a single legal entity, British Waterways (Scotland), has to seek its government financial assistance from Edinburgh. Within the annual report of BWB a new and detailed explanation of the affairs of the Scottish Canals appeared in 2002.

BWB is responsible to the Department of the Environment Food and Rural Affairs in England and Wales and to the Department of Enterprise, Transport and Lifelong Learning in Scotland. It reports annually on how it is carrying out agreed policies and provides accounts for the expenditure of government grants and other monies it receives. In the year 2003–4, BWB earned £88.3 million from its operations out of a total income of £197.4 million (A range of activities which included property rents, leisure boating, angling, water charges and tolls produced this income). The balance came from government grants and other forms of public support. Historically, earned income, although it varies from year to year, has been around 40 per cent of the total.

Consequently, except when it has benefited from property sales, BWB usually runs at an operating loss.

The 2003–4 expenditure was £201 million which produced an operating loss of £3.8 million. This was ameliorated by other income, mostly property sales of £7.6 million. In 2003–4, therefore BWB had a loss of £1.8 million.

However it should be noted that BWB undertakes, each year, a planned programme to reduce the considerable burden of maintenance arrears which it inherited from the British Transport Commission. There are two categories of arrears; 'backlog' and 'statutory'. Backlog arrears need urgent attention for safety reasons. Statutory arrears are those necessary to prevent assets falling into the backlog category. Despite commendable progress in these areas BWB is likely to have to carry this burden for some years. Scotland's arrears in both categories was assessed at over £14 million in 2002. The Scottish Executive has committed itself to providing grant funding to eliminate these arrears in due course.

A similar pattern in income and expenditure may well arise for the Scottish canals in the future. It is unlikely that in the short term BW(S) will earn enough from external sources to make a profit and it will look to the Scottish Executive to balance its books. Appendix XXVII details the financial results for BW(S) for the years 1999–2000 to 2003–4. They are inevitably distorted by the ongoing expenditure, supported by grants, on the Millennium Link and perhaps only the final years of this period give a clue to the future pattern. If this is the case then a greater level of support

Maryhill
Maryhill has the lines of a traditional puffer but she is not. She is a holiday cruising boat. She is only two-thirds the size of the Forth and Clyde's greatest invention but that means she can travel through the Union and cruise from Bowling to Edinburgh.

from the Scottish Executive may well be needed even if the expectation that BW(S) will earn more in the future through its commercial activities is realised. Grants of £8.9 million per annum have been indicated through to the 2005–6 financial year.

While the expenditure on the opening of the Lowland canals allowed many of the problems of previous neglect there to be corrected, there are still many miles of canal where the channel needs dredging and the banks need attention. Let us not forget, that while the recent focus has been on the Lowland canals, the Highland canals have still to be cared for and the effects of wear and tear put right. In addition to the four operating canals, the fifth, the Monkland, although largely buried, is still an important water supply to the Forth and Clyde.

Following the trend set by the rest of BWB, the Scottish canal management has committed itself to exploiting the revenue raising possibilities of its waterways. For example it has moved to utilise its property holdings for commercial development. The Edinburgh Quay project, at the eastern terminus of the Union, which began in the Lochrin Basin in 2001, is a partnership with a private developer which will contain housing, office and retail properties.

Of direct interest, in looking to the future effect of the re-opening of the two Lowland canals, is the increase in leisure usage of them, as indicated by the number of boat licenses taken out:

TABLE 19. *Scottish Canals, boat licences, 2000–4*

Canal	2000–01	2001–02	2002–03	2003–04
Caledonian	1,241	1,256	1,274	1,291
Crinan	1,261	1,292	1,323	1,275
Lowland	86	192	323	348
Total	2,588	2,740	2,920	2,914

The result for the year 2002–3 included a period when the Falkirk Wheel had been open for less than a full year. Future interest will focus on the trend for the Lowland canals. While figures for the Highland canals show modest increases, it is important to recognise that a recent study demonstrated that 14 per cent of all tourist activity in the Great Glen area was attributable to the Caledonian. It is noteworthy that income from

the Falkirk Wheel visitor centre increased to £1.1 million in 2002/3 and in the summer of 2003–4 over 200 vessels per month were using the Wheel.

In October 2002, the Scottish Executive published a report setting out its views on its future strategies for the Scottish canals. It was called *Scotland's Canals – an asset for the future*.

As far as the physical structure of the waterways was concerned the paper outlined the prospect of BW(S) developing the canal network with new capital projects. Among these were the possibility of:

– a navigable link between Loch Lomond and the Forth and Clyde via the River Leven. Investigation of this possibility will require the rationalisation of complex issues with the Loch Lomond National Park, local authorities and River Leven and Loch users before the question of raising finance is addressed. This may well typify the way in which BW(S) will have to interact in the future.

– a barrage on the River Carron. The eastern entrance to the Forth and Clyde is restricted by tidal considerations to a few hours a day and this is likely to inhibit use of the canal. A tidal barrage, a much less complex issue than the Loch Lomond scheme, would improve the time span of access.

– an improvement to the water supply to the Crinan. This canal has suffered chronic water shortages almost from the time of its opening and in high summer the back pumping of water is a regular practice. Improving reservoir feed to the summit reach, for example, would be beneficial to canal operations.

Apart from the technical problems and the need to consult with other stakeholders, financial restraints

The Junction of Spiers Wharf to Port Dundas
Port Dundas was the historic terminus of the Forth and Clyde and it became separated from the Glasgow Branch due to 1960s infilling. Now a £5.8 million project intends to rejoin Spiers Wharf to the Port. The picture shows the techniques of modern canal making with cast concrete forming the walls and bottom of the waterway. The depth may be judged by the height of the man standing next to the van in the foreground. The new canal turns sharply East from Spiers Wharf and runs alongside the busy M8 motorway.

may dictate the rate of progress in realising these aspirations.

However it is encouraging to report that that BW(S) and other stakeholders, namely Glasgow City Council and the Waterways Trust, have come together to begin work on linking the Forth and Clyde at Spiers Wharf to Port Dundas, the historic terminus of the canal's Glasgow Branch. This link had been infilled for around 40 years and it is planned to open that part of north Glasgow, which for many years had seen no new investment in new developments. The canal link is to cost £5.6 million to which sum Glasgow City, the Waterways Trust and European funding bodies have contributed.

Otherwise the *Scotland's Canals* paper seeks to integrate BW(S) into the network of government agencies and semi-autonomous bodies that regulate and promote Scotland's development in the fields of leisure, recreation, education, tourism and business creation. It thus expressed a serious intent to have the newly established BW(S) play its part in the future regeneration and prosperity of those parts of the country through which the canals pass. The running themes of the document are partnership and integration. In bringing the Millennium Link to completion BW(S) demonstrated that it was capable of such important interaction with a range of private, public and voluntary bodies.

In the document the Scottish Executive and BW(S) recognised the need to reinforce the valuable community links that were developed in launching and implementing the Millennium Project. The sad example of the vandalism before the opening of the Falkirk Wheel highlighted a national problem the causes of which run deep and the solution to which goes well beyond the remit of BW(S). The vandalism of the approaches to the Wheel was a dramatic example of an ongoing problem. Non-paternalistic 'education' in the benefits of the canals to many aspects of community life was recognised as a priority objective. In the environs of the Forth and Clyde and the Union in particular, BW(S) intended to address the problems of rubbish dumping and the deliberate causing of damage.

Can the canals return to their prime role as the carriers of goods and people? Tourism and leisure pursuits apart, can the waterways again play a part in the transportation of the public for everyday purposes? The transport infrastructure is very different today from that of the early 19th century when they came into their own as the preferred method of personal travel. Yet road and rail service are not ideal in the central belt and in Edinburgh there is a debate about the introduction of 'congestion' charges for car users

entering the city. The Union runs from the western suburbs to the centre of Edinburgh and the possibility exists, at least in theory, that a regular canal service would attract custom. While the Forth and Clyde does not run directly to the centre of Glasgow, Port Dundas could be easily linked to the main commercial centres for the benefit of those who find the present journey from, say, Kirkintilloch or Clydebank, not exactly convenient. After all an omnibus ran from Port Dundas to the Tron in Argyle Street in the 1820s.

A freight revival is more problematic. Vessels on the Union could carry around 60 tons and the Forth and Clyde and Crinan could take ships of 100 to 160 tons capacity respectively. Only on the Caledonian could a cargo of around 550 tons be carried in a single bottom. The economics of shipping are healthier there than in the lowlands but cargoes are difficult to identify except, possibly the Highland's maturing forestry products. To take 100 tons off the roads in the central belt and thereby reduce heavy lorry movements, is an attractive concept, but delivery to, and movement from, the canal termini are like to involve costly double-handling. Bulk cargoes whose timescale of delivery is non-critical offer the best prospects. In continental Europe, where, admittedly the canal network is more extensive, goods vehicles are banned from some roads at weekends and there is positive discrimination in favour of canals by subsidising their freight charges. Scotland might learn from a study of these examples? The Freight Facilities Grant Scheme, extended from inland waterways to short sea and coastal voyages, under the Transport (Scotland) Act of 2001, could benefit the Crinan and the Caledonian as they both shorten sea routes.

The future management of the canals is going to be complex and will encompass areas of activity far beyond the relatively simple matter of ensuring that water flows through as and when required. The canals will not be driven by a single simple commercial purpose. What does Scotland expect from its substantial recent investment of public money in the canals? Measuring the return on that capital cannot only be in the future profit and loss statements. What sort of payback will it get and when will it get it? BW(S) lost money in 2000–4 but perhaps the pay back has started. What else did those 400,000 visitors to the Falkirk Wheel do when in Scotland?

Even after the back log of repairs is complete and the Scottish Executive has 'only' to keep the canals operating it is difficult to envisage that the Scottish canals will be self-supporting financially. The history of BWB, which has had from the 1960s to address the problem nationally, for all its success in diversifying its activities in England and Wales, has not become self-sufficient. What makes us believe that the Scottish experience will be significantly different? Faced with an excess of expenditure over income what value does the nation put on the amenity created by the canals, on the leisure time enjoyed on them, on the renewed urban landscape along their banks and by the flora and fauna

in and around them, to cancel out the negative cash value?

Scotland and the Scottish Executive have to be in the canal business for the long haul. There will be grumbles when subsidies rise as no doubt they will from time to time. What price do you put on the national pride of having retained such unique examples of industrial archaeology?

The 18th and 19th century entrepreneurs who built the canals with an eye for profit have left a legacy that they could not have imagined. They did not see themselves as altruists. They were capitalists and proud of it and made hard-nosed commercial decisions when they walked away from the canals. They would not have envisaged that history would say that they created one of the main engines of the industrial revolution in Scotland and hold them in high regard for it. Even less could they have envisaged that long after the commercial use for which they were built had disappeared, that in the 21st century, their canals would still have the potential to play an important part in many aspects of the lives of the people of Scotland.

APPENDIX I

Canal chronology

1763   Smeaton surveys route for the Forth and Clyde Canal.
        End of the Seven Year's War.

1768   Forth and Clyde Canal Act passed. Work on canal starts.
        First edition of the *Encyclopedia Britannica* published in Edinburgh.

1769   Watt surveys a route for the Monkland Canal.

1770   Monkland Canal Act passed and work starts on canal.

1771   Watt surveys routes for the Crinan Canal.

1773   Watt surveys a route for the Caledonian Canal. Work on Monkland stops due to lack of money.

1775   Work on the Forth and Clyde stops at Stockingfield due to lack of money.
        American War of Independence begins. (Ends 1783)

1776   Adam Smith publishes the *Wealth of Nations*. On the River Doubs the Marquis de Jouffroy d'Abbans sails the first steamboat.

1777   Glasgow Branch of the Forth and Clyde opens to Hamiltonhill.

1789   French Revolution began.

1790   Forth and Clyde completed from east at Grangemouth to west at Bowling and the Glasgow Branch extended to Port Dundas.

1793   Britain joins coalition against France in the French Revolutionary Wars.
        Crinan Canal Act passed. Work starts on the canal. The Forth and Clyde and the Monkland are joined together at Blackhill. Route for the Edinburgh and Glasgow Union Canal surveyed.

1798   British naval victory at the Battle of the Nile.

1801   Crinan opens in partially completed state. Telford makes a proposal for building of the Caledonian Canal. *Charlotte Dundas* trials mark the beginning of steam propulsion on the Forth and Clyde.

1803   Caledonian Canal Act passed.

1804   Work starts on the Caledonian Canal.

1805   British naval victory at Battle of Trafalgar.

1806   French victories at the Battles of Ulm and Austerlitz.

1809   Crinan completed.

1815   Napoloeon defeated at Battle of Waterloo.

1816   Management of the Crinan taken over by Commissioners of the Caledonian Canal.

1817   Act for the Edinburgh and Glasgow Union (the Union) Canal passed.

1818   Work on the Union starts.

1819   *Comet I* begins first steamship service through the Crinan Canal to Oban. *Vulcan*, the first iron-hulled vessel in Scotland, is built on the Monkland Canal.

1822   Caledonian opens with a restricted depth. Union Canal completed and joined to the Forth and Clyde.

1824   Monkland and Kirkintilloch Railway opens.

1825   Stockton to Darlington railway opens.

1829   J B Neilson patents the 'hot-blast' process of iron manufacture.

1842   Edinburgh and Glasgow Railway opens.

1846   Forth and Clyde and Monkland canal companies amalgamate.

1849   Union Canal taken over by the Edinburgh and Glasgow Railway.

1854   Crimean War begins.

1856   Steam lighterage begins on the Forth and Clyde and with it the 'puffers' are born.

1859   Construction of the Suez Canal begins.

1865   Union Canal and Edinburgh and Glasgow Railway taken over by North British Railway.

1867   Forth and Clyde and Monkland taken over by the Caledonian Railway Company.

1894   Manchester Ship Canal opens.

1895   Kaiser Wilhelm (Kiel) Canal opens. Widened and deepened in 1905.

1914   World War I begins.
The Forth closes to commercial navigation for duration of World War I.
The Panama Canal is completed.

1919   Control of the Caledonian and the Crinan vested in the Ministry of Transport.

1923   London Midland & Scottish Railways (LMS) take over Caledonian Railway Company and London & North Eastern Railways take over North British Railway Company.

1933   Traffic ceases on the Union.

1935   Traffic ceases on the Monkland.

1936   Union Canal locks at Falkirk filled in.

1939   World War II begins.

1942   LMS petitions to have the Monkland closed.

1948   British Transport Commission take over control of all canals.

1950   Monkland formally abandoned and is piped in at Blackhill in 1954.

1961   Infilling and piping of the Monkland begins around Coatbridge.

1962   British Waterways Board forms to take control of all UK canals.
Forth and Clyde closes to all traffic.

1965   Union closes.

1968   Caledonian and Crinan designated as 'commercial' waterways and Forth and Clyde, Monkland and Union as 'remainder' waterways.

1973   Historic Scotland begins 'listing' features of the Scottish canals.

1993   The Millennium Commission established by the Lottery Act.
British Waterways apply to the Millennium Commission for funding for the re-opening and rejoining of the Forth and Clyde and Union: the 'Millennium Link'.

1997   Millennium Commission agrees to partially fund the Millennium Link.

1999   Scottish Parliament reconvenes.

2001   Forth and Clyde re-opens, 'sea to sea', to leisure traffic. Funding of the Scottish canals is devolved to the Scottish Executive.

2002   Union and Forth and Clyde are joined at the Falkirk Wheel and re-opens for leisure traffic.

APPENDIX II

Scottish canals: dates and costs

Name	Began	Opened	Actual Cost	Estimated Cost	Length (Miles)	No. of Locks	Year Last Used	Year Abandoned
Caledonian	1804	1822	£905,000	£475,000	60	29		
Crinan	1794	1801	£140,000	£69,000	9	15		
Forth & Clyde	1768	1775/ 1790	£330,000	£147,000	39	41	1962	1962*
Monkland	1770	1773/ 1793	£120,000	£20,000	12	0	1935	1950
Union	1817	1822	£462,000	£264,000	32	11	1933	1965**

Notes

1. Length quoted excludes side cuts.
2. Actual cost is the amount spent up to the opening date.
3. The Forth and Clyde reached Stockingfield in 1775 and was extended to Bowling in 1790.
4. The Monkland reached Jermiston in 1773 and was extended to join the Forth and Clyde in 1793.
5. * Re-opened in 2001
6. ** Re-opened in 2002

APPENDIX III

Principal canal dimensions (as built)

	Length (miles)	Summit Height (ft)	Summit Length (m)	No. of Locks	Lock Surface Dimensions (ft)	Canal Depth (ft)	Canal Width (ft) (top x bottom)	Major[5] Aqueducts
Forth & Clyde	38	156	15	39	70 x 20	8	60 x 30	1
Monkland	9[1]	246	9[1]	0	70 x 14	4	32 x 16	
Crinan	9	69	0.8	15	112/96 x 27/24	8	56/84 x 30/48	
Caledonian	60	106	4	29[2]	170 x 40	15	110 x 30/50	
Union	32	242	32	11	69 x 12.5	5	37 x 20	3

Notes:

Summit height is measured as above sea level.

1. Monkland was originally built to be lockless from Sheepford to Glasgow. When extended to the Calder and linked to the Forth and Clyde it acquired some two miles of extra length and two locks at Sheepford, four pairs of locks at Blackhill and a regulating lock at Port Dundas.

2. Including four regulating locks at which there was little or no level change. The second lock at Gairlochy was added in 1843.

3. See Appendix IV for details of the aqueducts.

APPENDIX IV

Aqueducts and alterations

1. Aqueducts

Canal	Crossing	Date	Arches	Length (ft)	Height (ft)
Forth & Clyde	R. Kelvin	1790	4	400	70
Union	R. Almond	1822	5	420	76
Union	R. Avon	1822	12	810	86
Union	Water of Leith	1822	8	500	75

2. Alterations

The following is a list of major improvements, as distinct from repairs, made to the to the canals in the years following their opening to traffic.

A. Forth & Clyde

Date	Structural Change
1806	A regulating lock was added to the east end of the basin at Port Dundas. The banks were raised on the Cut of Junction to improve water depth.
1812	Carron basin was built.
1836	A half-mile cut was made to Whitecrook on the Clyde, opposite the River Cart. A new reservoir at Lily Loch and a basin at Port Dundas were made.
1841	Port Dundas and Grangemouth basins were extended.
1842	Cut of Junction was deepened. Hillend reservoir was extended and new reservoirs were made at Roughrigg and Bogfoot.
1846	Bowling basin was extended.

B. Monkland

Date	Structural Change
1793	Canal extended east to the River Calder through new locks at Sheepford and West to the Glasgow branch of the Forth and Clyde.
1798	New reservoir at Hillend was completed.
1806	Banks raised to match the water depth on the cut of Junction on the Forth and Clyde. Four staircase pairs of locks constructed at Blackhill to link up with the Forth and Clyde.
1836	New reservoir made at Lily Loch, the cost of which was shared with the Forth and Clyde (40%).
1841/42	The depth of the Hillend Reservoir was increased. New double line of locks at Blackhill completed.
1843	The Drumpellier Railway was built and opened to supply coal to the canal (up to 900 barges per annum).
1851	The Blackhill Inclined Plane was completed. Largely used to return empty barges up to the Monkland from the Forth and Clyde to save water.

C. Crinan

Date	Structural Change
1816	The repairs and alterations made at this date truly completed this canal. All the lock gates were either repaired or renewed and the banks were straightened. The eastern entrance was deepened, a new sea lock made at Crinan and the Ardrishaig pier was lengthened.
1835	The Loch-an-Add reservoir depth was increased by five feet.
1837	A new pier was built at Ardrishaig
1838	Ardrishaig entrance was deepened.
1846	The reservoirs at Loch an Faolinn and Glen Clachaig were joined to improve water supply to the summit reach.
1857	New piers and jetties were constructed at Ardrishaig and Crinan.
1930	Sea locks and reservoirs were extensively repaired.

D. Caledonian

Date	Structural Change
1844	A second lock was made at Gairlochy.
1850	The canal banks were raised at Dochgarroch and Aberchalder.
1960	The mechanisation of all locks was begun.
1964	The sea lock and basin at Corpach was modified to allow ships of 1,000 tons deadweight to use them in anticipation of the planned paper mill coming into operation.

APPENDIX V

The Glasgow, Paisley and Johnstone Canal

After a meeting held in Glasgow in 1804, at the instigation of the then Earl of Eglinton, £20,000 was subscribed for a canal to link the south bank of the Clyde with Ayrshire. Eglinton had extensive estates in the Ardrossan and Kilwinning areas which were known to be rich in coal. Such luminaries as Rennie and Jessop had been involved in assessing the possibilities of a canal and new ports on the Ayrshire coast at Saltcoats or Ardrossan. Eventually Ardrossan was settled on as the outlet to the sea.

Telford produced a modified scheme in 1805, diverting the route between Glasgow and Johnstone so that it became lockless. It was proposed that the canal would rise to an 18-mile summit reach which passed through mineral-rich ground without any more locks until it came within two miles of the sea. An act was passed in 1806 for a canal from Ardrossan to Glasgow, at Tradeston, with branches to several existing industrial sites. A share capital of £140,000, with powers to borrow a further £30,000, was authorised.

Work began in 1807 but only £44,000 of capital was raised. Loans had to be raised by the committee of management and £71,000 more was scraped together on their personal credit. All of this money was used up in building the canal between Glasgow to Johnstone; it did not proceed beyond this point. The Glasgow to Paisley section was opened in 1810 and Johnston was reached in 1811. The waterway, as built, was lockless, four feet deep, 13 feet wide at the bottom and 25 feet wide at the top. There was an aqueduct 240 feet long over the River Cart and two substantial tunnels of over 200 feet in length. Eglinton tried twice to raise government loans or grants to finish the canal, at an estimated cost of a further £144,000, but did not succeed.

By 1815 the canal had an active goods trade of around 22,000 tons per annum. Passenger traffic opened up at much the same time and 46,000 people were carried in 1817. The Paisley section has to be credited with developing the 'swift' type of passage boat in the 1830s which was later adopted by the other Scottish canals. The passenger traffic reached a peak of 373,000 in 1835 but even at this time the canal was not profitable enough to repay its debts consistently or to pay dividends to its shareholders. The canal suffered from severe competition from railways in the 1840s and in 1843 it gave up its passenger traffic for an annual payment of £1,367 from the railways. Thereafter it fell into decline.

In 1869 an act vested the canal company in the Glasgow and South Western Railway which took over its outstanding debts and some of its shares. The railway increased its hold on the canal over the next few years and the decline continued. In 1881 there was no opposition to an act closing the canal.

APPENDIX VI

Canal barges: steam and horsepower costs

(Details taken from the records of Wm Baird, Gartsherrie Iron Works, 1867)

1. Capital Costs

	Hull	Machinery	Total	Deadweight	Cost/Ton
Steam-lighter	£413.60	£494.25	£907.85	67 tons	£13.55
Horse-drawn scow	£270.90	£0	£270.90	56 tons	£4.84

2. Operating Costs per Journey

	Journey	Machinery[1]	Hull[1]	Horse	Wages[2]	Others[3]	Total	Cargo	Cost/Ton[4]
Horse-drawn	Gartsherrie to	£0	£0.40	£0.66	£0.96	£0.40	£2.42	56 tons	**£0.043**
Steamer	Bowling	£0.61	£0.51	£0	£1.14	£0	£2.26	67 tons	**£0.034**
Horse-drawn	Gartsherrie to	£0	£0.60	£1.00	£1.43	£0.50	£3.53	56 tons	**£0.063**
Steamer	Grangemouth	£0.91	£0.76	£0	£1.72	£0	£3.39	67 tons	**£0.051**

Notes:

1. These costs took into account depreciation, interest on the capital and consumables such as rope, repairs and coal for the steamers; in this case four hundredweights per journey. No provision was made for insuring the vessels. The costs quoted are time-based, i.e. dependent on the time taken for the various journeys. The capital cost of the steamer hull (£413) was 50% higher than that of the horse-drawn scow, yet the quoted 'Hull' cost for the Bowling trip of £0.51 is only 27% higher than that of the scow. This is because, as may be expected, the steamer would complete more journeys.

2. The wage for the crew was paid on a tonnage-delivered basis. Wages were higher for the steamers because more cargo was carried and the expense of an 'engine boy' was included.

3. These are miscellaneous expenses for the horse such as stabling.

4. The final cost per ton included the canal dues charged. In these examples pig iron was carried and amounted to £0.033 for the Bowling trip and £0.063 for the voyage to Grangemouth. The latter reflected the longer distance on the Forth and Clyde from Glasgow to Grangemeouth than from Glasgow to Bowling.

It is recorded that for this year, 1635 steamer voyages were completed to 1354 by scow. This implies that Bairds shipped around 185,000 tons of pig iron in 1867.

APPENDIX VII

Number of puffers by year of building

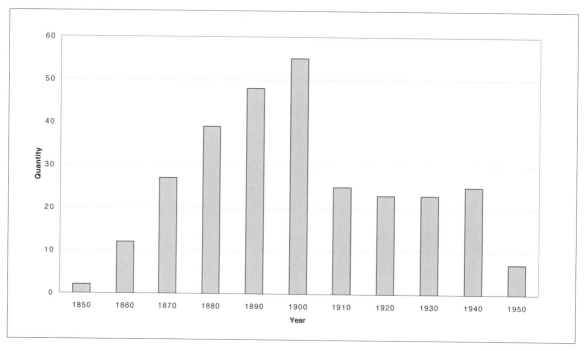

Notes

1. In the two decades following the first puffer many were not new vessels but modified, existing, iron scows. It has been reported that as many as 70 puffers were operating on the Forth and Clyde by the mid-1860s but most of these would have been modified scows.

2. During World War I few puffers were built due to the shortage of building materials and the fact that the eastern end of the Forth and Clyde canal was closed. Post-war tonnages never reached the levels of pre-1914.

3. The 1940's figure includes only those VICs that traded in Scotland after World War II.

4. By the 1950s puffers were built which were designed principally for the West Highland trade and were too large for the Forth and Clyde locks. Their greater deadweight compensated for their smaller numbers.

APPENDIX VIII

Forth and Clyde Navigation: extracts from the Financial Accounts

The Accounts for the year to 31st December 1815

Profit and Loss Statement	(£)	Balance Sheet	(£)
Expenditure		*Assets*	
Ordinary Expenses	6,737	Canal property	393,899
Officers' salaries	1,781	Debtors, deposits	38,170
Lock-keepers etc, wages	1,500	**Total**	**432,069**
Miscellaneous costs	1,907		
Canal repairs etc	6,300	'Account of stock'	
Property tax	1,371	Shares @ £325 each	421,525
Dividends	22,698	Dividends due	7,633
Surplus of revenue	4,604	Sundries due	2,911
Total	**46,898**	**Total**	**432,069**
Revenue			
Tolls	39,356		
Passage Boats	2,829		
Track boats	736		
Dues and Rents	3,977		
Total	**46,898**		

Notes on the 1815 Statement

1. In modern accounting practice the profit of £27,302 (£22,698+£4,604) would have been smaller because of a depreciation charge. On the other hand capital spent on improvements would probably not have been charged against revenue (thus increasing the profit) but would have been capitalised. Profit was not taxed as it would be today.

2. The dividend is equal to £17.50 per share.

Analysis of 1815 Toll Revenue

	£	% of total	% E to W	% W to E
Port Dundas to Clyde	2,729	6.9	6.9	
From Forth to Clyde	4,848	12.3	12.3	
From Forth to Port Dundas	16,725	42.5	42.5	
From Clyde to Port Dundas	418	1.1		1.1
From Clyde to Forth	9,261	23.5		23.5
From Port Dundas to Forth	2,998	7.6		7.6
Intermediate Traffic	2,377	6.1		
Total	**39,356**	**100.0**	**61.7%**	**32.2%**

Toll revenue showed a bias to the westward movement of materials, and into Glasgow (Port Dundas) in particular. Sea-to-sea traffic was 35.8% of total income.

Extracts from the Balance Sheet for the year to 31 December, 1791

Assets

Line of the old canal	£200,039
Line of the new canal	£83,849
Properties	£10,586
Debtors	£11,392
Total	**£305,866**

Accounted for by:

Creditors	£39,040
Loan[1]	£50,000
Shares[2]	£216,826
Total	**£305,866**

Notes on the 1791 Statement

1. This loan was the £50,000 from the proceeds of the Forfeited Estates.
2. This values the 1,297 shares (issued at £100 each) at £167.20 each.
3. No profit and loss statement is available for this year.
4. The 'line of new canal' is the extension from Glasgow to Bowling.

Comments

1. The net worth of the company rose from £306,000 to £432,000 in the period 1791 to 1815.
2. Broadly speaking, in today's values, the 1791 and 1815 net worth of the company is £70,300,000 and £99,400,000 respectively.

APPENDIX IX

Forth and Clyde Canal: number of passengers, 1809–48

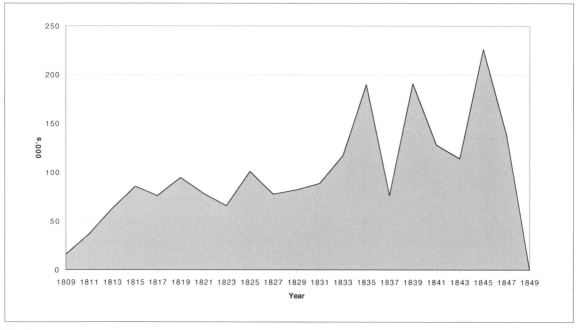

Key Dates

1822   Union Canal opens.

1842   Edinburgh and Glasgow Railway opens.

1843   Price war between railway and canals begins.

1846   Night-passage boats between Glasgow and Edinburgh are withdrawn.

1848   All passenger boat services are withdrawn in March 1848.

APPENDIX X

Forth and Clyde: profit ratio, passenger boats, 1809–48

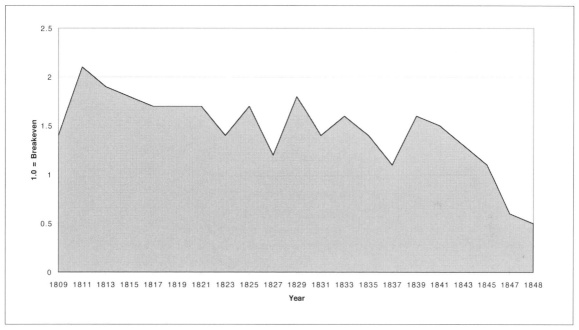

Notes

1. When the profit ratio fell below 1.0 (after 1845) the operation became loss-making.

2. The average passenger fare in 1840 was 7p.

3. The average passenger fare in 1842 was 5p.

4. The average passenger fare from 1844 to 1848 was 2p.

APPENDIX XI

The Aitken 'Queen' fleet (1893–1939)

1. Vessels

A. SS *Fairy Queen (I)* (1893-97), 45 grt., 20 hp.

B. SS *Fairy Queen (II)* (1897-1912), 48.5 grt., 10 hp.

C. SS *May Queen* (1903-18), 55.3 grt., 22 hp.

D. SS *Gipsy Queen* (1905-39), 75 grt., 10.6 hp.

E. MV *Fairy Queen (III)* (1923-31), 38 grt., 40 bhp.

2. Brief History

George Aitken had served on the Taylor's *Rockvilla Castle* and his son James, who had a thriving grocery business in Kirkintilloch, decided to restart sailing excursions on the Forth and Clyde. In 1893 he introduced the *Fairy Queen (I),* capable of carrying 200 passengers, to the public. She ran excursions from the industrial gloom of Glasgow to the pleasant countryside at Craigmarloch near the Townhead Reservoir, west of Castlecary, where passengers could and did picnic. Refreshments of a non-alcoholic variety were available and there was music on board.

She was well received and was eventually replaced by the larger, 260-passenger, *Fairy Queen (II)* in 1897. Demand grew and a second ship, *May Queen*, built at McGregor's yard in Kirkintilloch, joined the service. She was followed by a third, *Gipsy Queen*, in 1905 and the next seven years were the high point of canal cruising. They were very popular with clubs, societies and Sunday schools. The facilities at Craigmarloch, which became the eastern limit of the cruises, were developed and improved with play areas for children and a tearoom, called The Bungalow, for lunching, dining and dancing.

Fairy Queen (II) was withdrawn in 1912 and not replaced. The cruises continued during World War I as they were seen as a necessary leisure relief to the stresses of the conflict. *May Queen* was sold in 1918 and the fleet was not enlarged until 1923 when the motor vessel *Fairy Queen (III)* arrived. But the great days were over and in any case the diesel vessel did not have the same aesthetic appeal as the steamers and she was withdrawn in 1931. The cruises continued on a reduced schedule with only the popular *Gipsy Queen* until the outbreak of World War II. She went to the breakers in early 1940. Thereafter what leisure 'cruising' there was on the canal took a very different form.

APPENDIX XII

Monkland Canal: Blackhill inclined plane, number of movements, 1854–84

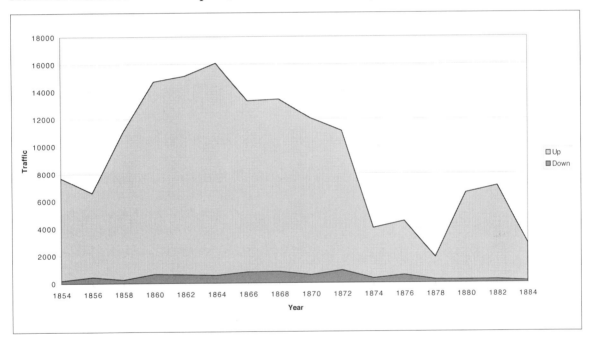

Notes

1. The peak number of movements occurred in 1864 when 16,057 barges were lifted back up from the Forth and Clyde to the Monkland. These were mostly empty. Very few went down eg 831 in 1868.

2. The inclined plane replaced a railway, first built in 1772. Goods, mostly coal, were transferred from barges to wagons, which ran downhill under gravity.

3. Assuming the 16,057 barges carried around 60 tons of cargo it suggests that in 1864 around 1,000,000 tons were transported between the Monkland and the Forth and Clyde.

A P P E N D I X   X I I I

Union Canal: tolls earned, 1830 to 1920

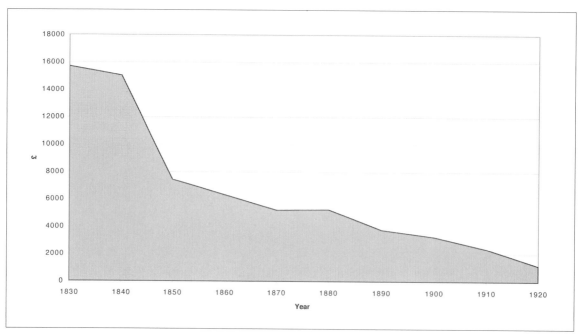

Notes

1. From 1842 until it was taken over by the Edinburgh and Glasgow Railway in 1849, the Union conducted a price war with the railway company.

2. These figures do not include income from passenger services and other minor sources but are only for goods carried.
   The above graph represents the downward trend in the canal's basic commodity trade.

APPENDIX XIV

Forth and Clyde and Monkland: tonnages, 1800 to 1925

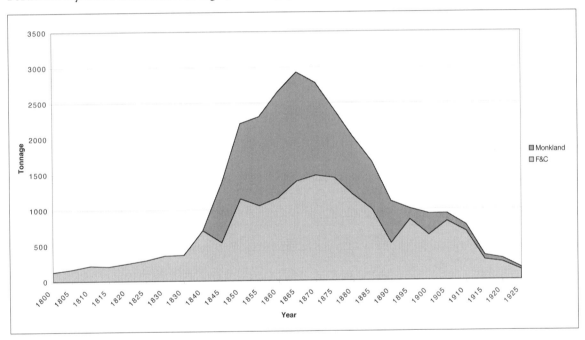

Notes

1. The amalgamation of the Forth and Clyde and the Monkland took place in 1846.
2. After 1900 the Monkland was in serious decline due to the exhaustion of its neighbouring mineral fields. Competition from the North British Railway began to have an effect from about 1879 onwards.
3. The Blackhill Inclined Plane, opened in 1850 to improve the link between the two canals, closed in 1884 because its extra capacity was no longer required.
4. The Forth and Clyde did not recover from the closure of the Forth Estuary during World War I.

APPENDIX XV

Crinan Canal, number of ship passages 1840 to 1925

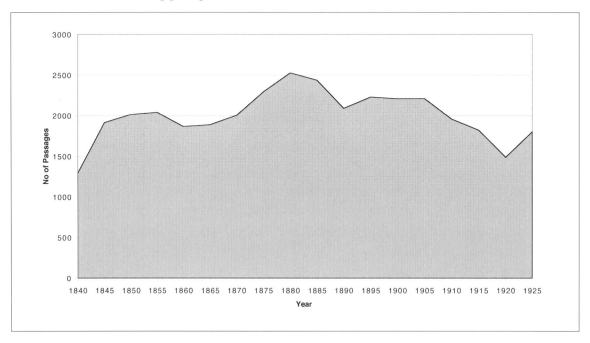

APPENDIX XVI (a)

Caledonian Canal: number of ship passages, 1825 to 1890

Notes (1825-90)

1. The canal was closed for repairs from September 1844 till May 1847. During this period there was a healthy internal trade.

2. The falling off in the number of internal passages after 1860 may be attributed to the availability of other forms of transport.

   The railways in particular, started to make an impact in the Highlands after this date, making it quicker and cheaper to travel between Glasgow and Inverness.

APPENDIX XVI (b)

Caledonian Canal: number of ship passages, 1890 to 1965

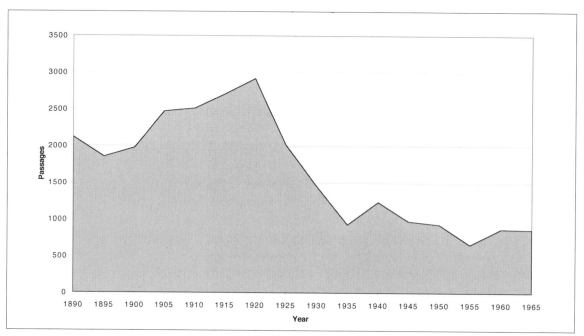

Notes (1890 to 1965)

1. Of the 2014 passages recorded in 1925, over 600 were the twice-daily run of the internal mail steamer between Fort Augustus and Inverness.
2. The Glasgow to Inverness sailing services ended in 1927.
3. The number of fishing boats using the canal fell from around 1,400 in 1928 to under 400 a decade later.

APPENDIX XVII

Crinan Canal: profit ratio, 1820 to 1905

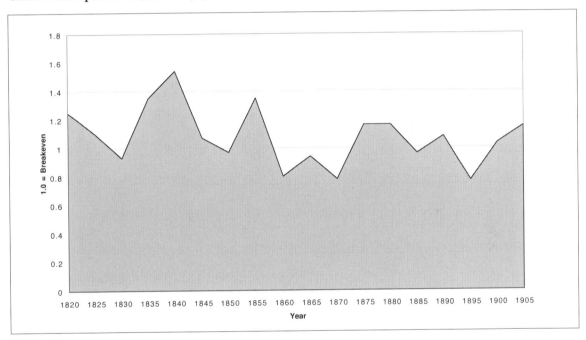

Notes

1. The profit ratio of less than 1.0 indicates that the year in question was loss-making.
2. The Crinan was mostly in surplus between 1835 and 1845. Thereafter it lost money as often as it made it. Had it been privately owned it would seldom have returned dividends to its shareholders.
3. The aggregate ratio for the period of the chart above is 0.97 i.e. just below breakeven.

APPENDIX XVIII

Caledonian Canal: profit ratio, 1835 to 1945

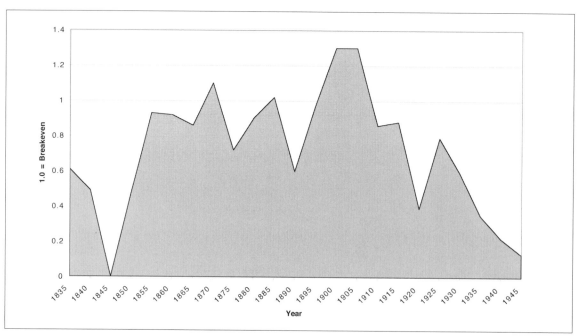

Notes

1. A profit ratio of less than 1.0 indicates a loss for the year in question.
2. Since the canal was in public ownership the managerial policy was to attempt to breakeven. But on the eve of World War II costs were running at about five times the amount of income.
3. Between 1825 and 1840 the ratio lay in the range from 0.56 to 0.79. The canal was closed for two and a half years from 1844 to 1847 and £220,000 was spent on reconstruction.
4. At frequent intervals, e.g. in 1890, there was an injection of cash in the form of a government grant to pay off accumulated deficits or to pay for repairs to the fabric of the canal.

APPENDIX XIX

Forth and Clyde Canal: income, 1779 to 1800

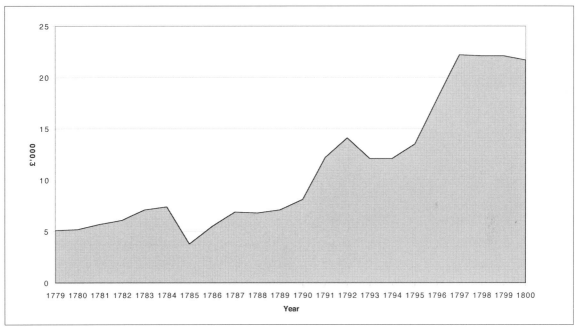

Notes

1. From 1775 the canal ran from Grangemouth to Stockingbridge. The Glasgow Branch was opened in 1777.
   Bowling was reached in 1790 and by 1793 the junction with the Monkland had been constructed.
2. It is likely that income was greater then running costs from about 1790.
3. There was a noticeable improvement in income from 1793, the date of the junction with the Monkland.

APPENDIX XX

Forth and Clyde Canal: income 1810 to 1940

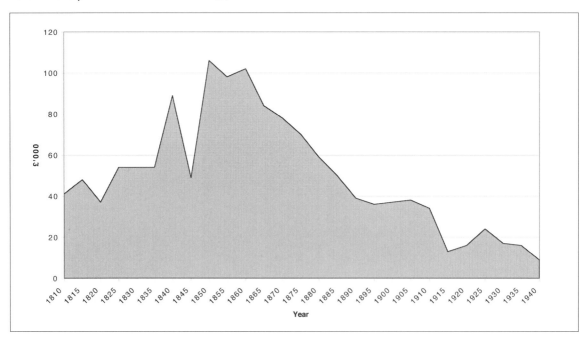

Notes

1. The Forth and Clyde took over the Monkland in 1846 and thereafter the income shown above is for the two canals.

2. The Forth and Clyde was closed at its eastern end from 1914 to 1918.

APPENDIX XXI

Forth and Clyde Canal: profit ratio, 1800 to 1910

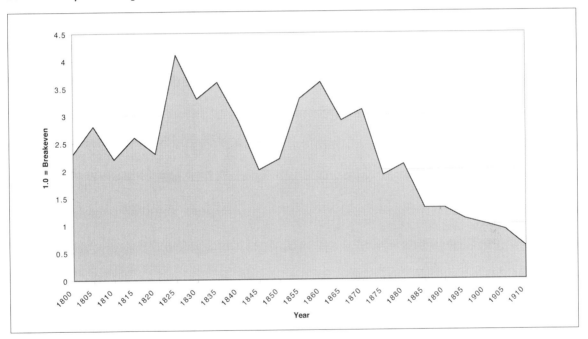

Notes

1. When the profit ratio is less than 1.0 the canal is losing money.

2. The peak tonnages carried occurred in 1868. Thereafter there was a general downturn in income and a more dramatic decline in the use of the Monkland.

APPENDIX XXII

Forth and Clyde Canal: income, costs and dividend, 1800–60

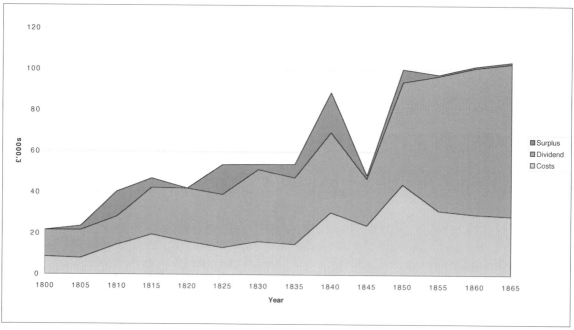

Notes

1. The sum of the costs, dividend and surplus equals the total income.
2. The first dividends were paid in 1800. Previous to that the shareholders had no direct return on their investment.
3. In 1820 the company went into deficit by £5,000 to maintain the dividend level of the previous year.
4. In 1846 the Forth and Clyde took over the Monkland and the figures after this date are for the two canals combined.
5. From 1845 onwards large dividends were paid and very little surplus taken into reserves.
6. The Forth and Clyde was taken over by the Caledonian Railway in 1866.

APPENDIX XXIII

Union Canal: profit and loss, 1832–45

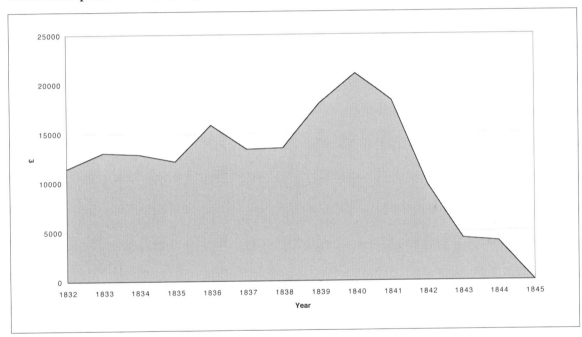

Notes

1. Profit is defined here as the surplus left after taking costs from income. In general terms this surplus would be used for the payment of dividends.

2. The Edinburgh and Glasgow Railway opened in February 1843 and was in direct competition with the Union.

3. Having benefited from increased activity during the construction phase of the railway (1839-41), the canal cut its rates drastically after 1840. Its commodity rates in 1845 were only half of those it was charging in 1837.

4. The Union paid a dividend to its shareholders only once after 1842. It was taken over by the Edinburgh and Glasgow Railway in 1848.

APPENDIX XXIV

Union Canal: income, average tonnage rates, 1837–46

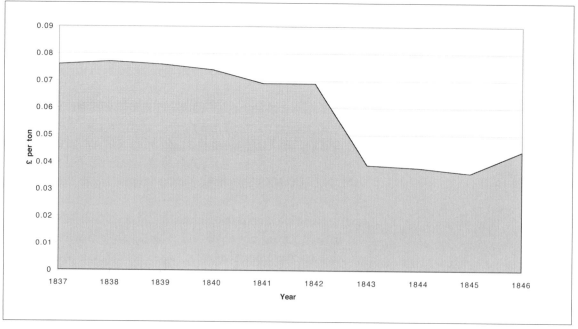

Notes

1. The Edinburgh and Glasgow Railway opened in competition to the canal in 1842.

2. The amount of stone carried by the canal trebled during the construction of the railway (1839-41) but the rate was dropped from £0.034 to £0.024 per ton.

3. The partial recovery in 1846 was due to increasing the coal rate from £0.049 to £0.074. It had been £0.108 in 1837 before the price war with the railway began in earnest. Coal was typically 40% of the tonnage carried on the canal.

APPENDIX XXV

Scottish Canals (under BTC Control): tonnages, 1948–61

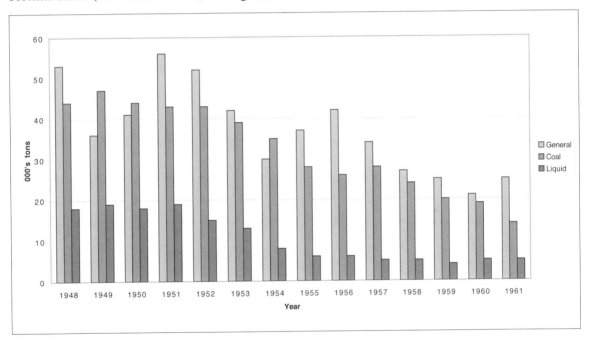

Notes

1. In this period the Monkland and the Union were closed to traffic and there was little movement on the Forth and Clyde. The quantities moved on the Forth and Clyde had dwindled to nothing by 1955 and prior to this most of the traffic was on the Highland canals.

2. All categories, general merchandise, coal and bulk liquids were declining over this period.

3. During this time the Crinan was of greater economic significance than the Caledonian. It carried greater numbers of commercial vessels and yachts and much the same number of fishing vessels. In most years the Crinan carried twice the tonnage of the Caledonian.

APPENDIX XXVI

Millennium Link Project

A. Millennium Link: Major Reconstruction Elements

Canal	Location	Construction Work
Union	A801 road, Lathallan Road, Vellore and Greendykes Road M8 motorway at Broxburn	Canal diverted and bridge built. New bridges built. Canal re-aligned and bridge built.
Union	Wester Hailes, Edinburgh	1.1 miles of canal re-instated and nine bridges built. Estimated cost of £9.5 million.
Union	Falkirk	Falklirk Wheel and associated locks and basins built at junction with Forth and Clyde. Estimated cost of £17.5 million.
Union	Lemington Bridge, Edinburgh	Bridge restored.
Forth & Clyde	Grangemouth	New canal link to River Carron and the Forth made and two new locks built. Estimated cost of £4.5 million.
Forth & Clyde	Falkirk, Bainsford Locks 11 and 16	Four bridges and three new locks constructed. Estimated cost of £5 million.
Forth & Clyde	Bonnybridge	New opening bridge built.

Canal	Location	Construction Work
Forth & Clyde	Castlecary and A80 trunk road	Two new fixed bridges.
Forth & Clyde	Wynford and Auchinstarry	Two new bridges constructed.
Forth & Clyde	Twechar and Hillhead	Two new bridges built.
Forth & Clyde	Townhead	New fixed bridge made.
Forth & Clyde	Cadder	Bridge raised.
Forth & Clyde	Glasgow (Balmuidy Road, Clevenden Road, Blairdardie Avenue and Duntreath Road).	Four fixed bridges made and Lock 36 rebuilt.
Forth & Clyde	Dalmuir, Kilbowie Road, Sylvania Way and Argyll Road	New drop-lock constructed and three fixed bridges built.
Forth & Clyde	Erskine Ferry	Opening bridge restored.

B. Reconstructed Canals: Dimensions (feet)

	Forth & Clyde	Union
Width of channel	20.8	12.6
Depth of channel	6.0	3.5
Air draft at bridges	9.7	8.9
Max. vessel length	66.0	70.0
Max. vessel breadth	19.0	12.0
Max. vessel draft	5.3	3.0

C. Funding of the Millennium Project

Funding Body	Grant (£m)	% of total Grant
Millennium Commission	32.20	41.08
Scottish Enterprise	18.70	23.85
British Waterways	9.30	11.86
European Regional Development Fund	8.59	10.96
City of Glasgow Council	2.35	2.99
City of Edinburgh Council	1.70	2.17
North Lanarkshire Council	1.28	1.63
Falkirk Council	0.55	0.71
West Lothian Council	0.55	0.71
East Dunbartonshire Council	0.44	0.56
West Dunbartonshire Council	0.33	0.42
Private/voluntary sector	2.40	3.06
Total	**78.39**	**100.00**

APPENDIX XXVII

British Waterways (Scotland): operating profit 1999 to 2004

Year	£ Million 1999/2000	2000/2001	2001/2002	2002/2003	2003/2004
Income					
Direct income	24.76	33.31	12.82	4.33	3.98
Government grants	7.27	10.54	8.60	12.64	12.64
Total	**32.03**	**43.85**	**21.42**	**16.97**	**16.62**
Expenditure					
Renovations/					
Repairs	28.13	37.96	16.98	6.17	4.92
Operating Costs	1.59	3.96	4.79	9.84	5.76
Others	2.76	2.88	3.66	4.75	5.79
Total	**32.48**	**44.80**	**25.43**	**20.76**	**16.47**
Profit (Loss)	**(0.45)**	**(0.95)**	**(4.01)**	**(3.79)**	**(0.15)**

Notes

1. Direct income includes grants from the Millennium Commission for the Millennium Link and influenced the figures for 1999/2001.

2. The Scottish Executive took over the grant provision in 2001/2002 when the restored canals came into operation.

3. Sale of investment properties and earned interest have tended to reduce losses and/or improve profits.

4. Operating costs rose from 2001/2002 when the restored canals came into operation.

5. The fall in renovation costs after 2001 reflected the completion of the Millennium Link.

6. The trading losses are underwritten by the British Waterways Board.

REFERENCES

GENERAL

British Waterways Board, *Annual report and Accounts*, 1963/1982, ZLIB/28/1-16, National Archives, Kew.

Waterways of the British Waterways Board, 1968, RAIL 1029/78, National Archives, Kew.

Waterways of the British Waterways Board, 1974, RAIL 1029/93, National Archives, Kew.

British Waterways Board, Annual Report and Accounts, 1999/2004.

Our Plan for the Future, 2001/5, British Waterways Board.

Our plan for the Future, 2003/7, British Waterways Board.

Waterways for People, 2003, British Waterways Board.

Allen et al, *Coatbridge – Three Centuries of Change*, ISBN 0 946120 00 5.

Committee of Inquiry into Inland Waterways, H.M.S.O., 1958.

British Waterways Board, *The Future of the Waterways*, Interim Report, H.M.S.O., 1964.

Bowman, AI., *Kirkintilloch Shipbuilding*, ISBN 0 904966 08 9.

Management Reports of the Estates Forfeited, Volume 11, E786/43 and Volume 54, E702/4, National Archive of Scotland, Edinburgh.

Haldane, J., *New Ways through the Glens*, ISBN 01 899863 05 2.

Macdonald, D., *The Clyde Puffer*, ISBN 0 7153 7443 5.

Paterson, L., *The Light in the Glens*, ISBN 0 948905 78 6.

Martin, D., *The Monkland and Kirkintilloch and Associated Railways*, ISBN 0 904966 41 0.

Scotland's Canals – an Asset for the Future, 2002, the Scottish Executive.

CALEDONIAN CANAL

Applications for Funds for Repairs, 1911, T/1/11297, National Archive, Kew.

Applications for Funds for a Deep-Sea Canal, 1913, T/1/11668, National Archive, Kew.

Annual Reports to the House of Commons, 1802/1822, BR/CCL/1/1, National Archives of Scotland, Edinburgh.

Annual Reports of the Commissioners of the Caledonian Canal, 1823/1891, BR/CCL/1/4 to 7, National Archives of Scotland, Edinburgh.

Annual Reports of the Commissioners of the Caledonian Canal, 1837/1967, BW1/1/14/1 to 15, Highland Library Service, Inverness.

Annual Statistics, 1958/1961, BW1/4/2/2 to 5, Highland Library Services, Inverness.

General File, 1886/1966, BW2/4/2/4/1, Highland Library Services, Inverness.

Revenue and Expenditure Reports, 1890/1948, BW2/2/2, Highland Library Services, Inverness.

Shipping Lists, 1820/24, BW1/4/3/2, Highland Library Service, Inverness.

CRINAN CANAL

Note: After 1818 reports on the Crinan Canal were included in those made by the Commissioners of the Caledonian Canal. See above.

Annual Reports, 1939/45, BW2/1/3/1 to 3, The Waterways Trust, Ellesmere Port.

Engineering Reports, 1794/1800, CRI/1/4/1, National Archives of Scotland, Edinburgh.

Financial Ledgers,1950/1979, BW2/2//1/3, The Waterways Trust, Ellesmere Port.

List of Ships, 1845/1920, BR/CRI/4/1 to 8 and BR/CRI/4/19, National Archives of Scotland, Edinburgh.

Minutes of Meetings of Subscribers, BR/CRI/1/1, National Archives of Scotland, Edinburgh.

Revenue and Expenditure, 1858/1928, BR/CRI/23/6 to 10, National Archives of Scotland, Edinburgh.

Vessel Returns, 1795/1858, BW2/1/5/1, The Waterways Trust, Ellesmere Port.

EDINBURGH AND GLASGOW
UNION CANAL

Minutes of the Goods, Passengers and Traffic Committee, 1848/65, Edinburgh and Glasgow Railway, BR/EGR/73 to 74, National Archives of Scotland, Edinburgh.

Minutes of Shareholders Meetings, 1845/65, Edinburgh and Glasgow Railway, BR/EGR/1 and 2, National Archives of Scotland, Edinburgh.

Traffic Statements, 1962-5, Edinburgh and Glasgow Railway, Br/EGR/4-9, National Archives of Scotland, Edinburgh.

Directors Reports to Shareholders, 1867/8, North British Railway Company, NBR/1/76, National Archives of Scotland, Edinburgh.

Minutes of Meetings of Directors, 1864, North British Railway Company, NBR/1/117, National Archives of Scotland, Edinburgh.

Alternative Routes for the Canal, 1813/16, AO37-64, Falkirk H.R.S., Callender House, Falkirk.

List of Ships and Goods at Port Downie, 1823/30, AO53/14, Falkirk H.R.S., Callender House, Falkirk.

List of Ships at Lock 16, 1910/41 and 1951/60, Falkirk H.R.S., Callender House, Falkirk.

Passenger Fares, 1830/5, AO09.003/03-5, Falkirk H.R.S., Callender House, Falkirk.

Objections of Wm Forbes of Callender Estate to the Route of the Canal, GD/171/1044-1078, Falkirk H.R.S., Callender house, Falkirk.

The following are all in the records of the Edinburgh and Glasgow Union Canal held at the National Archives of Scotland, Edinburgh, under the reference numbers given below:

Accounts Record, 1909/12, BR/EGU/23.

Agreements between Edinburgh Corporation and the North British Railway for Alterations to the Canal, 1909/12, BR/EGU/4/8.

Accounts, 1835/1848, BR/EGU/23/1-2.

Income and Expenditure,1837/1847, BR/FCN/1/23.

Minutes of the General Assembly of Proprietors, 1822/47, BR/EGU/1/8.

Minutes of the Management Committee, 1816/1821,
    BR/EGU/4/6/1-5.
Minutes of the Management Committee, 1822/47,
    BR/EGU/1/1-7.

FORTH AND CLYDE CANAL

Minutes of the Joint Committee, 1857/66, Caledonian
    Railway Company, BR/CAL/1/91-2.
Minutes of the Meetings of Shareholders 1845/1923,
    Caledonian Railway Company, BR/CAL/1/1-6.
*Arbitration on Acquisition of the Forth and Clyde
    Canal, 1846/1865,* Edinburgh and Glasgow
    Railway, UGD/8/6/12, Glasgow University
    Archive Service.
Pricing Agreements with Forth and Clyde Canal, 1861,
    Edinburgh and Glasgow Railway, UGD/8/6/10,
    Glasgow University Archive Service.
Annual General Meeting Notice, 1866, Forth and Clyde
    Navigation, UGD/8/2/2, Glasgow University
    Archive Service.
Dividend Book, 1802/16, Forth and Clyde Navigation,
    BW/4/2/1, Glasgow University Archive Service.
Trade Book, 1937/39, BW/5/3/1/1, The Waterways Trust,
    Ellesmere Port.
Traffic Dues, 1930/1962, BW/4/2/10. The Waterways
    Trust, Ellesmere Port.
Forth and Clyde Local (Subject) Plan, 1964, PA5/202,
    Glasgow City Libraries and Archives.
Forth and Clyde local (Subject) Plan, 1980, PA5/85 and
    PA5/202, Glasgow City Libraries and Archives.

The following are all in the records of the Forth and
Clyde Navigation held at the National Archives of
Scotland, Edinburgh, under the reference numbers
given below:

*Minutes of the Annual general Meetings of the
    Proprietors, 1774/1852,* BR/FCN/1/30-32.
*Minutes of the Meetings of the Governor and Council,
    1787/1862,* BR/FCN/1/14, 25-29.
*Minutes of the Meetings of the Management
    Committee, 1775/1850,* BR/FCN/1/1,11,33-90.
*Minutes of the Meetings of the Committee of Council,
    1825/1850,* BR/FCN/1/65-90.

MID-SCOTLAND SHIP CANAL

Print of Lecture, (1910), D.A. Stevenson, DTC.6/478,
    Glasgow City Libraries and Archives.
Report of the Mid-Scotland Ship Canal Committee,
    H.M.S.O., (Cmnd. 3657).
Miscellaneous Papers, DTC/6/606/3-12, T-CN18/64
    and DTC6/478, Glasgow City Libraries
    and Archives.

MONKLAND CANAL

Blackhill Inclined Plane, Transactions of the Royal
    Scottish Society of Arts, 1856, Volume IV.
Diary of James Watt, 1770/74, TD729/36, Glasgow City
    Libraries and Archives.
Income and Expenditure, 1837/45, UGD8/2/8,
    Glasgow University Archive Service.
Income and Expenditure, 1846, BR/FCN/1/86,
    National Archives of Scotland,
    Edinburgh.

Infilling of Canal, 1951/68, UC.5/4/09, North Lanarkshire Archives, Cumbernauld.

Objections to Infilling of Canal by Coatbridge Tinplate Co., 1946, U2.3/101, North Lanarkshire Archives, Cumbernauld.

Minutes of the Management Committee, 1770/1806, BW5/1/2, The Waterways Trust, Ellesmere Port.

Minutes of the Management committee, 1838/46, BR/FCN/1/93, National Archives of Scotland, Edinburgh.

Tonnages, 1863/1921, TD 729/36, Glasgow City Libraries and Archives.

Monkland and Kirkintilloch Railway, 1837/46, UGD 8/2/8, Glasgow University Archive Services.

Wm Baird and Co., Board Papers and Accounts, 1824/1974, UGD164/1/1, Glasgow University Archives.

Wm Baird and Co, Cost of Boating, 1861-3, U8.10/05, North Lanarkshire Archives, Cumbernauld.

INDEX